Advance Praise for
The Liberating Path of the Hebrew Prophets

"This is a wise-hearted book, a wisdom text for our times. To read it is to go on a journey of love for the world. Grounded in the biblical prophetic tradition and in dialogue with contemporary prophetic voices, it is a pouring forth of lessons for living with spiritual exuberance. Give it to your friends; read it in community; teach it to your children." —**Sandra Lubarsky**, Professor Emeritus of Sustainable Communities, Northern Arizona University

"Nahum Ward-Lev has mastered the uncommon skill of being at once profoundly wise and practically useful. He's written an invaluable guide to social transformation. This book provides wisdom and hope for our day!" —**Joan Borysenko**, New York Times bestselling author, *Minding the Body, Mending the Mind*

"Ward-Lev tracks the prophetic stream throughout the Hebrew Bible and on into the present. What surfaces is the relational energy of transformation as experienced in the presence of a liberating God. The whole is a treasure for the Abrahamic family." —**Larry Rasmussen**, Reinhold Niebuhr Professor Emeritus, Union Theological Seminary

"The practice of facilitated dialogue, relationship building based on mutuality, and deep listening are fundamental building blocks of peacemaking and conflict resolution. Ward-Lev sets these practices in a deep historical context which gives them new life and clarifies how radical and indispensable they have been for centuries and continue to be in the present social and environmental climate. I don't believe humanity can heal or move forward without a deep understanding of these practices." —**Roberto M. Chene**, Director, Intercultural Leadership and Conflict Resolution Albuquerque, N.M.

"As a political organizer, this book meets a perpetual longing in my work— to know our dreams and our agonies were shouted into existence centuries before we named them, and to experience that inheritance of political struggle as a source of connection and resilience. The problems of our day can feel grueling and demoralizing, but alienation—from each o⁺ʰ God, from our ancestors—worsens their wear or antidote to that wear and that alienation. It is a **Zahav**, Community Organizer, Jews for Racial

"In 1962 the great Abraham Heschel responded of the Cuban Missile Crisis with his now-classic st _._ prophetic tradition. Ward-Lev's study can have similar impact, animating hope in our dark time. I warmly recommend it to Christians to build literacy in the first half of our Bible, and its wisdom for our work and witness." —**Ched Myers**, Bartimaeus Cooperative Ministries

"This book resounds with the voices of poets, prophets, philosophers, and inspired leaders. With honesty, creativity, and warmth, Rabbi Ward-Lev invites us into revolutionary ways of being in relationship that are themselves potent medicine in these times." —**Adam Horowitz**, Chief Instigator, U.S. Department of Arts and Culture

"This is an extraordinary work of great clarity and scholarship. I hope this book is read by leaders worldwide, because our future may depend on the wisdom embedded in these pages." —**Larry Dossey**, author, *One Mind*

"The two most critical issues facing humanity today, our relationship with the earth and a just response to refugees and the poorest among us, are cogently addressed by Ward-Lev, brilliantly weaving together the two strands. Standing in a long prophetic lineage, he passionately invites us to let the earth bring forth its energies for healing and to summon from the human soul a new vision for justice." —**John Philip Newell**, author, *The Rebirthing of God*

"This well-researched book opens the door for both believers and non-believers to join together in facing genuine concerns about recent authoritarian political dangers that threaten our society. Ward-Lev also presents a Biblically based alternative to the extreme individualism and base materialism which undermine our capacity to treat the other as human. It is modern midrash in the best sense of that term." —**Lewis Barth**, Professor Emeritus of Midrash and Former Dean, Hebrew Union College

"Rabbi Ward-Lev invokes his passionate curiosity to reveal fresh, timely insights and precious tools. It would be hard to imagine more essential, on-target wisdom than this generous offering. This book is a precious gift. If we use it wisely, it will nurture the global healing we all yearn for." —**Wayne Muller**, author, *Sabbath*

"I was profoundly moved by the fresh and provocative interpretations offered on some of our best known biblical narratives, and even more by Rabbi Ward-Lev's way of connecting his reading of the Bible to the greatest personal, societal and global challenges we face today." —**Ruth Sohn**, Director of Rabbinic Mentoring, Hebrew Union College

"Nahum's work on the prophets has opened up entirely new ways of thinking for me. This is the best kind of scholarship: deep engagement with the text grounded in a clear-sighted appreciation for the implications for us as we confront the challenges in the world today. If you're looking for a fresh perspective, this is it." —**Rick Ufford-Chase**, Former Moderator of Presbyterian Church (U.S.A), Co-Director, Stony Point Retreat Center

THE LIBERATING PATH OF THE HEBREW PROPHETS

THE LIBERATING PATH
OF THE HEBREW PROPHETS

Then and Now

NAHUM WARD-LEV

ORBIS BOOKS
Maryknoll, New York 10545

ORBIS BOOKS
Maryknoll, New York 10545

Fathers and Brothers
MARYKNOLL™

Founded in 1970, Orbis Books endeavors to publish works that enlighten the mind, nourish the spirit, and challenge the conscience. The publishing arm of the Maryknoll Fathers and Brothers, Orbis seeks to explore the global dimensions of the Christian faith and mission, to invite dialogue with diverse cultures and religious traditions, and to serve the cause of reconciliation and peace. The books published reflect the views of their authors and do not represent the official position of the Maryknoll Society. To learn more about Maryknoll and Orbis Books, please visit our website at www.maryknollsociety.org.

Library of Congress Cataloging-in-Publication Data

Names: Ward-Lev, Nahum, author.
Title: The liberating path of the Hebrew prophets : then and now / Nahum Ward-Lev.
Description: Maryknoll, NY : Orbis books, [2019] | Includes bibliographical references and index.
Identifiers: LCCN 2018051790 (print) | LCCN 2018053708 (ebook) |
   ISBN 9781608337910 (e-book) | ISBN 9781626983298 (pbk.)
Subjects: LCSH: Liberty—Religious aspects—Judaism—History of doctrines. |
   Bible. Old Testament—Criticism, interpretation, etc.
Classification: LCC BM645.F7 (ebook) | LCC BM645.F7 W37 2019 (print) |
   DDC 296.3—dc23
LC record available at https://lccn.loc.gov/2018051790

To my Beit Midrash companions on the learning journey

Let justice roll down like a river

Righteousness like a mighty stream

—Amos 5:24

Another world is not only possible

She is on her way. . . .

On a quiet day, if I listen very carefully,

I can hear her breathing

—Arundhati Roy

You are not obligated to complete the work

but neither are you free to desist from it

—Talmud

Contents

Foreword by Walter Brueggemann xi

Acknowledgments xv

A Note on Translation xix

Introduction: A Stream Runs through It xxi

Part One
Prophetic Wisdom for Societal Transformation

1. A Journey in Love 3

2. The Prophets and Deuteronomy: A Societal Revolution 13

3. The Liberation Journey 19

4. The Way of Relationship 31

5. Telling the Essential Story throughout Time 39

6. Headwaters: The Prophetic Stream in Creation 45

7. Journey Partners: God and Abraham 55

8. Rivalry and Resolution in Genesis 65

9. Exodus: A Women's Liberation 79

10. Force and Transformation 87

11. The Reluctant Prophet and the Unprepared People 93

12. Head for the Hills: Origins of the Liberation Journey 99

13. A Scribal Tradition 107

Part Two
Contemporary Reflections on Prophetic Wisdom

14. A Mighty Stream: Contemporary Prophetic Critique 119

15. A Listening Lineage 133

16. We Make the Road by Walking: Life as Journey 137

17. Dialogue Is the Way 145

18. Dialogue against Oppression 155

19. The World Is Built with Love (Ps 89:3) 163

20. Enacting a Love Ethic 169

21. The Exquisite Lightness of Being 179

22. The Art of Stars and Stones 183

23. The Love That Binds Us 199

Appendix A. Spiritual Practices for Prophetic Action 205

Appendix B. Chapter Reflections 213

Selected Readings 221

Index 227

Foreword

It is a delight to read and an honor to comment on this moving textual study by Nahum Ward-Lev. The book in a singular a way serves to connect the dynamism of the old covenant tradition and the prospect and reality of faithful covenantal living in contemporary culture. At the outset, Ward-Lev solves the difficult problem of how to translate the divine name by rendering it as the "Living Presence." By this happy phrase we are on the alert for a lively agent who has a purpose, a will, and a capacity for transformation. The identification of the God of Israel (whose primary narrative is the exodus story) indicates that this God will not long remain allied with or patron of any settled authority or sociopolitical structure that contradicts the divine purpose of freedom and justice.

Ward-Lev has in fact done nothing less than to offer a theological exposition of the covenantal tradition that has at its core the teaching of Deuteronomy and the critical tradition of the prophets. This exposition deftly identifies and characterizes five dimensions of that theological claim.

1. The movement of the narrative from Pharaoh's Egypt to the land of promise via the wilderness yields the dominant metaphor of "*journey*," as noted in the title of the book. Ward-Lev declares, "We are each called to a liberation journey for which we are never fully prepared. That journey characteristically entails a departure from a settled circumstance and an entrenched authority to a risky life of venturesome freedom."

2. The journey constitutes participation in and with the *mystery* of the living God who exercises agency, who variously enacts rescue and judgment, and who finally will not be mocked. While the tradition has great clarity about this living God, the pluralistic elusiveness of the tradition shows that this God can never be caught or domesticated in a formula, a ritual, or an ideology. This witness to mystery illuminates why the tradition

is vigorously opposed to idolatry, because idolatry is an attempt to dispel the mystery and gain control over divine power.

3. The journey alongside mystery is the celebration of and participation in a *relationship*. Ward-Lev shows how engagement with this living God is one of mutuality, thus a contradiction of every top-down authority, whether of the unilateral sovereignty of God or of any human political construct. The exercise of mystery by this Living Presence yields a different polity of mutuality.

4. This mutuality between incommensurate partners is an ongoing *dialogue* in which both parties—Israel or the world alongside God— have a vigorous voice. For that reason the relationship depends upon serious, engaged listening. Ward-Lev's exposition of Moses exhibits him as a great listener to the new impulses that shape his life toward risky emancipation.

5. This collage of journey, mystery, relationship, and dialogue is finally shaped in ancient Israel by *the covenant at Sinai*. As a result the Torah of Sinai is not a flat, top-down decree (as it is mistakenly understood in so much thoughtless religion), but it is a venue for interaction in fidelity with Moses fully holding up the other end of the conversation. This covenantal shape of life, perforce, always concerns the "other," the one who is unlike self, Israel unlike God, and neighbor unlike neighbor.

This book revolves, so it seems to me, around two magisterially expressed chapters. First, Ward-Lev focuses on the dynamism of the tradition of Deuteronomy. He shows in a compelling way how the covenantal tradition is preoccupied with a neighborly economy that resists and refuses settled hierarchal powers. This tradition funded the prophetic sequence in the eighth and seventh centuries, and later supplied the essential resources for the formation of Judaism in the Torah-based work of Ezra.

Second, Ward-Lev shows the way in which the creation narratives in Genesis function as the counterpoint to the Deuteronomic understanding of history. Thus the "bring forth" addressed to a rich inventory of creatures in Genesis is clearly parallel to the "bring forth" of Israel from Pharaoh's Egypt. In both creation and history, God "brings forth" in a transformative way to an emancipated, flourishing life. In both cases, the Living Presence is an emancipatory agent who intends the flourishing of creation and the flourishing of Israel by way of the divine blessing. The God who blesses creation is the God who blesses the family of Abraham.

I should add a special comment on a quite distinctive chapter on "necessary force" that is required for historical living, a necessary force that takes the form of violence. Ward-Lev eschews all romanticism and pietism about the historical process and sees that in some circumstances violence is required. He also shrewdly notes, however, that "God learns the limitation of violence," a hard learning for the Living Presence as it is for the creatures of the Living Presence. Violence is necessary, but its limitations are acute in a world designed for just freedom.

Before he finishes his historical exposition of the tradition, Ward-Lev reflects on the decisive role of the ancient scribes in the formation of the biblical tradition. Even though the scribes were characteristically linked to established power, it is an undeniable wonder that they continued to prize and transmit this subversive tradition that surely undermined the very power in which they were ensconced. Thus this subversive covenantal tradition has its own say, exactly through the work of the scribes and, we may believe, partly in spite of the scribes themselves. It is not unexpected that Ward-Lev would trace a defining connection between the tradition-generating scribes and the subsequent rabbinic tradition that has continued to enliven the tradition and keep it pertinent and effective in always newly emerging circumstance.

As a Christian I welcome this rich exposition of the Jewish tradition. As in Judaism, it is a continuing challenge among Christians to take seriously the dynamism and ongoing vitality of the tradition. Thus this book will be of immense value to Christian readers who want to understand both the deep Jewish roots of the Christian covenantal-prophetic tradition and the inherently subversive urgency of the Christian tradition.

Having lined out this subversive tradition, in which the content is matched by the dynamism of interpretive energy, it is not surprising (but very welcome) that Ward-Lev has extended his discussion to contemporary performances of this tradition. Moses had declared, "Not with our ancestors did the LORD make this covenant, but with us, who are all of us here alive today" (Deut 5:3).

In citing this glorious company of these contemporary figures of daring faith and risky living, Ward-Lev demonstrates how it is that the old covenant pertains, even now, to all of us who are here alive today!

Ward-Lev is not finished when he ends his shrewd exposition of the ancient prophets. His discussion artfully opens the prophetic tradition to its compelling contemporaneity. In the latter part of his elegant manuscript, Ward-Lev, in the interpretive trajectory of Buber, Heschel, and Levinas, sees that the "prophetic" consists in a journey of liberation that is increasingly committed to relationships of mutuality. Coming to terms with "the other" is growth in dialogic capacity that opens up until then unimagined new social possibilities. For that exposition Ward-Lev mobilizes such variant voices as Maya Angelou, William Barber, Wes Jackson, Mary Oliver, and Alice Walker. His exposition effectively connects the ancient tradition with contemporary practitioners who enact life-giving alternatives to the reductions of technological flatness.

For this Christian reader, this remarkable presentation makes clear that being "prophetic" means to move increasingly into a world of relationships. This means, conversely, that the conventional stereotype of "prophetic" as bashing people with a radical agenda of social justice is a false construal. The prophets rather attest to an alternative way in a world that is rooted in holy mystery and expressed in concrete neighbor love. Such a life is one of risk so that Ward-Lev can judge that God "is fundamentally in support of falling forward." Those in the prophetic company may try and fail in the enactment of new futures, but they try again and then yet again.

I finished this book with waves of wonder and gratitude. Ward-Lev, in his generous way, invites to hope, possibility that is on offer only outside the dominant regime of fear and control.

Walter Brueggemann
Columbia Theological Seminary
October 7, 2018

Acknowledgments

As I wrote this book, I felt supported and carried by a mighty stream. I am profoundly grateful. The book grew out of hundreds of Beit Midrash conversations, lively exchanges of twenty adults of diverse faiths who gathered weekly to study a sacred text. Many diverse voices make for strong Torah. I appreciate each of the people who participated in the Beit Midrash conversation over the years. If you sat around that table, somewhere your voice is in this book.

I am deeply grateful to Walter Brueggemann, a contemporary prophet. Walter's many books on the Hebrew Bible have inspired and guided me for over three decades. In recent years, his friendship and his confidence in my work have been immeasurably important to me.

Several treasured friends provided me with wise and heartfelt support throughout the writing process. Mark Gordon and I have walked together talking about this book for hundreds of miles, in the mountains and in the city. Mark gave me the great gift of telling me how he was applying the teachings in this book to his inspired work with people living with disabilities. My teaching brother, John Philip Newell, told me many moons ago that I had a worthy book in me and that I should write. Years later, I listened. Thank you, Philip, for your confidence in me and for your ongoing support. I am grateful to Ruth Sohn for her encouragement throughout the writing process and for suggesting that I add a chapter on spiritual practices for the liberation journey. Wayne Muller has been my trusted guide through the world of book publishing. His wisdom and generous heart helped me to stay on course and stay connected to my own heart through the challenging process of finding the right publisher for my work. Finally, Rick Ufford-Chase provided me with an opportunity to present my material to his community and encouraged me to send my manuscript to Orbis, a recommendation I so much appreciate.

I have been blessed with editing support from many thoughtful people during the writing process. Emily Wichland commented on the earliest draft of the book and continued to support me with wise counsel as the manuscript moved forward toward publication. Lib O'Brien, Lucy Moore, and Roberto Chene responded to specific questions I had about some chapters. Martha Franks was my trusted companion for the first strong editing of the manuscript. I am deeply indebted to her for helping me think through many of the ideas in the book and for frequently challenging me to take another step forward in my thinking. Along the way Martha and I had a lot of fun, and she taught me a thing or two about writing. I am ever so grateful for Henry Carrigan, who brought his fine eye for clarity of expression to the entire manuscript and helped me prepare the manuscript for final submission.

I feel fortunate and honored that Orbis Books is publishing my work. For over four decades, Orbis has published books that bring forward the liberating insights and teachings found in biblical Scriptures. Thank you to Ched Myers, who introduced me to Robert Ellsberg, the publisher at Orbis. Heartfelt appreciation to Robert for seeing the value in my manuscript and taking a chance on a first-time author.

I appreciate David Mandel for generously granting me permission to include biblical translations from the Soncino Collection and for permitting me to substitute "the Living Presence" for "the Lord" in those translations.

Fr. Francis Dorf, of blessed memory, was my cherished soul friend for nearly thirty years. As we shared our spiritual journeys with each other, I had the blessed opportunity to explore many of the ideas in this book in the context of our lived experience.

I am the fortunate beneficiary of the enthusiastic support of my much loved family. My in-laws, Don and Micky Mann; my sister, Nancy Walch; and my brothers-in-law, Richard Walch, Barney Scout Mann, and Charlie Mann, all had a hand and a heart in bringing this book into print. I feel so blessed that they have been my companions along this journey. I am grateful to my daughter, Eliana, for her love and support. I pray that this book will make a little contribution to the world that she and her peers will inhabit.

I wish to honor here my parents of blessed memory, Richard M. Ward and Shirley Ward, and my grandparents of blessed memory, Sam and Evelyn Ward and Alex and Winnie Hamburg. I inherited from them the disciplines of mind and heart that helped me to write this book.

My wife, Shelley, the love and light of my life, supported me with unbridled encouragement and insightful feedback throughout the journey of writing this book. Her generous heart, brilliant mind, and passion for social justice touched every page. Shelley possesses the courage to be my toughest editor. She has a tremendous facility to track and bring focus to a complex flow of ideas. My gratitude to Shelley is as deep as the love we share.

A Note on Translation

In most English translations, God's Name, the four letter Tetragrammaton, is usually translated as "the Lord," a rendering that is in keeping with the rabbinic tradition of pronouncing "Adonai" (my Lord) when reading the Tetragrammaton in the Bible. In rabbinic times, when Caesar was the lord of the land, the rabbinic representation carried great meaning, indicating that God was the true lord. In contemporary times, the word "Lord" carries a connotation of domination that does not fit the character of the God of liberation we meet in the Bible.

Seeking an alternative to "the Lord," I have chosen to translate God's Name as "the Living Presence." This translation reflects the meaning of the four letters of the Tetragrammaton—*yud, hey, vav,* and *hey.* Combining those letters in different orders, one can form the Hebrew word "to be" or "being" in the perfect, present, and imperfect tenses. The four letters of God's Name seem to refer to "being" itself, to "Being" or "Being-ness" that transcends time. My use of "the Living Presence" is also guided by God's interaction with Moses at the burning bush. When Moses asks God for God's Name, God replies, "I will be what I will be" (Exod 3:14). With this response, God both informs Moses that God's nature cannot be defined by any limiting quality, such as a name, and God assures Moses that God will be with him throughout time. Looking for a term that reflects this sense of "Being" or "Being-ness" accompanying human beings and creation throughout time, I chose the term "the Living Presence."

With the noted exceptions, translations of biblical verses come from the Soncino Classics Collection. In those verses in the Soncino Collection, where the term "the Lord" appears, I have substituted the term "the Living Presence." The author's translations have been marked with a dagger (†) following the notation of the biblical chapter and verse.

All the author's translations conform to the definition of Hebrew words found in *The Brown-Driver-Briggs Hebrew and English Lexicon of the Old Testament.*

Introduction
A STREAM RUNS THROUGH IT

*The intent of Torah study is to transform
ourselves so that we might transform the world.*

Wisdom. Courage. Vision. The world needs these powerful human resources today. We are facing life-threatening forces of destruction, including global climate change, proliferation of nuclear weapons, environmental degradation, accelerating inequity between the few who are privileged and the many who suffer in poverty, growing numbers of failed states, and the rise of authoritarian regimes in formerly democratic societies. In the face of these grave dangers, humankind needs to take wise, courageous, and visionary action to create the conditions in which all life can flourish.

I am a rabbi. For many years I have devoted myself to gathering people around the Hebrew Scriptures to study the sacred text. Given my training and experience, when I felt the need to search for wisdom, courage, and vision to respond to grave global challenges, I turned to the Hebrew prophets.[1]

Over two and a half millennia ago, the Hebrew prophets arose in an era that is resonant with our own. A growing gap between the rich and the poor caused widespread suffering and political instability. The major

---

[1] The term "Hebrew prophets" refers to the fifteen prophets whose verbal testimony is preserved in books bearing their names in the Hebrew Scriptures. These same prophets are also referred to as the "writing prophets." Other prophets, such as Nathan and Elijah, appear in the Bible. The text records some of their words and deeds, but an entire book of the Bible is not dedicated to their ministry. A note on usage: when I capitalize "Prophets," I am referring to the biblical books. When writing about the individual prophets themselves and their actions, I use the lower case, "prophets."

institutions were failing to protect people from the overwhelming power of privileged elites, and political leaders seemed unwilling and incapable of averting impending disaster.

In the face of these profound crises, the Hebrew prophets lived the wisdom, courage, and vision that I believe is desperately needed now. They possessed the wisdom and courage to proclaim the unsustainability of the current order, a reality that others ignored. At the same time, they possessed the vision that enabled them to transcend the brokenness of the moment to articulate an alternative society in which all would be well.

I want the wisdom, courage, and vision I find in those ancient prophets for myself and for all of us. It takes wisdom and courage to face squarely the depth of injustice and structural oppression in the current societal order and to call out that the status quo is fundamentally immoral and unsustainable. We all need wisdom and courage to face the full truth of our situation and to take bold action in the face of entrenched powers to bring about systemic change.

Our day also begs for vision. We need vision to make our way forward. We can become so deeply discouraged and disheartened by the brokenness of our societal structures as well as the enormous challenge of pursuing justice that we fail to see the great opportunity of the moment. We need moral imagination to see beyond the current order, to perceive the profound possibilities of the moment, and to begin to enact an alternative future.

In search of the wisdom, courage, and vision articulated by the Hebrew prophets, I wanted to invite companions to join me in studying the prophetic testimony. I was very fortunate to have those good companions right at hand. For the last eighteen years, I have led a Beit Midrash,[2] a spiritual learning community of twenty people, including Jews, Christians, and people who don't identify with a faith tradition. In the Beit Midrash, we are committed to the deep study of Jewish texts and to incorporating the wisdom of those texts into daily life. The Beit Midrash meets weekly for two and a half hours from September to June each year. In each session, a spirit of adventure and vulnerability, together with careful listening to the text and to each other, has led to insightful and heartfelt conversation. Our study has been both intellectual and personal, engaging the heart and soul as well as the mind.

In the fall of 2011, I invited the Beit Midrash to study the Hebrew prophets with me. I told my students that I had turned to the prophets seeking wisdom, courage, and vision for our time. I remember saying

---

[2] Beit Midrash is the traditional rabbinic term for a place of study and for the study endeavor itself. The term means "house of exploration," an expression that carries the sense of adventure that characterizes a Beit Midrash.

that I had increasingly found those ancient prophets speaking across the millennia to the present moment. To my joy, my students received my invitation with enthusiasm.

In our study, we followed the lead of the great scholar of the Hebrew Prophets, Abraham Joshua Heschel. In the introduction to his book *The Prophets*, Heschel states that he turned to the Prophets to find an alternative to contemporary thought. As a doctoral student in philosophy at the University of Berlin in the 1930s, Heschel began to understand that the catastrophe that had engulfed the Germany of his day was the external manifestation of fundamental flaws in common ways of thinking. Describing his experience in Berlin, Heschel wrote,

I was slowly led to the realization that some of the terms, motivations, and concerns which dominate our thinking may prove destructive of the roots of human responsibility and treasonable to the ultimate ground of human solidarity. . . . It became clear to me that the most important philosophical problem of the twentieth century was to find a new set of presuppositions or premises, a different way of thinking.[3]

Heschel looked for a new set of premises, a new way of thinking, in the Hebrew Prophets.

For four years in the Beit Midrash, we studied Heschel's writings alongside the Prophets. In our fifth year, we studied contemporary prophets, including Paulo Freire, Martin Buber, Gustavo Gutiérrez, Beverly Wildung Harrison, Martin Luther King Jr., and bell hooks. The work of these liberation thinkers developed themes we had found in the Prophets and applied these themes to contemporary challenges.

Eight years after forming the Beit Midrash, I gathered a second Beit Midrash group to study the book of Genesis. As I sat in those two circles, week after week, I began to see similar themes emerge in the Prophets and Genesis. This resonance between the texts grew until I came to see that Genesis is also a prophetic work, written in a different form. Energized by this insight, I examined other books of the Torah.[4] Through many different stories and literary styles, I saw what I now call the "prophetic stream" flowing powerfully through the Torah and Prophets. The prophetic stream parallels the action of the prophetic

---

³ Abraham Joshua Heschel, *The Prophets* (New York: Harper Collins, 1962), xxviii.

⁴ The Hebrew Bible includes three sections: Torah, Prophets, and Writings. The Torah consists of five books: Genesis, Exodus, Leviticus, Numbers, and Deuteronomy.

word. It is characterized by a movement toward freedom and justice and by a critique of imperial power and imperial thinking. Biblical texts carrying the prophetic stream articulate alternative, more egalitarian presuppositions and values.

This book traces the movement of the prophetic stream both in the Hebrew Bible and in the work of contemporary prophets. The first section of the book describes the flowing of the prophetic stream in the Torah and the Prophets, detailing the basic premises and themes that define its movement. The second section draws upon the writings of contemporary prophets to further develop these premises and themes.

In the first section of the book, the exploration of the flow of the prophetic stream uncovers a core biblical theme: Israel's liberation journey with God. The Hebrew Scriptures came into being to chronicle and guide this liberation journey, to explore the dynamics of the journey with God toward a more just and inclusive society.

In the Bible, the flow of the prophetic stream begins with creation. The creation stories in Genesis present each new phase of the evolving creation as a liberation from the constraints of the phase that preceded it. On each day of creation, God animates the physical world to transcend the limitation of the day that preceded it, bringing forth a more diverse, dynamic, and interrelated world.

The same energy of liberation then flows into the journeys of individual people. The liberation journey shapes the lives of the patriarchs and matriarchs as well as Judah, Joseph, Miriam, and Moses, and then ultimately shapes the trajectory of the entire people Israel. Each of these biblical persons and then the whole people Israel are called out by God to "go forth" on the long liberation toward a less oppressive and more just society. As we peer deeply into the lives of these biblical characters and the people, the "new set of premises" and the "different way of thinking" that Heschel found in the Prophets becomes clear.

This exploration of the biblical texts reveals two premises that are central to the prophets and to the prophetic stream: (1) God calls each individual and society to an ongoing liberation journey, and (2) the primary dynamic of the liberation journey is the free movement toward mutual relationship. These two interrelated premises have profound implications for how we perceive and live our lives. A society founded on these premises will inevitably evolve toward being a more just, inclusive, and healthy civilization.

The second section of this book unpacks these two premises—liberation journey with God and the centrality of mutual relationship—to ask how these propositions speak to our lives today. To guide our study, we explore the ways that contemporary liberation thinkers such as Paulo Freire, Martin Buber, Martin Luther King Jr., Beverly Harrison, Gustavo Gutiérrez, and bell hooks, among others, develop these premises. Akin to the biblical prophets, these modern prophets develop those two premises to challenge modern thinking and to offer guidance for how we can live in ways that promote human flourishing and global well-being.

At the end of the book, you will find two additional resources. The first appendix describes spiritual practices for the liberation journey. These practices support our journey by cultivating the inner resources that enable us to act with wisdom, courage, and vision. I invite you to turn to these practices either while you are reading this book or at its conclusion. The second appendix contains a reflection for each chapter. In the Beit Midrash, we frequently use reflections to help apply the insights we found in the Scriptures to our daily lives. These reflections offer you the opportunity to delve more deeply into a key concept in each chapter and to explore what this concept means in your life. After completing a chapter, you might it helpful to turn to the corresponding reflection.

When I first sat down to write this book, I had three clear goals in mind. I wanted to lift up the wisdom, courage, and vision in the prophetic testimony. I wanted to highlight the prophetic themes that run throughout the Torah as well as the Prophets, and to translate those themes into terms that could help us respond to contemporary challenges. And I wanted to present the Torah and the Prophets as I understood them, as sacred texts fundamentally concerned with human liberation. As I worked on the book over time, I discovered that the book wanted to go further than I had envisioned. The book wanted to speak in more detail about how we walk the liberation journey and with more specificity about the perspectives, priorities, and practices that would shape a society that supports the flourishing of all its members. I have done my best to write the book that wanted to be written.

Sitting—in Beit Midrash and while writing this book—has felt to me like walking, like moving forward step by step on a great adventure, learning the perspectives and processes that support the liberation journey. I write this book to share this journey with you. I write with the intention that you might join my Beit Midrash companions and me on our journey, so that you might share in the challenge and inspiration that we have found in Scripture. In my experience, many contemporary people, religious and secular, are hungry to find wisdom, courage, and vision that speaks directly to the challenges of our day. In our Beit

Midrash study, we have found these powerful human resources in the Hebrew Scriptures. It is my pleasure to be able to offer them to you.

The journey begins by falling into step with the prophet Amos, the first of the Hebrew writing prophets.

Part One

Prophetic Wisdom for
Societal Transformation

CHAPTER I

A Journey in Love

The Bible says that in the days of King Uzziah of Judah, in the middle of the eighth century BCE, a Judean shepherd named Amos left his flock in Tekoa and set out on foot for Beth El, the cultic center of Israel twenty-four miles to the north. A flock of sheep is all that shepherds have; they rarely leave their flock behind. On the pilgrimage festivals, Amos might take a sheep to the great Temple in Jerusalem, twelve miles to the north of Tekoa. But why would a Judean herdsman walk past Jerusalem and continue to Beth El, the cultic center of Israel, a foreign kingdom?[1] What could possibly lead a shepherd to abandon his flock and make such a journey?

Perhaps the prophet set out on his journey because of the divine revelations he had received. Indeed, God had appeared to Amos in visions, terrifying appearances of devastating locusts and devouring fire consuming land and sea. The visions were an alarming warning of impending disaster. God had also spoken to Amos, telling him to bring this warning to the people Israel. One might therefore conclude that Amos went to Beth El in obedience to God.

This understanding underestimates both the man and the God he served. Amos was not a passive messenger of the divine word. From the outset, Amos stood up to God; he entered into dialogue with God, pleading for the people. When God revealed to Amos these two terrible visions of Israel's destruction, Amos cried out, "O God, Living Presence, forgive, I beseech you! How shall Jacob stand? He is so small!" (7:2).

---

[1] After the death of King Solomon in 960 BCE, his kingdom was divided into two separate political entities, Israel to the north and Judah to the south. In 722 BCE the Assyrian Empire overran Israel and took her people into exile. In 586 BCE the Babylonian Empire destroyed the southern kingdom, Judah.

Not once, but twice, after the vision of locusts and the vision of fire, Amos responded to the divine revelation with the same impassioned cry, "O God, Living Presence, forgive, I beseech you!" (7:5). Twice God relented. Like Moses who stood up to God and pleaded for the lives of the people who worshiped the Golden Calf, Amos did not simply accept God's decree. The prophet engaged God in dialogue about the fate of Israel.

God then revealed a third vision to the prophet. This third vision was decisive for Amos. After this vision, Amos did not resist. He immediately set out on the long, dusty journey to Beth El. The prophet went to inform the people what God revealed to him.

What did God reveal to Amos?

> Thus he showed me; and behold, the Living Presence stood upon a wall made by a plumb line, with a plumb line in his hand. And the Living Presence said to me: Amos, what do you see? And I said, a plumb line. Then the Living Presence said, Behold, I will set a plumb line in the midst of my people Israel. (Amos 7:7–8)

In this third revelation, Amos is again in dialogue with God, again an active participant in the vision. The image of God holding a plumb line to a wall decisively animates Amos. He responds to this image because it speaks not only to danger but to the causes of the danger. Amos now sees deeply into the relationship between God and Israel, which is to say deep into the fabric of reality. Amos perceives that the wall, a symbol for the kingdom of Israel, was "made by a plumb line," upheld by uprightness, by justice. He sees that justice is an essential aspect of societal stability. He understands that in the absence of justice, the kingdom will certainly fall. The fall will not be because God has moved to destroy the kingdom, but because the kingdom, made crooked by its abandonment of justice, was destroying itself: "And the high places of Isaac shall be desolate, and the sanctuaries of Israel shall be laid waste" (Amos 7:9).

Amos sets off for Beth El to warn the people. But that is not all. God also gave Amos a positive vision, an instruction for how the people can preserve themselves and their communal life:

> Seek the Living Presence and you shall live. . . . Seek him who made the Pleiades and Orion and turns the deep darkness into morning and makes the day darken into night. . . . Seek good and not evil, that you may live. . . . Hate the evil and love the good and establish justice in the gate. (5:6, 8, 14, 15)

Amos, animated by the grave understanding that the present order cannot stand, also bears an alternative vision for the future: seek the Living Presence, seek good and not evil that you may live. Burdened and energized, he leaves his flock behind and sets out for Beth El to bring God's word. The shepherd of Tekoa heads north in the name of the Shepherd of Israel.

Amos embodies the qualities found in all the writing prophets in the Hebrew Bible.[2] The prophets are people who are imbued with God's love for creation and consequent passion for justice. The encounter with this love and concern brings forth from the prophet the courage to face what others turn away from—the unsustainability of a society that oppresses the poor. At the same time, the soaring possibilities present in God's loving attention to the world fires the prophet with the imaginative power to present the people with an alternative, life-giving future. Engagement with divine love, courage to condemn oppression, and imagination to envision an alternative future are three qualities that define the prophetic experience.

These qualities arose in the biblical prophets in response to the events of their day. The historical period of the prophets, from around 740 to 520 BCE, was a time of shattering social crisis and political instability that ultimately led to the destruction of both Israel and Judah.[3] During those two centuries, the small farmers in Israel and Judah, who had been the backbone of Israelite society, were increasingly losing their hereditary holdings to large landowners. The imposition of heavy taxes and harsh debtor laws allowed wealthy elites to seize the lands of small farmers who often then became indentured servants. The king, rather than protecting the common people, profited from the creation of ever-larger estates. Premonarchic Israel had been a relatively egalitarian society. By the eighth century BCE, a small class of large landowners and merchants had set themselves above the small farmers who had been the backbone of Israelite society.[4]

While these elites treated the impoverishment of common laborers as an acceptable condition of society, the prophets would not turn aside from this human suffering. Seeing the situation as if through God's eyes and carrying God's word, the prophets proclaimed that economic injustice

---

[2]   The writing prophets are the prophets whose words are recorded in the Hebrew Scriptures in books bearing their names. In one of those books, Isaiah, contemporary scholars have identified two separate prophets, and perhaps three.

[3]   All the writing prophets, except Malachi, ministered between 740 and 520 BCE.

[4]   Rainer Albertz, *A History of Israelite Religion in the Old Testament Period*, trans. John Bowden, vol. 1 (Louisville, KY: Westminster/John Knox Press, 1994), 159–63; Joshua Berman, *Created Equal* (New York: Oxford University Press, 2008), 87.

and the oppression of the poor were intolerable and abhorrent. The growing inequality was, in the prophetic perspective, an existential crisis. For the prophets, the very identity of the people, the essence of their covenant with God, was to embody an alternative to oppressive imperial systems, to become a more just and equitable society than the neighboring kingdoms. From this perspective, both kingdoms, Judah and Israel, had utterly failed in their covenanted mission as they increasingly mirrored the stratified, oppressive, and unjust regimes of nearby Canaanite kingdoms as well as more distant great empires.

Animated by God's love for creation and God's passion for justice, the prophets confronted the princes and the privileged, decrying the greed and insensitivity of these elites. Amos, the first of the writing prophets, was unstinting in his condemnation:

> They sold the righteous for silver and the poor for a pair of shoes. They pant after the dust of the earth on the head of the poor, and turn aside the way of the humble. . . . Hear this word, you cows of Bashan, who are in the mountain of Samaria, who oppress the poor, who crush the needy, who say to their masters, Bring, that we may drink! . . . You trample upon the poor, and you take from him exactions of wheat, you have built houses of cut stone, but you shall not dwell in them; you have planted pleasant vineyards, but you shall not drink wine of them. (2:6–7; 4:1; 5:11)

Isaiah and Micah were contemporaries of Amos. While Amos confronted the king and the high priest in the northern kingdom of Israel at the height of its wealth and regional dominance, Isaiah and Micah condemned the arrogant elites in Judah, the southern kingdom, at the apex of its power.

> Your princes are rebellious, and companions of thieves; everyone loves bribes, and follows after rewards; they judge not the orphans neither does the cause of the widow reach them. (Isa 1:23)

> Hear, I beg you, O heads of Jacob, and you princes of the house of Israel: Is it not for you to know justice? You who hate the good and love the evil, who tear off their skin from them and their flesh from off their bones. (Mic 3:1–2)

These prophets also brought God's judgment on the human judges who responded to the bribes of the wealthy and failed to protect the vulnerable and the poor:

For I know your many transgressions, and your mighty sins; you who afflict the just, you who take a bribe, and turn aside the poor at the gate.⁵ (Amos 5:12)

Their heads judge for bribes. (Mic 3:11)

Amos, Isaiah, Micah, and the rest of the biblical prophets did not shrink from bringing God's word against the priests in the holy Temple, priests who assuaged the guilt of the privileged and ignored the suffering of the poor. The prophets proclaimed that the Temple sacrifices were meaningless in the face of injustice, or worse than meaningless. The rituals were a threat to the extent that they falsely assured the people of God's blessing during a time of great peril.

When Amos journeyed to Beth El, he confronted Amaziah, the high priest of his day. Amos faced Amaziah and said,

And the high places of Isaac shall be desolate, and the sanctuaries of Israel shall be laid waste; and I will rise against the house of Jeroboam [the Israelite king] with the sword. (7:9)

The high priest, confident in the overwhelming power of his position, attempted to dismiss the prophet:

Amaziah said to Amos, O you seer, go, flee away to the land of Judah, and there eat bread, and prophesy there. But never again prophesy at Beth-El; for it is the king's sanctuary, and the royal house. (Amos 7:12–13)

Amos would not be dismissed. He stood firm in the word that God had sent him to deliver. He spoke personal judgment against Amaziah, who sought to banish the prophetic word and to exempt the king's sanctuary from the justice of God:

Then answered Amos, and said to Amaziah . . . the Living Presence took me while I followed the flock, and the Living Presence said to me: Go, prophesy to my people Israel. And, therefore, hear the word of the Living Presence; You say, Do not prophesy against Israel, and do not preach against the house of Isaac. Therefore, thus says the Living Presence; Your wife shall be a harlot in the city, and your sons and your daughters shall fall by

---

⁵ Judicial sessions often took place at the city gates.

the sword, and your land shall be divided by line; and you shall die in an unclean land; and Israel shall surely go to exile away from its land. (7:14–17)

In Judah, the southern kingdom, Micah also denounced the collusion of the priests in the oppression of the people. He dismissed the belief that Temple rituals could save the kingdom while the poor continued to suffer. Micah was the first prophet to proclaim the destruction of Jerusalem and the holy Temple:

Their priests teach for hire, and their prophets divine for money; yet they lean upon the Living Presence, and say: Is not the Living Presence among us? No evil can come upon us! Therefore, because of you, Zion shall be plowed like a field, and Jerusalem shall become heaps of rubble, and the mountain of the house like the high places of the forest. (3:11–12)

Isaiah was equally dismissive of the belief that ritual sacrifice could protect the nation from the consequences of social injustice. Making a deeply disturbing association, he equated the priestly rituals to the abominations of Sodom and Gomorrah.

Hear the word of the Living Presence, rulers of Sodom; give ear to the Torah of our God, people of Gomorrah. To what purpose is the multitude of your sacrifices to me? said the Living Presence; I am full of the burnt offerings of rams, and the fat of fed beasts; and I delight not in the blood of bulls, or of lambs, or of male goats. When you come to appear before me, who has required this at your hand, to trample my courts? Bring no more vain offerings; incense of abomination they are to me; as for new moons and sabbaths, and the calling of assemblies, I cannot bear iniquity along with solemn meeting. Your new moons and your appointed feasts my soul hates; they are a trouble to me; I am weary of enduring them. (1:10–14)

In words that are as challenging in our time as they certainly were in his day, Isaiah proclaimed what God desires: "This is the fast I desire: to unlock fetters of wickedness and untie the cords of the yoke, to let the oppressed go free, to break off every yoke" (58:6). God does not want ritual fasting. God wants *liberation* from oppressive societal structures. God calls upon people, in Isaiah's time and in ours, "to share your bread with the hungry and to take the wretched poor into your home" (Isa 58:7).

In response to the prophets' impassioned pleas and repeated critique, the kings, large landholders, and priests made a fateful choice. Instead of seeking to address the injustices in the society, they did everything in their power to hold on to the status quo. As Walter Brueggemann highlights in his influential work *The Prophetic Imagination*, the royal regime rejected any possibility of a more just and inclusive society. The political elites, supported by the priests, maintained that the current order was the only alternative: God in heaven had blessed the present state of society. As Micah describes, "They lean upon the Living Presence, and say: Is not the Living Presence among us? No evil can come upon us!" (Mic 3:11).

The prophets arose in Israel and Judah to shatter complacency. They sought to alert the people to the disaster that the elites were courting. They brought God's judgment against the excessive wealth and privilege of the princes and the priests and the cruelties they inflicted on the poor. They proclaimed that an oppressive society will inevitably crumble; neither the privileged few nor their wealth would endure.

God's fearsome warnings were not the entirety of the prophetic testimony. The prophets also spoke of a God who yearned to forgive. They envisioned a pardoning God beckoning to a potentially repentant people. The prophet Jeremiah, living in Jerusalem shortly before the destruction, held out the possibility of averting the disaster through repentance. "Perhaps the House of Judah . . . will return from their wicked ways, and I will pardon their iniquity" (36:3).[6]

Isaiah articulated a detailed process of repentance and forgiveness:

Wash yourselves, make yourselves clean; put away the evil of your doings from before my eyes; cease to do evil. Learn to do well; seek judgment, relieve the oppressed, judge the orphan, plead for the widow. Come now, and let us reason together, said the Living Presence; though your sins be as scarlet, they shall be as white as snow; though they be red like crimson, they shall be as wool. If you are willing and listen well, you shall eat the good of the land. (1:16–19)

In other passages, the prophets went even further and envisioned God working to support the people's repentance. Jeremiah articulated God's promise that God will act to bring about a change of heart in the people: "I will give them a heart to know me, that I am the Living Presence; and they shall be my people, and I will be their God; for they shall return to me with their whole heart" (24:7).

---

[6] Translation from *Tanakh* (Philadelphia: Jewish Publication Society, 1985).

Alongside forgiveness, the prophets also offered the people a hopeful vision of an alternative future. As in the case of Amos, each prophet articulated a vision of a transformed, more inclusive, and just society. Micah foresaw a day when the people had renewed their sacred covenant with God, and had returned to pursuing justice in their communities. On that future day,

> Many nations shall come, and say, Come, and let us go up to the mountain of the Living Presence, and to the house of the God of Jacob; and he will teach us of his ways, and we will walk in his paths; for the Torah shall go forth from Zion, and the word of the Living Presence from Jerusalem. (Mic 4:2)

The most beautiful vision of the renewed covenant is found in the words of the northern kingdom prophet Hosea, a younger contemporary of Amos. Hosea is the prophet who offers the most intimate image of God's longing for Israel and God's anguish in the face of the people's betrayal. God had instructed Hosea to marry a "wife of harlotry" (Hos 1:2) so that he would know the profound hurt that Israel's infidelity brought upon God. God's pain was as deep as the most profound human agony. Yet for both Hosea and God, love and hope persist. Despite Hosea's personal suffering and his empathy for God's suffering, the prophet could envision a time when God and Israel would be reunited. Employing the evocative imagery of a new marriage rebinding God and Israel, Hosea brings the people these words of hope and healing:

> Therefore, behold, I will allure her, and bring her into the wilderness, and speak tenderly to her. And I will give her vineyards from there, and the valley of Achor for a gate of hope; and she shall sing there, as in the days of her youth, and as in the day when she came out of the land of Egypt. And it shall be at that day, says the Living Presence, that you shall call me My husband. . . . And I will betroth you to me forever; I will betroth you to me in righteousness, and in judgment, and in grace, and in mercies. I will betroth you to me in faithfulness; and you shall know the Living Presence. (2:16–18, 21–22)[7]

Amos, Isaiah, Micah, and Hosea are just four of the fifteen prophets whose words have been preserved in Scripture. Each of these prophets possessed extraordinary vision. Perceiving their world as if through

---

[7] 2:14–16, 19–20 in the KJV.

God's eyes, these prophets were able to maintain a sustained focus on the suffering of the poor, to see the disaster that would inevitably come in the wake of profound, endemic injustice. At the same time, lifted by divine inspiration, each prophet possessed the moral imagination to transcend the brokenness of his[8] own day and envision an alternative society. Even in the midst of crisis and imminent disaster, the prophets could see an inclusive economic and social order in which all beings would flourish.

These then are the three qualities inherent in every prophet and in the prophetic stream: an encounter with divine love and concern for the world, courage to name oppression, and moral imagination to articulate an alternative future.

The rise of the prophets at their moment in history marks the emergence of the prophetic stream into a consciously articulated human word. Lifted up by this stream of liberating energy, carried by the waters of transcendent possibilities, these prophets articulated the transforming power of the prophetic stream in words that would animate liberation struggles worldwide, millennia into the future.

The Bible presents this liberating flow in several forms—narrative, statute, and prophetic word—to help people who study the text perceive the movement of the prophetic stream beyond the Bible, most especially in their personal and public lives. While most of us are not yet prophets, we also know the presence of a great love, a love that includes the entire world. Awakened by that love, we too are aggrieved in the face of human oppression. A voice within us calls out, "This is wrong and cannot stand." We yearn for a world in which all can flourish. Fueled by our own particular yearning, we occasionally entertain visions for how some small part of our world can be liberated into greater possibility. Moral imagination lives in us, even though we may not give our imaginings the attention that they deserve.

The biblical prophetic stream comes along to awaken our anguish, to lift up our yearnings, and to fuel our moral imagination. I have written this book to articulate the work of this stream in the Bible and to explore how it is flowing in our personal and collective lives.

---

[8] The Bible mentions five prophetesses: Miriam, Deborah, Isaiah's wife, Huldah, and Noadiah. In the Talmud, Megillah 14a, the Rabbis identify seven prophetesses: Sarah, Miriam, Deborah, Hannah, Abigail, Huldah, and Esther.

CHAPTER 2

The Prophets and Deuteronomy

A SOCIETAL REVOLUTION

Beginning in the eighth century BCE, for two hundred years, the Hebrew prophets revealed God's judgment and God's vision to the people Israel.[1] During those two centuries, the prophetic stream in the Hebrew Bible attained its full liberating power, like an underground river coming to the surface and bursting forth out of the earth. This stream was the wellspring of a societal revolution.

The revolutionary and liberating effect of prophetic thought may be seen most clearly when the Prophets and the book of Deuteronomy, roughly contemporary works, are placed side by side.[2] Much like the Prophets, Deuteronomy emerged in response to the external and internal threats that confronted the kingdom of Judah. As in the Prophets, the prophetic stream flows mightily in Deuteronomy.

Most biblical scholars date the initial writing of Deuteronomy to middle and late seventh century BCE, during the reign of King Josiah, in the middle of the prophetic age. Josiah was a child when his father, King Amon, was assassinated in 640 BCE. The child-king Josiah had

---

[1]   The first prophet, Amos, appeared in Israel in the middle of the eighth century BCE. The last three prophets—Haggai, Zechariah, and Malachi—ministered to the people after the return from Babylonian exile around the year 535 BCE. Of those latter three prophets, Malachi lived about a century after his peers, in the last third of the fifth century BCE.

[2]   Biblical scholars still vigorously debate the dating of Deuteronomy. Some scholars contend that the earliest form of Deuteronomy was written as early as the eighth century. Many scholars date the development of the book from late in the seventh century BCE. Recently, the scholarly consensus is moving toward dating the completion of Deuteronomy to the Persian Period, after the return from the exile late in the fifth century.

been installed in power by a traditionalist group of scribes, priests, and other elites who opposed the assimilationist policies of Josiah's father and long-reigning grandfather, King Manasseh. Manasseh had alienated these traditionalists by becoming a vassal of the Assyrian Empire and by introducing Assyrian gods into the Temple. The young King Josiah did not disappoint the traditionalist group that had supported his rise to power. He cleansed the Temple of the foreign gods that his grandfather and father had embraced and went on to initiate a physical renovation of the Temple itself. During the renovation, the high priest "found" a sacred scroll in the Temple.[3] Upon hearing the words of the scroll, King Josiah was aghast, "for our fathers have not listened to the words of this book" (2 Kgs 22:13)—that is, have not kept the civil statutes and religious practices set forth in the scroll. The young king immediately became even more vigorous in his religious reforms, based on the content of the scroll.[4]

The reformation that King Josiah embarked on after reading the scroll paralleled many of the laws and practices found in Deuteronomy, leading contemporary scholars to think that the scroll found in the Temple was an early form of Deuteronomy. For example, Josiah assembled the people to hear the scroll read and to renew the covenant set forth in the scroll, an act directly reminiscent of the Deuteronomic account describing Moses convening the people to recovenant with God at the end of their journey in the wilderness.[5] In words that again evoke Deuteronomy, Josiah committed to keep the provisions of the covenant "with all his heart and all his soul" (see 2 Kgs 23:25; Deut 6:5). The actual reforms instituted by King Josiah correspond, almost without exception, to the provisions of Deuteronomy.[6] Unfortunately, King Josiah's reformation came to an abrupt end when the king was killed attempting to resist the advance of Pharaoh Necho at Megiddo in 609 BCE.[7]

After King Josiah's death, Deuteronomy continued to evolve during the sixth century BCE, a span of time that included the mounting Babylonian threat to Judah and ultimately the Babylonian destruction

---

[3] Most scholars think that the scroll was likely written during Josiah's reign to be "found" in the Temple.

[4] 2 Kgs 22:1–23:24.

[5] Deut 29:1–2.

[6] Mark E. Biddle, *Deuteronomy* (Macon, GA: Smyth and Helwys Publishing, 2003), 2–3. For further discussion on the compositional history of Deuteronomy, see also Richard Nelson, *Deuteronomy* (Louisville, KY: Westminster John Knox Press, 2002), 6–7, and Duane Christensen, *A Song of Power and The Power of Song* (Winona Lake, IN: Eisenbrauns, 1993), 3–61.

[7] 2 Kgs 23:29–30.

of the Temple and the exile to Babylon in 586 BCE. This was a period of significant political instability and imperial devastation. The authors of Deuteronomy, some of whom witnessed the Babylonian destruction and the exile that followed, were all too familiar with the brutality of foreign imperial power, as well as with the injustice and abuse of power inside Judah. These biblical scribes had good reason to critique both imperial power abroad and the power of kings, princes, and judges at home.

Thus, Deuteronomy and the testimony of the prophets share a similar outlook: they were working with the same existential crisis. They responded to the political and religious disintegration, and ultimately the destruction, of the kingdoms of Israel and Judah. Both literary creations asserted that corruption and injustice within Judean society had brought on the devastation. The growing gap between the rich and the poor and the assimilation of foreign gods had assisted the invasion of imperial power by weakening the kingdoms from within. The kingship and the Temple had failed the people and had met with destruction.

The depth of the catastrophe and the bleak despair that followed must have made it seem to the surviving Judeans that their communal journey was at an end; there was no way forward. For the people of Judah, the Temple in Jerusalem had been more than a religious institution. The Temple was the house of God and the embodiment of God's promise to preserve the people on the land. The sacrifices in the Temple were the ritual that purified the people and the land, clearing the way for God's blessings to flow upon them. How could God have allowed the savage barbarians to destroy God's holy Temple? As the people were taken away in exile in 586 BCE, they had lost the central symbol and ritual practice that bound them together as a people and that connected them to God. Their grief is preserved in psalm:

> By the rivers of Babylon, there we sat down, we also wept, when we remembered Zion. We hung our lyres on the willows in its midst. For there those who carried us away captive required of us a song; and those who tormented us required of us mirth, saying, Sing us one of the songs of Zion. How shall we sing the song of the Living Presence in a foreign land? (Ps 137:1–4)

This great devastation presented both an existential and an institutional crisis to the surviving community, in Babylon and later among the exiles who returned to Judah. In the shadow of the fall of the Temple and the kingship, society could no longer be ordered as it had been. The institutions that supported political stability and religious practice had been destroyed.

In the despair of this historical moment, a remarkable thing happened. The words of the prophets and Deuteronomy were collected, held sacred, and given a new role among those who returned from the exile. The texts were used to help the people understand the devastation that had befallen them. Not only that, but, with astonishing creative power in the midst of a great political and religious void, these texts envisioned a way forward. The prophets and the authors of Deuteronomy stepped into the hollowness of profound loss and articulated an attainable future, a radically new vision for Judean society.[8]

When Deuteronomy and the prophetic witness are recognized as parallel efforts responding to the same existential crisis, several common elements emerge. Both Deuteronomy and the prophets are fundamentally disturbed by, and seek to remedy, the growing gap between the rich and the poor. In both texts we find elaborate exhortations, and in Deuteronomy legal statutes, on behalf of the poor, debtors, indentured servants, immigrants, widows, orphans, and animals. Concern for the poor is expressed in terms of God's special care for the widow, orphan, and stranger.

All the Hebrew prophets focus on these vulnerable people in society. In this passage from Jeremiah, the prophet links the future of the community to the treatment of the poor:

> For if you thoroughly amend your ways and your doings; If you thoroughly do justice between a man and his neighbor; If you oppress not the stranger, the orphan, and the widow, and shed not innocent blood in this place, nor walk after other gods to your harm; Then will I make you dwell in this place, in the land that I gave to your fathers, forever and ever. (7:5–7)

---

[8] The early prophets, men such as Amos, Hosea, Isaiah, and Micah, did not witness the destruction of the kingdoms. But they had seen the profound injustice of society and had foreseen the likely destruction. The prophets Jeremiah, Ezekiel, and Second Isaiah experienced the exile. The latter prophets, Haggai, Zechariah, and Malachi, labored to renew the devastated community after the return from Babylon. The book of Deuteronomy evolved during this same period of collapse and renewal. All these writings, the prophets and Deuteronomy, were ultimately collected sometime after the return to Judah. These texts were brought together to help a devastated community redefine and reconstitute itself. The second book of Maccabees states that the fifth-century Judean governor Nehemiah "found a library and collected books about the kings and prophets." (2:13–15). The book of Nehemiah describes how Ezra the Scribe read the "Torah of Moses" before the people at around the same time (8:1–3) See also Joseph Blenkinsopp, "The Formation of the Hebrew Canon: Isaiah as a Test Case," in Lee McDonald and James Sanders, eds., *The Canon Debate* (Peabody, MA: Hendrickson, 2002), chap. 4.

In Deuteronomy, in eleven distinct passages, the text reminds the people of God's concern for the widow, orphan, and stranger, including this passage: "[God] executes the judgment of the orphan and widow, and loves the stranger, giving him food and garment. Love you therefore the stranger; for you were strangers in the land of Egypt" (10:18–19). Deuteronomy's focus on the needs of the poor is again evident in the wording of the Fourth Commandment:

> In it [the Sabbath] you shall not do any work, you, nor your son, nor your daughter, nor your manservant, nor your maidservant, nor your ox, nor your ass, nor any of your cattle, nor your stranger who is inside your gates; that your manservant and your maidservant may rest as well as you. (5:14)

Deuteronomy also introduces the sabbatical year, radical new legislation that redistributes wealth to address the needs of the poor. Every seventh year indentured servants are to be set free, debts forgiven, and the land left to go fallow. The poor were permitted to eat the produce of the land.[9]

In the political realm, Deuteronomy shared the prophet's suspicion of the king, setting in place statutes to limit royal privilege and power. Instead of aggrandizing himself with horses, wives, and wealth, Deuteronomy requires the king to spend his time writing and reading the Torah "that his heart not be lifted above his brothers" (17:20).

This heightened concern for the disadvantaged is the most salient common element found in Deuteronomy and the Prophets. But the radical common vision of these texts goes deeper. The prevailing social concern in both Deuteronomy and the prophetic writings is rooted in an alternative worldview, in new assumptions that shape the social consciousness of these texts. These revolutionary categories of thought would, in time, radically reorient every aspect of Israelite society. Like the movement of a great river wearing away mountains and irrigating the altered landscape, this new thinking would, in time, bring down structures of domination and nurture more inclusive social relations. This worldview is the "new thinking" that Abraham Heschel sought in *The Prophets*, his book addressing the crisis of the 1930s.

This alternative worldview has vast power—the power to reshape a society—as it did over the centuries in postexilic Judah. In like manner, it has the power to reshape and bring healing to much that ails contemporary societies, especially those societies where the Hebrew Scriptures are held sacred.

---

9   Deut 15.

Two interrelated assertions about life and society pulse at the heart of the radically new worldview put forward in the Prophets and Deuteronomy. First, the people Israel, and by implication all people, are on a liberation journey with God. Second, the core dynamic of the liberation journey is learning to engage in increasingly mutual relationship. The next two chapters explore these two assertions.

CHAPTER 3

The Liberation Journey

People commonly think that the central story of the Torah is the people Israel's journey to the promised land. Not quite so! In both the Prophets and in Deuteronomy, the concluding book of the Torah, the focus is on the journey *toward* the promised land. The dynamics of the journey and the direction of the journey—out of slavery and toward freedom—are more important than arriving at the destination.

In Deuteronomy, the emphasis on the journey itself, and not its destination, is evident in the narrative arc. In the text, Moses recounts in some detail the journey out of Egypt and through the wilderness. At the conclusion of Deuteronomy, the Torah ends and Moses dies in the wilderness. This surprising and even disturbing ending keeps the focus on the journey, not on the arrival in the promised land.

The emphasis on the journey is also clear in the rituals that Deuteronomy enjoins. In expectation of the day when the people will eventually settle into the promised land, Deuteronomy instructs the people to continue to walk the exodus journey, physically and spiritually. Three times a year, at the time of the great festivals—Passover, Shavuot, and Sukkot—the people are to make a pilgrimage to "the place that God will choose" to appear before the Living Presence.[1] Generations after the settlement in the land, Deuteronomy requires the people to get on their feet and take to the road, to renew the journey with God each spring (Passover), summer (Shavuot), and fall (Sukkot).

At each of these three festivals, the people are instructed to relive some aspect of the liberation journey. In the spring, for Passover, Deuteronomy requires the people to relive the exodus, annually recalling the story of liberation while eating the bread of affliction. The people are to recall the exodus as if they had personally experienced the liberation.

---

[1] Deut 16:2, 6, 7, 15, 16.

Hence, in Deuteronomy when Moses instructs the people to observe the Passover rituals, addressing a population that had not experienced the exodus, he adjures them to eat "the bread of affliction . . . that you may remember the day when you came out of the land of Egypt all the days of your life" (16:3). The Passover ritual is not a reenactment done to honor a memory; it is participation in an ongoing journey.

Seven weeks after the festival of participation in the exodus, at the end of the spring rains, the people are instructed to set out once again on a pilgrimage. At this season of Shavuot, the festival of first fruits, the people are required to bring the first fruits of their harvest in a basket to the Temple, to give the basket to the priest and then to retell the liberation story:

> And the priest shall take the basket from your hand, and set it down before the altar of the Living Presence your God. And you shall speak and say before the Living Presence your God, A wandering Aramean was my father, and he went down into Egypt, and sojourned there with a few, and became there a nation, great, mighty, and populous. The Egyptians dealt ill with us, and afflicted us, and laid upon us hard slavery; And when we cried to the Living Presence God of our fathers, the Living Presence heard our voice, and looked on our affliction, and our labor, and our oppression; And the Living Presence brought us out of Egypt with a mighty hand, and with an outstretched arm, and with great awesomeness, and with signs, and with wonders; And he has brought us to this place, and has given us this land, a land that flows with milk and honey. And now, behold, I have brought the first fruits of the land, which you, Living Presence, have given me. (Deut 26:4–10)

Finally, for Sukkot, the fall harvest festival, Deuteronomy instructs the people to celebrate the festival outside in flimsy harvest booths, reminiscent of the booths they dwelt in during their journey in the wilderness.[2] Sukkot, the festival of fulfillment and thanksgiving, was not to be celebrated in the security of home, but rather in a temporary dwelling like those that the Israelites inhabited during the journey across the wilderness. The people are instructed to find fulfillment in a temporary structure and to give thanks for the journey, a journey with God.

The Hebrew prophets also place the people's present experience in the context of the exodus journey. In imagery and rich poetic verse, the

---

[2] Deut 16:13.

prophets remind the people of God's liberating deeds, delivering them from Egypt and covenanting with them in the wilderness:

When Israel was a child, then I loved him, and called my son out of Egypt. (Hos 11:1)

The Living Presence of hosts shall stir up a scourge for him . . . as his rod was upon the sea, so shall he lift it up as he did in Egypt. (Isa 10:26)

Go and cry in the ears of Jerusalem, saying, Thus said the Living Presence; I remember you, the devotion of your youth, your love like a bride, when you went after me in the wilderness, in a land that was not sown. Israel is holy to the Living Presence, and the first fruits of his produce . . . And they did not say, Where is the Living Presence who brought us up out of the land of Egypt, who led us through the wilderness? (Jer 2:2–3, 6)

And I caused them to go out of the land of Egypt, and brought them into the wilderness. And I gave them my statutes, and made my judgments known to them, by whose observance man shall live. (Ezek 20:10–11)

Addressing a people who had lost their way, the prophets offer a historical perspective on the present crisis. They envision the people's future as a renewal of the age-old liberation journey with God, a return to the wilderness passage of their ancestors. At a time of crisis, says the prophet,

A voice cries, Prepare in the wilderness the way of the Living Presence, make straight in the desert a highway for our God. (Isa 40:3)

Therefore, behold, the days come, says the Living Presence, that it shall no more be said, As the Living Presence lives, who brought the people of Israel out of the land of Egypt; but, as the Living Presence lives, who brought the people of Israel from the land of the north, and from all the lands where he had driven them; and I will bring them back to their land that I gave to their fathers. (Jer 16:14–15)[3]

---

[3] A number of other prophetic passages envision the people's current hardship as a stage in the exodus journey. See Amos 2:10; Hos 13:5; Isa 43:14–21; 44:26–28; 63:11–16; Jer 23:7–8; 31:1–6, 30–34; 32:36–41.

This reimagining of the liberation journey is part of the revolution in thought that was developed in Deuteronomy and the Prophets in the shadow of the impending destruction of the Temple or in its immediate aftermath. To help the people integrate and survive that great disaster, Deuteronomy and the Prophets offer the people a fundamental shift in communal self-understanding, a renewed emphasis on the exodus journey. The king and the Temple had failed to provide justice or physical security for the people. In response to the inevitable collapse of these great Israelite institutions, the prophets and the Deuteronomic authors step into the breach and offer a new way forward. The key to this new way is a reconceptualization of the exodus from an event in the past to an ever-present process, an ongoing journey, a liberation journey with God.

In this visionary reformation of Israelite society, the people's lived relationship with God—keeping God's statutes—replaces the temple sacrifices as the central religious practice. Hence, in addition to highlighting the exodus journey, both Deuteronomy and the Prophets move to minimize the importance of the temple and ritual sacrifice.

In Deuteronomy, the text restricts sacrifice to a single site that God will choose. No longer will people be able to offer sacrifice at a local temple. As the biblical scholar Jeffrey Tigay notes, "The law must have been extraordinarily disruptive to popular religion since most of the public lived far from the Temple and could not often travel there, and would have to decrease, delay or forgo vital services that it provided to them."[4] Maimonides likewise held that the centralization of the cult in Jerusalem served to minimize the role of sacrifice in the people's religious lives. Two modern biblical scholars concluded that the central purpose of the book of Deuteronomy itself was to curtail the Temple cult.[5]

Deuteronomy both limits access to the Temple and makes the people's liberation journey a central aspect of the sacrificial cult. Most of the references to the cult and sacrifice in Deuteronomy relate to the three pilgrimage festivals—Passover, Shavuot, and Sukkot—times in which the people take to the road to renew their exodus journey.

The prophets also minimized and even critiqued the role of the Temple. In the following passages, Amos and Jeremiah express the prophetic judgment on the sacrificial cults:

> I hate, I despise your feast days, and I will not smell the sacrifices of your solemn assemblies. Though you offer me burnt offerings and meal offerings, I will not accept them; nor will I regard the

---

[4] Jeffrey Tigay, *Deuteronomy* (Philadelphia: Jewish Publication Society, 1996), 459.

[5] Ibid., 460.

peace offerings of your fat beasts. Take away from me the noise of your songs; for I will not listen to the melody of your lutes. But let justice roll down like waters, and righteousness like a mighty stream. Did you bring me sacrifices and offerings during the forty years in the wilderness, O house of Israel? (Amos 5:21–25)

For I did not speak to your fathers, nor charge them in the day that I brought them out of the land of Egypt, concerning burnt offerings or sacrifices; But this thing I charged them, saying, listen to my voice, and I will be your God, and you shall be my people; and walk in all the ways that I have charged you, that it may be well with you. (Jer 7:22–23†)[6]

With the exception of the prophet Ezekiel, the prophets hardly ever mention the priests and the Temple cult, except to condemn the priests for participating in injustice.[7]

They have become fat and sleek; indeed, they overpass the deeds of the wicked; they judge not the cause of the orphans, that they may prosper; and they do not judge the right of the needy. Shall I not punish for these things? says the Living Presence; shall not my soul be avenged on such a nation as this? An appalling and

---

[6] I use the word "charge" for the Hebrew word מצוה (*mitzvah*) instead of the more common "command" because "charge" carries the sense of entrusting someone with a task. "Charge" implies a reciprocal relationship that honors the independent agency of the one charged, whereas "command" implies the power to make someone do something. In the context of Deuteronomy and the Prophets, "charge" more faithfully carries the relational intent than "commandment."

[7] The prophets Ezekiel, Zechariah, and Jeremiah envisioned a future Temple, but these references to the Temple are notable exceptions in prophetic writings. Ezekiel, both a priest and a prophet, exhibits an exceptional interest in the Temple, foreseeing in detail both its desecration and its renewal. He offers an elaborate vision of the Temple rebuilt (chaps. 41–42). Zechariah, who like Ezekiel was likely a priest, and who lived in Judah at the time of the rebuilding of the Temple (521–516 BCE), also mentions the Temple (chap. 6). Jeremiah, in his "Book of Consolation," briefly mentions both the kingly line of David and the priests (33:14–17). Walter Brueggemann writes that the Davidic dynasty is mentioned in Jeremiah, and I would add the priests as well, because "God's good inclination toward the dynasty and family of David belongs to Israel's central stock of promises. It is therefore included here among the many ways in which Israel voices its hope. Indeed, this chapter seems to want to collect all Israel's possible ways of speaking of God's good future" (*A Commentary on Jeremiah* [Grand Rapids: Eerdmans, 1998], 318).

horrible thing is committed in the land; The prophets prophesy falsely, and the priests bear rule by their means. . . . For from the least of them even to the greatest of them every one is greedy for gain; and from the prophet even to the priest every one deals falsely. (Jer 5:28–30; 6:13)

Hear this, O priests; and listen, O house of Israel; and give ear, O house of the king; for yours is the judgment, because you have been a snare on Mizpah, and a net spread upon Tabor. And the revolters are deep dyed in slaughter, and I am rejected by them. (Hos 5:1–2)

In place of the Temple sacrifices, the prophets focused on the people's journey with God.

And I will bring you out from the peoples, and will gather you out of the countries where you are scattered, with a mighty hand, and with a stretched-out arm, and with fury poured out. And I will bring you into the wilderness of the people and there will I remonstrate with you face-to-face. (Ezek 20:34–35)

In response to the collapse of venerated institutions, Deuteronomy and the Prophets limited the importance of those institutions and offered the people a new way of thinking, placing the exodus, now understood as ongoing liberation journey with God, at the center of the people's cultural identity and religious practice. In the same imaginative interpretation with which Deuteronomy and the Prophets reconstrue the exodus as an ongoing process, these innovative texts also deepen the understanding of the exodus, portraying liberation as an inner as well as an outer journey. In these biblical texts, the essential dynamic of the liberation journey is reconfigured from a physical outward journey to now also include an inward journey, an internal liberation journey, a learning journey with God.

The internal learning journey includes all the people. While the prophets specifically condemn the political, religious, and economic elites for oppressing the poor, they do not require change only from the elites, or conclude that the poor are without responsibility. They hold all Israel responsible for the corrupted state of the society. They call upon all Israel to learn from God and to change their ways. In this social vision, the well-being of the society is not founded on the beneficence of the elites but on the learning of all the people, elites and poor alike: "And the Living Presence charged me [Moses] at that time to teach you [Israel] statutes and ordinances, that you might do them in the land that you are crossing into to possess" (Deut 4:14†).

Deuteronomy and the Prophets teach that learning stands at the heart of Israel's relationship with God. Teaching and learning are essential to civic well-being. This is an extraordinary, creative reimagining of how a community can flourish. Instead of attributing the iniquities of the society to the sinful nature of the people, these texts perceive the injustice and idolatry of Israelite society as a sign of a failure to learn, an indication of a need for more teaching. Sinful behavior is not innate to people's nature, but rather the product of bad learning. We can see this understanding in the oft-quoted verse, "They shall beat their swords into plowshares, and their spears into pruning hooks; nation shall not lift up sword against nation, nor shall they learn war anymore" (Isa 2:4). In Isaiah's vision, the violence of warfare is a learned behavior and not an inherent flaw in human nature.

God's faith in the people's inherent capacity to learn is the foundation of Israel's liberation journey. The path of liberation is a learning way. In the long course of this journey, Israel will inevitably go astray, get lost, run amuck. But ultimately God holds faith that Israel will learn and pursue a path that will lead to communal well-being.

The connection between learning and communal well-being is evident throughout Deuteronomy. Time and time again, Moses informs the people that God charged him to "teach" God's ways. In turn, the people are charged to learn Torah (teaching) and to teach it to their children.[8] Most famously, Moses says,

> Hear, O Israel; The Living Presence our God, the Living Presence is one. You shall love the Living Presence your God with all your heart, and with all your soul, and with all your means. These words, which I charge you this day, shall be upon your heart. You shall teach them diligently to your children, and shall speak of them when you sit in your house, and when you walk by the way, and when you lie down, and when you rise up. (Deut 6:4–7†)

Deuteronomy wove the reading of the Torah into the ritual life of the people. Every sabbatical (seventh) year, when the people are gathered in Jerusalem to celebrate Sukkot, the entire Torah shall be read in the presence of all the people.[9]

---

[8] See Deut 4:1, 9, 10, 14; 5:28; 6:1, 7; 11:19; 17:11; 20:18; 24:8; 31:19; 33:10.
[9] Deut 31:10–11.

As set forth in Deuteronomy, the king must have an especially intimate relationship with the Torah. He is charged to write his own copy
of it and to learn from it all the days of his life.

> And it shall be, when he sits upon the throne of his kingdom, that
> he shall write for himself a copy of this Torah in a book from that
> which is before the priests the Levites; And it shall be with him,
> and he shall read in it all the days of his life; that he may learn
> to fear the Living Presence his God, to keep all the words of this
> Torah and these statutes, to do them. (Deut 17:18–19)

The prophets, especially the later prophets, also understand the people's relationship with God as a learning process. In these texts, God
appears as a teacher calling on the people to learn God's ways:[10]

> Learn to do well; seek judgment, relieve the oppressed, judge the
> orphan, plead for the widow. (Isa 1:17)

> Those who erred in spirit shall come to understand, and those
> who murmured shall learn a lesson. (Isa 29:24)

> And many nations shall come, and say, Come, and let us go up to
> the mountain of the Living Presence, and to the house of the God
> of Jacob; and he will teach us of his ways, and we will walk in his
> paths; for the Torah shall go forth from Zion, and the word of the
> Living Presence from Jerusalem. (Mic 4:2)

Out of the crucible of catastrophe, Deuteronomy and the Prophets
brought forth a radical reworking of Israelite tradition, reimagining the
people's communal life as an ongoing liberation journey with God, an
outward physical journey, and an inward learning journey. This fundamental shift of Israelite identity and practice from a devotion to institutions to a commitment to a liberation journey served the people on multiple levels. First, the emphasis on the exodus journey with God enabled
the people to integrate the loss of the king, Temple, and land into their
self-understanding. During and immediately after the Babylonian exile,
the destruction of the Temple and the kingdom must have seemed to
augur the end of Israelite society. The prophetic view, in a breathtaking
exercise of healing imagination, reframed the destruction and exile as

---

[10] See Isa 2:3, 4; 26:9, 10; 28:9; 29:24; Jer 9:19; 10:2; 12:16; 31:33; Ezek
44:23; Mic 4:2, 3; Hab 4:3.

a painful but necessary stage on a journey. On this journey, God had redeemed the people who had suffered in Egypt. So, too, God would deliver the people from Babylonian oppression and exile and bring them back to the land. The prophetic journey enabled the people to recognize and accept the reasons for their great loss and inspired them to raise their eyes and envision a more fruitful future.

Second, the prophetic emphasis on learning and journey presented a trenchant critique of the static worldview of the apparently victorious Babylonian empire. Stability and immutability are the professed currencies of every empire. Life envisioned as a journey is anathema to such currencies. The prophetic message consistently undermined the static imperial worldview, insisting that every empire would fall to God, a God who is ever on the move.

Third, the prophetic and Deuteronomic perspective empowered the people by removing the priests as an intermediary between them and their God. In the prophetic message, God's primary concern is the fidelity of the people, their commitment to learn from God, to walk in God's ways. The people were no longer dependent upon the priests and the Temple institution to receive God's favor. The people could heal their relations with God through their own learning and by their own right actions. In the view of the prophet Isaiah, the people themselves would become as priests by keeping God's ways: "You shall be named priest of the Living Presence; people shall call you servants of our God" (Isa 61:6[†]).

Finally, in shifting the focus from static institutions to the movement of a journey, the prophets offered the people a true insight into the depths of their personal and communal lives, a liberating truth that holds for contemporary lives as well. In the lives of all people, whether three millennia ago or today, when we slow down and quiet our tender hearts, looking deeply into our lives, reflecting on the many roads we have taken, we can see that over time we have walked a meandering path whose coherence is often seen only in hindsight, but a coherent path nonetheless. Looking inside, we witness that certain themes, issues, and longings have been moving inside us, moving us along, sometimes fitfully, over the months and years of our lives. We see that our lives have been, and are, a journey.

In this journey of our lives, it is as if we have been carried along by an inner stream of longing and yearning. Drawn forward by the movement of this stream, we aspire to be more of who we might be. This yearning to transcend present limitations leads us, as it led the Israelites, into new territory, a wilderness in which we might become more than we have been.

This stream of yearning is an aspect of the felt presence of the Infinite One in our finite lives. Deep in our souls, we are touched by a quality of something transcendent, something beyond. Touched ever so gently by the transcendent, we respond with personal aspiration. We yearn to learn, to grow, to become.

It is as if the Holy One whispers inaudibly into a person's ears to stimulate the yearning to leave one's personal Egypt, to leave behind strictures that limit participation in life, and to become who that person can be in the next moment. The Rabbis have a beautiful teaching along these lines. In the midrash[11] we are told that God sends an angel to each blade of grass, an angel that whispers to the green blade, "Grow, grow, grow." So, too, in the human soul: become, become, become. This is the voice of the God whose name is "I will be what I shall be" (Exod 3:14).

A relationship with God or devotion to God is inevitably a journey. How else could it truly be? We humans are finite beings who are graced to be in relation to the Infinite, whose souls are touched by the transcendent. In the depths of this meeting, we humans inevitably aspire to be more than we have been.

In a recent journal entry, I explored my own sense of this journey:

> I woke up at some point in my life, woke up to the somewhat surprising realization that I find myself to be on a journey, a journey that I did not consciously choose, a journey whose real origin I cannot fathom and whose end I cannot perceive. I do have some sense of the direction, but even here the pathway of this journey is most clear in hindsight. Yet the movement along this pathway is the energetic core of who I am. Sometimes I feel drawn on the journey, at other times impelled, often both. In any case, I am deeply energized to take the next step. This journey is truly a mystery to me, but at the same time the journey may be the most real or deeply rooted aspect of my life. I can discern some qualities that consistently remain with me along the path of this journey: curiosity, fascination, creativity, love, relationship, adventure, courage, persistence. While the journey winds and turns, the direction, when I am at my best, always seems to be toward relationship, love, and wholeness.

As I contemplate my life as journey, as I trace where my footsteps have taken me, I see that my journey in the world is a journey into rela-

---

11 Midrash is a genre of rabbinic literature consisting of stories based on biblical texts. The term "midrash" is also used to refer to one such story. The plural of midrash is "midrashim," a term I use later in this book.

tionships: with people; with trees, brooks, mountains, and meadows; with light and dark; with dogs and butterflies; with birdsong and folk song; with all the myriad ways the Infinite is expressed in the finite. While the exact why and wherefore remain a mystery, the direction of my journey is relationship.

A liberation journey inevitably leads into the territory of relations. A journey becomes rich and worthwhile as one comes upon and meets people, places, flora, fauna, art, and the like. A liberation journey implies greater freedom to meet and a greater capacity to respond and be changed in the meeting. In this way, the twin assertions at the core of prophetic thinking are intertwined. For the Prophets and Deuteronomy, relationship—increasingly mutual relationship—is the hallmark of the liberation journey with God. So, let us now look at the development of the second assertion: the core dynamic of the liberation journey is the development of increasingly mutual relationship.

CHAPTER 4

The Way of Relationship

The Prophets and Deuteronomy brought forward the understanding that life is a liberation journey, an understanding that enabled the people to survive the catastrophe of Israel's loss of the land, the king, and the Temple. These texts also define the direction of that journey—toward greater mutual relationship. In exploring the journey toward mutual relationship, the Prophets and Deuteronomy highlight three relational dynamics: covenant, love, and dialogue. Each of these dynamics contributes to the flow of the prophetic stream.

Covenant

The Hebrew Bible is an exploration of the covenant relationship between God and Israel. All the stories and statutes in the Scriptures relate to this covenantal relationship. Deuteronomy and the Prophets are no different than other biblical books in this regard; the covenant remains central. Indeed, in the days of King Josiah, Deuteronomy was called the book of the covenant (2 Kgs 23:2).

While upholding the reality of the covenant, Deuteronomy also needed to change its terms. The traditional covenantal understanding was that God promised to protect Abraham and his descendants, unconditionally and forever. This understanding did not accord with the increasing political instability and vulnerability that Judah faced from the eighth to the sixth centuries BCE. Reflecting the perilous times in which it developed, the covenant in Deuteronomy is neither unconditional nor eternal. Deuteronomy reimagines the covenant as a mutual relationship requiring Israel to perform certain deeds to merit God's favor. In place of God's unconditional promise, Deuteronomy understands that Israel must keep God's way to enjoy the fruits of God's bounty.

The conditional covenant envisioned in Deuteronomy is a more relational pact than the unconditional Abrahamic covenant. God's promises in Deuteronomy are contingent on the people's compliance with God's directives for justice. This conditional covenant requires ongoing dialogue between God and the people. In Deuteronomy God enters a more dialogical relationship with Israel. They are now journeying together.

The prophets also present a conditional covenant in which God's promises are contingent on the standard of justice that the people uphold in their society. This understanding of contingency developed over generations of prophetic ministry, from Amos, Isaiah, and Hosea in the eighth century BCE; to Jeremiah, Ezekiel, and Deutero-Isaiah in the sixth century BCE; to Zechariah and Malachi, who lived among the returnees to Judea in the late sixth and fifth centuries BCE.

The prophet Jeremiah, in particular, warned the people of Judah that God's promise to their forefathers would not protect them against the consequences of injustice. In the course of his ministry, Jeremiah vigorously confronted the false prophet Hananiah, who relied on the earlier understanding of covenant to assure the people that God would certainly bring down their enemy, the Babylonian Empire. Jeremiah saw that Hananiah's assurances put the people in great danger. He condemned Hananiah: "The Living Presence did not send you, and you have assured this people with lies" (Jer 28:15†).

Understanding the covenant to be mutual and contingent, Jeremiah reminded the people that they must keep the covenant in their day or ruin would befall them: "Thus says the Living Presence God of Israel; Cursed be the one who will not listen to the words of this covenant" (Jer 11:3†). When the people did not listen to his words, Jeremiah foretold the destruction of Jerusalem.

The impending devastation was not the end of the story, though. Jeremiah also offered the people a stunning vision of a future time in which the covenant would be renewed:

Behold, the days come, says the Living Presence, that I will make a new covenant with the house of Israel, and with the house of Judah; Not according to the covenant that I made with their fathers in the day that I took them by the hand to bring them out of the land of Egypt; my covenant which they broke, although I was their master, says the Living Presence; But this shall be the covenant that I will make with the house of Israel; After those days, says the Living Presence, I will put my Torah in their inward parts, and write it in their hearts; and will be their God, and they shall be my people. (Jer 30:30–32)

In his vision Jeremiah took another step forward in understanding the mutuality of the covenant. The prophet envisioned a covenant that would be far more intimate than the earlier relationship, which set forth the external behaviors required of Israel. In the new covenant God's teaching would be placed internally in the very fibers of Israel's heart.

Love

The love between God and Israel is the second quality of mutual relationship developed in both Deuteronomy and the Prophets. Deuteronomy is the only place in the Torah where we are repeatedly told that God loves Israel and that Israel is enjoined to love God.[1] In the other four books of the Torah, we find the word "love" used only once to describe the relationship with God. In Deuteronomy, the mutual love between humans and God appears sixteen times, as in these passages:

And now, Israel, what does the Living Presence your God require of you, except to hold the Living Presence your God in awe, to walk in all his ways, and to love him. (Deut 10:12)

He [God] will love you, and bless you, and multiply you; he will also bless the fruit of your womb, and the fruit of your land. (Deut 7:13)

The prophets also proclaim God's love for Israel and, reciprocally, God's longing for Israel's love. As noted earlier, this yearning for Israel is highly developed in the book of Hosea:

And I will betroth you to me forever; I will betroth you to me in righteousness, and in judgment, and in grace, and in mercies. I will betroth you to me in faithfulness; and you shall know the Living Presence. (2:21–22)[2]

Hosea is not alone in proclaiming the love between God and Israel, as seen in the following passages:

In his love and in his pity he redeemed them, and He bore them, and carried them all the days of old. (Isa 63:9).

---

[1] God loves Israel: See Exod 20:6 (Ten Commandments) and Deut 7:7, 13; 10:15. Israel is enjoined to love God: See Deut 5:10; 6:5; 7:9; 10:12; 11:1, 2, 22; 13:14; 19:19; 30:6, 16, 20.

[2] Hos 2:19–20 in the KJV.

The Living Presence has appeared to me, far away, saying, I have loved you with an everlasting love; therefore, I have remained true to you. (Jer 31:2)[3]

And when I passed by you, and looked upon you, behold, your time was the time of love; and I spread my skirt over you, and covered your nakedness; yes, I swore to you, and entered into a covenant with you, says the Living Presence God, and you became mine. (Ezek 16:8)

In the generations immediately before and after the disasters that brought down Israel and Judah, the prophets understood that the people's journey with God could not be sustained by the worship of a distant, commanding God. The people needed a far more intimate and relational connection to God. The prophets responded to the people's need; they brought God's healing word of profound love for Israel. The prophets articulated that the liberation journey is a journey in love, toward love.

Dialogue

Covenant establishes a relationship. Love provides the intimate quality of the relationship. Dialogue is how an intimate relationship evolves from day to day. The Prophets and Deuteronomy both hold up dialogue as an essential aspect of Israel's relationship with God.

A dialogue requires listening on both sides. Deuteronomy and the Prophets emphasize that Israel must listen to God, just as God listens to Israel. The charge "to listen" appears only once in Exodus, Leviticus, and Numbers. In Deuteronomy the injunction "to listen" appears more than a dozen times. For example,

The Living Presence shall greatly bless you in the land which the Living Presence your God is giving you for an inheritance to possess it. Only if you carefully listen to the voice of the Living Presence your God, to take care to do all these charges which I charge you this day. (Deut 15:4–5[†])

And most famously: "Listen Israel, the Living Presence your God the Living Presence is One" (Deut 6:4[†]). This verse in Deuteronomy, the central affirmation of Jewish liturgy, is followed by the verse, "You shall

---

[3] Jer 31:3 in the KJV.

love the Living Presence your God with all your heart, all your soul and all your means" (Deut 6:5†).

In these two verses the Torah makes the connection between listening and love. When the people listen to God and hear God's profound caring for all of creation, the most natural response is love. Listening to God opens the human heart to hearing and feeling the love present in God's Presence. Feeling that love, a person responds with love.

The entreaty to listen is also central to the prophetic message, appearing numerous times in prophetic books, as in the following two texts: "Perhaps they will listen, and turn every man from his evil way" (Jer 26:3); "Give ear and hear my voice; listen and hear my speech" (Isa 28:23).

Most often in the Prophets, God grieves the failure of the people to listen. Sometimes the prophetic call to listen is voiced as a warning, as in this passage from Jeremiah:

"Thus says the Living Presence; If you will not listen to me, to walk in my Torah, which I have set before you, to listen to the words of my servants the prophets, whom I sent to you, sending them from early in the morning, but you have not listened, then will I make this house like Shiloh, and will make this city a curse to all the nations of the earth." (26:4–6)

Seeking mutual relationship, God also listens. God hears the cries of the people in Egypt, leading to the exodus. God also hears the pleas uttered by Hagar, Rebecca, Hannah, and Ruth, among others. God listens to Abraham about Sodom and Gomorrah. On two separate occasions, God hears a plea from Moses and forgives the people.[4] Deuteronomy and the Prophets present a God who listens to the people:

And the Living Presence heard the voice of your words, when you spoke to me; and the Living Presence said to me, I have heard the voice of the words of this people, which they have spoken to you; they have well said all that they have spoken. (Deut 5:25)[5]

And when we cried to the Living Presence God of our fathers, the Living Presence heard our voice, and looked on our affliction, and our labor, and our oppression. (Deut 26:7)

---

[4] At Mount Sinai and in the incident of the twelve spies.
[5] Deut 5:28 in the KJV.

Then shall you call upon me, and you shall go and pray to me, and I will listen to you. (Jer 29:12)

Call me and I will answer you. (Jer 33:3)

Therefore I will look to the Living Presence; I will wait for the God of my salvation; my God will hear me. (Mic 7:7)

Deuteronomy and the Prophets envision the covenant as a dialogical relationship in which God and Israel listen to each other. The covenant calls for two-way communication. Even the apparently commanding divine word proclaimed by the prophets is best heard dialogically. For example, God's call to do justice, to love mercy, and to walk humbly is too open-ended and undefined to be a final word. Rather, it is an invitation to a conversation with God about what exactly it means to do justice or to love mercy. Through the prophet Micah, God calls upon Israel to center its communal living on that conversation: "He has told you, humankind, what is good and what the Living Presence requires of you: only to do justice, and to love mercy, and to walk humbly with your God" (6:8†).

One can read Deuteronomy and the Prophets and miss the emphasis on listening because most translations mistakenly render the Hebrew root שמע (listen) as "obey." For example, here is the translation of a verse from Deuteronomy in the King James Bible: "Thou shalt therefore obey the voice of the Living Presence thy God . . ." (27:10).

Everett Fox, whose translation strives to be as close to the Hebrew as possible, translates the same verse as follows: "You are to hearken to the voice of YHWH your God . . ." (Deut 27:10). The rendering of the Hebrew root שמע as "obey" may reflect the influence of an imperial worldview behind the translation. Perhaps the translators of the King James Bible (KJV) read the word as "obey" because they conceived of God in the image of the English king, a distant and commanding figure who expected unquestioning obedience from his servants. Similarly, perhaps the many translations that have followed the lead of the KJV have employed the word "obey" because these translators envision a God who relates to humankind through domination. Over the centuries, until modern times, ruling elites have sponsored translations of the Bible. No wonder the Hebrew root is translated in these Bibles as "obey." Unfortunately, these English translations misread the Hebrew Scriptures and misrepresent the God found in these Scriptures.

The God who loves and listens, the God who seeks dialogue, is central to the critique of empire found in Deuteronomy and the Prophets.

The authors of these texts, who had witnessed the abhorrent violence of unchecked imperial domination, envision a God who embodied an alternative to imperial ways. These Scriptures present a ruler who seeks loyalty through support and concern rather than through domineering power, a sovereign who seeks devotion through mutual relationship— covenant, love, and dialogue. Given the critique of empire central to these texts, translating the word שמע as "listen" or "hearken" captures the sense and context of the Hebrew texts.

Listening is different than obedience; it relies on a more dialogical and intimate relationship. Listening implies that the listener will hear a message, thoughtfully process its content, and then respond. Obedience implies automatic compliance. When translations render the root שמע as "obey," they miss the mutuality intended in the text and misrepresent the relationship God seeks with humans. The God of Deuteronomy and the Prophets seeks freely given devotion, not blind obedience. God seeks a faithful relationship with discerning human beings as distinct from compliance by servants who have no agency of their own.

This distinction between freely given devotion and blind obedience has profound implications for both individual and communal spiritual life. The God of the Prophets and Deuteronomy is supremely powerful, but not domineering. This God does not seek mindless followers. Rather, this God seeks and offers listening relationship. God desires human beings who will attend to God's *mitzvot*, God's "charges."

I use the word "charge" for the Hebrew word מצוה (*mitzvah*) instead of the more common "commandment," because "charge" carries the sense of entrusting someone with a task as a duty or responsibility.[6] In this way "charge" implies mutual relationship and honors the independent agency of the one charged, whereas "commandment" implies power, the ability to make someone do something. In the context of Deuteronomy and the Prophets, "charge" more faithfully carries the relational intent than "commandment."

The etymological origins of מצוה (*mitzvah*) throw an interesting light on God's intention in "charging" the people. The Hebrew root צוה is derived from the Syriac "stone-heap" or the Arabic "guide-stone." In this sense God's *mitzvot* (charges) are guide-stones, signposts to show the right way on the journey, direction markers for how to remain in mutual relationship with God.

The placement of dialogue and freely given devotion at the center of sacred practice is not a slackening of religious demands. Dialogue

---

6 For the Hebrew root "צוה" translated as "to lay charge," see Frances Brown, S. R. Driver, and Charles A. Briggs, *The Brown-Driver-Briggs Hebrew and English Lexicon of the Old Testament* (Peabody, MA: Hendrickson, 1996), 845c.

increases those demands. A God who demands blind obedience lays out a narrow path to fulfill external obligations and does not require the hard work of changing the human heart. By contrast, the dialogical relationship described in Deuteronomy and the Prophets places much more responsibility on human shoulders to discern and freely act upon God's charges. This responsibility is the crucible for human growth, liberation, and flourishing. The God of the Hebrew Scriptures is more concerned with flourishing than obedience.

The crucial role of listening to God is the basis of the biblical opposition to idolatry. The fundamental fault of idolatry is that idolatry is essentially a human monologue. Idols don't speak and humans don't listen:

> Every man becomes stupid without knowledge; every goldsmith is put to shame by the carved idol; for his molten image is falsehood, and there is no breath in them. (Jer 51:17)

> What use is there in a carved idol whose maker has shaped it, a molten image, and a teacher of lies, that its maker should trust in his own work when he makes dumb idols? (Hab 2:18)

In idolatrous practice, people seek to control God or the gods—to receive some bounty or avoid some punishment—by making offerings. Idolatry involves people in a predefined set of behaviors that they hope will mollify, please, and bind the gods. Idolatrous practice seeks to silence the gods, to neutralize them, to control their behavior. Idolatry is a static system. Idolatrous people are speaking and doing people, but not listening and learning people. Idolatry does not call a person into the wilderness on a journey of liberation. By contrast, the people Israel are called to listen to God, and to learn, grow, and journey in response.

Empire and idolatry are both forms of settling in to a given status quo. Both these systems resist change; both are deaf to the promise of something new. Hence, empire and idolatry thrive on monologue. Dialogue unsettles empire and challenges idolatry. The Prophets and Deuteronomy, expressions of the prophetic stream, critique empire and idolatry by offering a radically subversive alternative centered on mutual relationship expressed through dialogue, love, and covenant.

CHAPTER 5

Telling the Essential Story throughout Time

The Hebrew prophets, as well as the writers of Deuteronomy, saw clearly what the elites of their time, and even the common people, did not want to see. Without radical change, the king and the Temple, the political and religious foundations of their society, were doomed to fail and bring the entire kingdom down with them. When the prophets attempted to alert the people to the present danger, proclaiming what no one wanted to hear, they were subjected to repeated reproach.

As Walter Brueggemann so eloquently taught, each of the prophets needed to engage in a battle of narratives. The "royal narrative," endorsed by the privileged class, focused on the value of institutions. In this worldview, the stability of the kingship and the Temple guaranteed the welfare of the people. The royal narrative held that the status quo was the natural and inevitable order of society. Even in the face of instability at home and threats from abroad, there was no realistic alternative to those institutions.[1]

The prophets proclaimed a different narrative. They saw that the injustice perpetrated by the king and the priests put the people at risk. Rejecting static institutions as the wellspring of the society's welfare, the prophets asserted that a return to the people's liberation journey with God was the only viable way forward.

In entering this battle of narratives, the prophets faced a bracing rhetorical challenge. The Israelite people placed more credence in the familiar status quo than in a radically alternative future. The contemporary order had the advantage of presenting a reality that was already

---

[1] Walter Brueggemann, *The Prophetic Imagination* (Minneapolis: Fortress Press, 2001), chaps. 2 and 3.

manifest, a world that people could touch and see. The prophets were called to bring forth a counternarrative, to envision what the people could not yet see. Each prophet's formidable task was to inspire people to leave behind the security of established institutions and to engage in a journey with an unseen God.

The prophets presented a compelling counternarrative by offering a broad vision of the present moment. The royal narrative served the status quo by articulating a narrow perspective on time, viewing the present social, political, and religious configuration as the one eternal reality. The prophetic narrative offered a radically different perspective, a deeply subversive vision that placed the present crisis in an infinitely broader context. We have already seen how the prophets placed the current threats to the kingdom in the larger temporal context of the exodus journey. Peering even deeper into the nature of things, the prophets made an even grander claim, placing the contemporary moment in the broadest possible context in time and space—the context of the work of creation itself.

Standing in the flow of the prophetic stream, the prophets envisioned all creation as a liberation event. They traced the lineage of the people's journey with God back to the Exodus, back further to Abraham's leaving Haran, and then all the way back to the first act of creation. In prophetic thought, the liberating power that had taken the people out of Egypt is the same power that propelled the evolving, ever-transforming journey of the created universe itself. The people's liberating journey with God is rooted in the liberating journey of the created world.

In this prophetic counternarrative, the prophet challenged the power of the king by calling the people to refocus their attention on another, far greater power—the power of their creator. The prophets called the people to turn away from the familiar security of their relationship to the king and the Temple, and to turn toward a far more enduring relational context, the people's age-old liberation journey with God. In the place of the royal narrative that focused on the unchanging present, the prophets proclaimed a cosmic narrative in which the God of liberation was at work through time.

In a sense, the prophets viewed the crisis of their day as a crisis of forgetting, and the way out as a process of remembering. The people had forgotten the journey with their God who called Abraham out of Haran, who took the people out of Egypt. They had lost touch with their God who brought forth life in the beginning and who continually brings forth new life each day.

In the following testimony delivered by Amos, God calls the people to remember the exodus from Egypt and the destruction of Sodom and

Gomorrah, and then the prophet attributes these two momentous events to the power behind creation itself:

> I have sent among you the pestilence after the manner of Egypt. . . . I have overthrown some of you, as God overthrew Sodom and Gomorrah. . . . Therefore thus I will do to you, O Israel; and because I will do this to you, prepare to meet your God, O Israel. . . . For, behold, he who forms the mountains, and creates the wind, and declares to man what is his thought, who makes the morning darkness, and treads on the high places of the earth, the Living Presence, the God of hosts, is his name. (4:10–13)

The prophet Jeremiah, addressing the people shortly before the destruction of Jerusalem in 586 BCE, pleaded with the people to put their trust in God. In many passages Jeremiah identified the God whose word he brings as the God of creation and Exodus. In his most succinct statement of that connection, Jeremiah brings this word of God: "I have made the earth, the man and the beasts that are upon the ground, by my great power and by my outstretched arm, and have given it to whom it seemed proper to me" (27:5). "Great power" and "outstretched arm" are clear references to both creation and the exodus.

The prophet Isaiah, addressing the people in exile, placed the creation and the exodus story in one narrative flow:

> Awake, awake, put on strength, O arm of the Living Presence; awake, as in days of old, in the generations of old. Are you not he who cut Rahab in pieces, and wounded the crocodile? Are you not he who dried the sea, the waters of the great deep; who made the depths of the sea a way for the ransomed to pass over? (51:9–10)

Rahab, the primordial sea monster and a derogatory name for Egypt, symbolizes both the initial chaos that preceded creation and the terror of Egypt. The prophet then links God's power to place a limit on the primordial waters of the great deep with God's providing a way for the people to cross the Sea of Reeds. Creation and exodus are joined as one unified story—a breathtakingly wide vision.

In the following passage, Isaiah again links the God of creation with the God who will take the people by the hand and lead them forth:

> Thus said God the Living Presence, he who created the heavens, and stretched them out; he who spread forth the earth, and that which comes out of it; he who gives breath to the people upon

it, and spirit to those who walk in it. I, the Living Presence, have called you in righteousness, and will hold your hand, and will keep you. (42:5–6)

In the next evocative passage Isaiah intriguingly weaves transformative images of the created world with terms of social transformation. "Shower, O heavens, from above, and let the skies pour down righteousness; let the earth open, and let them bring forth salvation, and let righteousness spring up also; I, the Living Presence, have created it" (45:8).

In order to counter the power of the entrenched royal narrative, the prophets proclaimed an alternative story, one engendered by extraordinary imaginative vision. They envisioned the exodus story, the people's core story, as a vast narrative arc that extended to include both the creation in the distant past and the challenges of the current day. In this imaginative expression, the prophets layered three divine acts: the power behind creation, the exodus from Egypt, and God's liberating hand at work in the present moment. They then interpreted each layer in the context of the process that preceded it. They viewed the exodus as an extension of God's mighty acts during the creation, and the current struggle as a continuation of the liberation out of Egypt. This act of prophetic imagination provided a compelling narrative, enabling the people to perceive the possibility of living outside of the oppressive structures of their day.[2]

Undergirded by this layering process, the prophetic message became both timeless and current: today is a day of creation, today is a day of exodus, today is a day to take God's outstretched hand and set off into the wilderness of an alternative future. The rhetorical power of the prophet lay, in part, in the ability to see and express the dynamics of creation and the exodus at work in the prophet's own day.

The prophetic understanding that creation as a whole is on a liberation journey has significant implications for our day. On a spiritual level, this perspective on creation can heal human alienation from the earth. Many of us were raised to think of the earth as an inanimate object, a large rock floating in cold, empty space. As humans we dream and aspire, but in this view we are alone on earth with our dreams and aspirations. The prophetic understanding offers our species a way out of our alienation, offers people a return home. Human beings would feel more at home on the planet were we to recognize that we are nested in a larger creation that shares our aspirations for more freedom, for enhanced

---

[2] Walter Brueggemann calls this layering of traditions a "thick traditioning process"; see *The Practice of Prophetic Imagination* (Minneapolis: Fortress Press, 2012), 23–24.

mutual relationship. Humans would feel ever more grounded in their liberation journey were we to understand that our species coevolved within a creation that shares in our journey. The great Catholic earth theologian Thomas Berry devoted his academic career to healing the relations between humans and the earth. He wrote:

> We are returning to our native place after a long absence, meeting once again with our kin in the earth community. . . . Scientific evidence confirms, with a magnificent overview, the ancient awareness that we live in a universe—a single, if multiform, energy event. . . . Every reality of the universe is intimately present to every other reality of the universe and finds its fulfillment in this mutual presence. . . . The universe is a communion of subjects rather than a collection of objects.[3]

This sensibility to a common companioned journey alongside all of creation is powerful medicine for the loneliness of the human soul. The return of the human soul to our common creative journey with the earth would, in turn, call upon humankind to heal the wounds we have afflicted on the world of which we are a part.

On a societal level, the awareness of an ongoing exodus through time places liberation work at the center of the human vocation. The prophets' understanding that the exodus must take place in every generation can be heard in our day as a moral imperative to counter racism, sexism, homophobia, xenophobia, and related oppressions—an imperative to work for a society in which all people can flourish.

Finally, on a rhetorical level, the prophets and the Deuteronomic authors wrote their moment in time into the narrative arc of the exodus story. Their testimony models the power of reimagining the exodus story into one's own day. The prophets teach us that the liberation narrative, the ongoing creation/exodus story, needs to be reimagined for every generation, releasing the flow of the prophetic stream to move a society forward. As inheritors of prophetic wisdom, we, too, can bring forth from ancient stories the new ideas we need to meet the challenges of the present moment.

---

[3] Thomas Berry, *The Dream of the Earth* (San Francisco: Sierra Club Books, 1988), 1, 65, 106; and Berry, *The Universe Story* (New York: Arkana Publishing, 1984), 243.

CHAPTER 6

Headwaters

THE PROPHETIC STREAM IN CREATION

The prophets' witness to God's liberating action in both history and the created world was not only their innovation. This perspective is also present in the scriptural accounts of creation in Genesis, which portray the creation as a process of liberation. In the context of the Hebrew Bible, the words delivered by individual prophets are the human articulation of a liberating energy that moves within creation through time. I call this transforming energy the "prophetic stream" because this flow, rooted in the divine presence, functions in the natural world just as the prophetic word functions in human society. It challenges the limitations of existing structures in order to bring forth new possibilities.

The prophetic stream is a divinely initiated energy that interacts with each form within creation to release its potential. This transforming energy enables the bringing forth, the exodus, of ever more mutually interrelated and more conscious entities.[1] The prophetic energy does not create totally new forms. Rather it works *in relationship with* existing forms to liberate their inherent potential.

The prophetic stream energizes possibility. Just as the prophetic testimony both articulates the fundamental brokenness of the present

---

[1] At first glance, it appears that the transforming energy of the prophetic stream works only on living beings and not on nonliving entities like rocks. It is more difficult to see the prophetic stream working on rocks because this transformation happens over such a vast period of time. However, when we step back and consider the world in geologic time, we witness a profoundly dynamic world in which everything is being built up or torn down. The hard granite rocks are being continually eroded into the minerals that make plant and animal life possible. Living beings are an emergent quality of inanimate elements like carbon, nitrogen, and potassium.

order and transcends the present moment to envision a radically alternative future, the prophetic stream continually engages with what is to explore what could be. We can recognize the prophetic stream flowing through our own lives when we reflect on our continuing deep desire to grow past our limitations and to participate more fully and consciously in life.

The prophetic stream flows in the biblical text from the very beginning of creation. In Genesis 1, God-infused energy, expressed as God's word, calls forth the potential of each day to transcend itself, to transform itself into a more complex form. Like the word of God articulated by the prophet, God's word in creation disrupts the given order to liberate a higher degree of existence that is potential within it.

The liberating flow of the prophetic stream is present in the first words that God speaks in Genesis. In Genesis 1:3, God says, "*V'y'hee*" (Let there be). This familiar divine proclamation raises several questions: Why does God say, "Let there be"? Why doesn't God simply form light? Why does God speak at all? What do words have to do with creating? To whom is God speaking?

This last question has a clear answer. Throughout Genesis 1, God is addressing the natural world. On the first day, God addresses the "emptiness and chaos" that preceded creation.[2] In later days God says, "Let there be," to the world that God has created up until then. An answer to the other questions appears when we recognize that God's work with creation is a process of call-and-response. God does not create in an imperial way, by imposing an external will on passive creation. Rather, using the invitation of words, God animates the created world on a journey to liberate its potential, to respond as a person responds in dialogue. God calls out and thereby energizes the potential for transformation. Creation responds by bringing forth a new and more differentiated and interrelated order of being.

This nonimperial, liberating nature of the creative process begins with God's work in relation to the primordial chaos. At the beginning of creation, when "the earth was unformed and void" (Gen 1:2), God does not destroy or overcome the chaos. Instead, life emerges out of God's close presence to the chaos. God's intimate connection to chaos is evident in the verse, "The spirit of God hovered over the face of the (chaotic) waters. And God said, 'Let there be light'" (Gen 1:3). With this word, God infuses the world with the prophetic stream, with a transforming creative energy that works with whatever is, including chaos, to bring

---

[2] The Hebrew יְהִי [let there be] is the third-person singular verbal form. Here God is speaking to the created world as a sovereign. Rulers commonly speak to their subjects in the third person.

forth increasingly differentiated, interrelated, and conscious forms of life. On each subsequent day, God calls out to animate creation's potential, and creation responds by bringing forth the next order of creation.

The complexity theorists teach us that all living systems exist in a narrow zone between disequilibrium (chaos) and closed-ended equilibrium. Living beings draw energy from a chaotic environment and use it for becoming. In the Bible, as in complexity theory, chaos often underlies the creative effort. The Genesis story tells us that we don't need to overcome the chaos. Rather, we are called to face the chaos, see it clearly for what it is, and, in relationship to that chaos, bring forth new ways of being. The prophet, who both faces the present chaos and envisions a more relational, life-affirming future, illustrates this activity.

The pattern embedded in the creation story reveals the action of the prophetic stream as it creates certain forms and then liberates their potential to be more differentiated and interrelated forms of being. On the first three days of creation, God creates light, upper waters (heavens) and lower waters (seas), and earth, respectively. On days four, five, and six, in response to God's activating word, the creations of those initial three days evolve into more differentiated and interrelated forms. On day four, the light of the first day actualizes its latent potential in the forms of sun, moon, and stars. On days five and six, God works with the creations of days two and three to bring forth their potential. On day five, God does not independently create sea creatures. Rather, God empowers the waters to "swarm with living swarms" (Gen 1:20). Similarly, on day six, God does not place cattle and crawling things on the earth. Rather, God empowers the earth to "bring forth of all kinds of living creatures" (Gen 1:24).

The creation story directly connects creation and liberation when it uses the verb phrase "*bring forth*" to depict the creation of animals on the sixth day. Scripture uses the very same phrase to portray the liberation of the Israelites from Egypt. Speaking to Moses, God says, "I will send you to Pharaoh, that you may bring forth my people the children of Israel out of Egypt" (Exod 3:10).[3] The creation of animals is parallel to the exodus from Egypt; both acts liberate constrained potential: the potential of the earth to take the conscious form of animals and the potential of the Israelites to be a free people who serve God.

The earth even brings forth cattle and insects whole—quite a stretch for the imagination! The Torah makes this leap to emphasize that God has infused immense creative potential in the physical world.

---

[3] "Bring forth" is also used in reference to the exodus in Exod 3:11, 12; 12:39; 13:16.

We find another example of the transforming, liberating energy of God in the biblical treatment of seeds:

And God said, Let the earth bring forth grass, herb yielding seed, and fruit tree yielding fruit after his kind, whose seed is in itself, upon the earth; and it was so. And the earth brought forth grass, and herb yielding seed after its kind, and tree yielding fruit, whose seed was in itself, after its kind; and God saw that it was good. (Gen 1:11–12)

"Seeds" or "fruit containing seeds" appears six times in these two verses. Clearly, the text is fascinated with seeds. What accounts for this fascination?

The seed is a model of transformation. There is no little broccoli plant in a broccoli seed. There is no little oak tree in an acorn. The seed is an amazing example of the potential hidden within even the tiniest things. Seeds, as small as they are, contain the possibility of enormous, transforming growth. For the biblical authors, seeds were fascinating because they embodied the prophetic energy of transformation.

The creation of the human dramatically displays God's cocreative partnership with the world. In Genesis 1:26 God says, "Let us make man." The use of the plural "us" raises a question. Why would a text devoted to setting forth the unparalleled power of the one God use the plural "let us" and thereby take the risk of introducing the possibility that other gods exist? The midrash on Genesis asks this very question. Whom did God address by saying "let us"? "R. Samuel b. Nahman said: With whom did He [God] take counsel? He took counsel *with* the works of each day, like a king who had a counselor without whose *knowledge* he did nothing."[4]

In the view of this midrash, the biblical text took the risk of speaking in the plural to underscore that God did not decide alone to create human beings, imposing them on the rest of a passive creation. Instead, God took counsel with the created world as an active companion in the creative process. God created the human in partnership with "the works of each day." The "knowledge" or creative bent of each day flowed into the formation of the human. Earth and water, plant and animal each gave forth its potential in this act of creation.

While all of creation is the fruit of a dialogue between God and the created world, human beings are the outcome of the most inclusive and conscious form of this dialogue. In creating the human, God took

---

4 *Genesis Rabbah* 8:3 (emphasis added).

counsel with the knowledge of all the earlier works of creation. The lines of dialogue between God and creation form the very fibers of a human being. When we quiet ourselves and listen, each of us can hear this dialogue between heaven and earth, the transcendent and the finite, at our core.

God's partnership with the created world reaches its pinnacle in the creation of the human being. In an astounding declaration, God proclaims the intent to create the human in "our image" (Gen 1:26). The Bible's depiction of how God created the human surprises the reader in two separate ways. The text again uses a plural "our," and then the text imagines the human created in the image of God.

A midrash understands "in the image of God" to mean that, like God, the human is empowered to "speak" to and "intimately relate" to the created world.[5] In other words, the human is empowered to mirror God's creative action as depicted in Genesis 1. In intimate relation to creation, God spoke the potential of creation into being. So, too, the human is given the power to speak—to engage consciously—in intimate relationship with the world and thereby bring forth its potential. Like God, the human is given the power to create in partnership with the natural world.

The role of the human as creator is reinforced by the repeated use of the word "create" in the verse describing the creation of the human, "God created human beings in [the divine] image, creating [them] in the image of God, creating them male and female" (Gen 1:27).[6] In Genesis 1, the text is very sparing with the word "create." With the exception of the first verse in Genesis, and the creation of the great Leviathan on the fifth day,[7] the text only uses "create" or "created" for the human. All other forms are "made," "formed," "brought forth," and "sprouted forth." Other than the Leviathan, only human beings are "created," with the word "create/created" appearing three times in one verse. The human was created to create. The prophetic stream flows within human creativity, but only when the human speaks as God did—consciously, relating intimately to the world.

After God created the human, God blesses the new creation in these words: "And God blessed them, and God said to them, Be fruitful, and multiply, and replenish the earth, and subjugate it; and have dominion

---

5 *Genesis Rabbah* 8:11.

6 Translation from Tamara Cohen Eshkenazi and Andrea L. Weiss, *The Torah: A Women's Commentary* (New York: Women of Reform Judaism, 2008).

7 Scholars believe that the text uses the word "create" for the Leviathan to emphasize that God created this great creature. In the *Enuma Elish*, the Babylonian creation myth, the Leviathan is itself a god.

over the fish of the sea, and over the birds of the air, and over every living thing that moves upon the earth" (Gen 1:28). This divine blessing is an important verse in our exploration of the Torah as a liberating text, as over the years many interpreters have used it to sanction human exploitation of the earth. Indeed, with this blessing, God appears to authorize human domination. However, when we read this verse in its context, in the context of God creating in partnership and intimate relationship with the world, we arrive at a very different understanding.

The key words in Genesis 1:28 are "dominion" and "subjugate." "Dominion" means to be lord and master over someone or something. "Subjugate" means to treat someone or something as a subject, someone who lives in subordinate relation to a sovereign. In Genesis 1:28 these two words must be understood in the context of how God exercises dominion and subjugation in the creation story. "*Dominion*" means to be a master as God is a master. "Subjugate" means to make the earth your subject in the very same manner that God has subjugated the earth. God is a benevolent and relational master and sovereign; God works cocreatively in partnership with the natural world to bring forth its potential. The same relationship now applies to human beings. God gives human beings the ability to work in conscious relationship to "bring forth" the creative potential of the natural world. The human is not given license to treat the world as if it were a passive object to control.

The cosmologist Brian Swimme understands the human role in creation in just this way. The clay of the earth has the potential to be a beautiful pot. The tree has the potential to be a violin. The dawn of day and the sunset can be "brought forth" as a poem or a painting. The human is blessed to work with the earth as a creator. In the likeness of God, the human creator liberates the potential and possibility of creation.[8]

Many great artists have seen their work as a vehicle of liberation. Johann Sebastian Bach said that he "discovered" music in the world rather than creating music de novo. Michelangelo famously said that he labored to liberate the figure that was already present in the stone. Michelangelo's *Prisoners*, half-completed sculptures now located in the Academia in Florence, are alive with this sensibility. The half-exposed figures seem caught in the very act of whirling off the excess stone so that their full shape may be liberated.

Admittedly, the unique role of the human in creation has often been terribly misunderstood. Blind to the partnership model that God set, human beings have read the scriptural text as permission to control and

---

[8] Brian Swimme, *The Universe Is a Green Dragon: A Cosmic Creation Story* (Rochester, VT: Bear and Company, 1984).

destroy creation. Humankind's ability to subjugate creation solely for its own perceived benefit has put virtually all life on the planet at risk. Two thousand years ago the Rabbis foresaw and addressed this danger. Making a pun with the word "*uredu*," translated as, "and have dominion" (Gen 1:28), "R. Jacob of Kefar Hanan said: Of him who is in our image and likeness God says '*uredu*' (and have dominion); but of him who is not in our image and likeness God says '*yerdu*' (let them descend)."[9]

This midrash understands that God granted human beings the capacity to bring forth new forms. When humans act in intimate relation *with* creation to bring forth new forms that serve the larger creation, they act in the image of God and will have dominion—that is, they shall be sustained in their creative role. On the other hand, when human beings fail to act in the image of God and instead exploit the natural world, they will be brought down ("let them descend").

Hebrew Scriptures contain a second creation story that offers a different perspective on creation but reiterates the themes of liberation and relational cocreativity. In Genesis 2, "The Living Presence God formed the earthling [*adam*] of the dust of ground [*adama*], and breathed into the nostrils the breath of life" (Gen 2:7[†]). Similarly to the first creation story, God creates in partnership with the earth. As every potter will testify, working with the earth is a cooperative process; the potter works *with* the clay. In this Genesis passage, God works with the earth to create the human. The eleventh-century Rabbi Rashi highlights the significant role the dust played in creating the human. Rashi comments that God collected the dust "from the four corners of the earth" so that the human would feel connected to all the earth.[10] Every part of the earth participated in creating the human.

The same verse that depicts God creating the human in partnership with the earth also wraps the entire creation story in a culminating liberation of potential: "And the Living Presence . . . breathed into the nostrils the breath/soul of life, and the earthling became a living spirit" (Gen 2:7[†]). At the beginning of creation in Genesis 1, the *Ruach Elohim*—the Wind/Spirit of God—hovers over the waters. This hovering divine Presence is the energy that animates the liberating unfolding of nature. In Genesis 2:7, God breathes the breath/soul of life into the human. Human breath now embodies divine breath, the Wind/Spirit of God. By the gift of this divine breath, humans become more than simply a part of the ever-transforming creation. Human beings have the power to be conscious agents of creative liberation, following in the ways of God.

---

[9] *Genesis Rabbah* 8:12.
[10] Rashi on Gen 2:7.

The biblical presentation of the process of creation bears striking similarities to the scientific theory of evolution. The first Chief Rabbi of Israel, Rav Kook (1865–1935), fully embraced evolution as God's way of working with the world. Kook wrote, "The doctrine of evolution that is presently gaining acceptance in the world has a greater affinity with the secret teachings of the Kabbalah than all other philosophies."[11]

There is certainly an affinity between evolution and traditional Jewish understandings of creation, but there is also a difference. Unlike the scientific explanation, the biblical account presents a Creator who energizes the evolutionary process and expresses delight at its unfolding. Life does not expend itself alone in an indifferent universe. Life unfolds in a responsive relationship with a creative energy that pervades creation.

The Genesis creation story also differs substantially from the Intelligent Design theory. Unlike Intelligent Design, the biblical God does not function like an architect constructing the world according to a preconceived design. In Genesis God cocreates; the Divine creates in relation with the physical world to liberate its potential. God creates in mutual relationship.

Mutual relationship implies freedom of all parties. There is no genuine mutual relationship with another if one party controls the other. At each stage of creation, when God says, "Let there be," God does not control but energizes creation to transcend itself and bring forth a creation that is more differentiated, interrelated, and conscious than in the earlier stage. God gives the potential for an indeterminate number of outcomes, but God does not exactly know what the outcomes will be. In creating, the divine energy moves in the world to liberate new forms of life without knowing exactly what those new forms will be.

God's surprise and delight at each stage of creation are captured in the repeated refrain, "God saw that it was *tov*" (Gen 1:4, 10, 12, 18, 21, 25, 31). The word *tov* is best translated in this context as "delightful" or "vital."[12] God was delighted by the vitality God saw in creation. There is a responsive surprise in God's delight. The Torah could have simply said, "God said it is good." The words "God saw" suggest immediacy in God's response. God's pronouncement is not the sober recognition of an expected result, as if a machine was working properly as planned. Rather, upon seeing, God was delighted. God had not foreseen the exact outcome at each state of creation.

Jewish thought has long wrestled with the understanding that God

---

11 Rav Kook, *Orot HaKodesh* (Jerusalem: Maggid, 2015), 2:437, 555.

12 Frances Brown, S. R. Driver, and Charles A. Briggs, *The Brown-Driver-Briggs Hebrew and English Lexicon of the Old Testament* (Peabody, MA: Hendrickson, 1996), 373b.

does not predetermine the future. Rabbi Akiba, second century CE, famously taught, "All is foreseen and freedom is given" (Avot 3:17). The medieval philosopher Maimonides elaborated more fully on the freedom God has given creation:

> It is beyond our understanding how God can be aware of an indeterminate future. His awareness is as removed from our universe as God Himself and thus in no way affects the reality of free will. Thus, our futures truly are our own to decide. God's knowledge of our eventual decisions is, so to speak, not yet a part of this world—and has not assumed a form that impinges on the independence of this world. And so, as far as our universe is concerned, the future is still wide open.[13]

Maimonides states, "God is aware of an *indeterminate* future." One way of understanding this proposition is to consider that God, being infinite, is aware of each of the infinite possible outcomes of any particular moment. The divine energy embodies all possibilities. At the same time, God cocreates with the world and therefore does not dictate which possibility will emerge. The infinite divine energy does not take the form of any particular possibility until it comes into finite being. The aspect of God that interacts with the finite world does not predetermine which possibility will arise until it is realized in the world. Freedom is an essential quality of the process of creation.

In the two creation stories, the activity of the divine word foreshadows the action of the prophetic word later in the Bible. Like the prophetic word, the divine word in Genesis addresses the reality of the status quo, working in relationship with current conditions to overcome limitations and to liberate inherent potential. These creation stories detail an ongoing developmental process in which the primordial chaos evolves, stage by stage, to become more mutually interrelated forms of life. From the moment God declares, "Let there be light," the very stuff of creation becomes laden with potential for transformation, laden with the potential for a liberation journey. From the outset of Genesis, to be a part of God's creation is to be on a journey of becoming.

---

[13] Maimonides, *Mishnah Torah Hilchot Tsheuvh* 5:5.

CHAPTER 7

Journey Partners

God and Abraham

The Abraham narratives are the next liberation story in the Bible. As with creation, the trajectory of Abraham's journey with God embodies the movement of the prophetic stream, the journey of continuing liberation and growing mutual relationship. When Abraham's journey joins with God's journey, they discover together how to bring blessings into the world.

Abraham's Journey

In the Torah, Abraham's journey begins when he is seventy-five years old. Generations of rabbis have wondered about Abraham's earlier life. In particular, they wanted to know what prepared Abraham for his journey with God. To answer this question, these rabbis read between the lines of Scripture and wrote midrashim that provide a more elaborate account of Abraham's journey.

The medieval Rabbi Maimonides asserted that philosophical speculation led Abraham to discover the existence of a single, transcendent God. The Chaldeans, among whom Abraham lived, believed the heavenly bodies were gods. In awe and fear of the power of their gods, the Chaldeans had carefully and accurately charted the stars, the earliest astronomers in human history. Abraham gazed upon these same stars, but his philosophical speculations led him to wonder, "How is it possible that this sphere moves constantly without there being a mover, or one to turn it, for it is impossible that it turns itself."[1] There must be a greater power that moves them, Abraham concluded. But what power? He was perplexed.

---

[1]   Maimonides, *Mishnah Torah Hilchot Avodah Zara* 1:3.

Maimonides continues the story:

In time, through his own comprehension, he apprehended the way of truth and understood the path of righteousness. He realized that there is one God who moves the spheres, who created everything, and that there is none beside Him. He knew that the whole world was in error and that the cause of their error was service to stars and images, so that they had lost their awareness of the truth. Abraham was forty years old when he recognized his Creator.[2]

Midrash HaGadol, a fourteenth-century midrashic collection, offered a more experiential understanding of Abraham's search. In this midrash, God responded to the profound disorientation Abraham experienced when he rejected the prevailing belief that the sun and the moon are gods. Noting Abraham's willingness to suffer cultural vertigo in search for a relationship with the true God, God spoke to Abraham's suffering: "When God saw [Abraham] in distress, He said to him, 'You love right relationship.'"[3]

In Abraham's search for the prime mover, God perceived a pursuit of right relationship. God further observed that in this quest for relationship, Abraham had discovered in the Creator the great relationship: the Love that extends to all creation. Abraham had encountered a Love that called Abraham to care for all of God's creation.

Abraham comes into clearer focus when we view him through the philosophical and experiential lenses offered by Maimonides and the *Midrash HaGadol*. For Maimonides, reason and logic led Abraham to smash the Chaldean idols, to see clearly that the heavenly orbs were not themselves divine—all the while experientially, as developed in the *Midrash HaGadol*, Abraham's philosophical iconoclasm left him disoriented, stripped naked of the belief systems that had provided meaning and cosmic order for his life.

In the crucible of his existential distress, as the *Midrash HaGadol* describes, Abraham felt God respond to his suffering. Abraham experienced that the power that moved the stars cared for his welfare. Abraham encountered an infinite God who was concerned with a finite, mortal human being, a God unlike the Mesopotamian gods who paid no heed to the common person. Reflecting on this breakthrough experience, Abraham understood that the love of the infinite God who cared about

---

2 Ibid.
3 *Midrash HaGadol*, Gen 12:1.

him could not be limited to caring *only* about him any more than the effect of the prime mover of the stars could be limited to only one star. The God whom Abraham encountered was beyond all such boundaries. This God loves and cares equally for every human being and for all of God's creation.

Abraham was forty years old, Maimonides tells us, when he recognized God. With his wife, Sarah, he set about teaching the way of the one God and converting people to the path of right relationship.[4] After thirty-five years at this spiritual work, at the age of seventy-five, Abraham may have thought that his wanderings were over.

The Torah now takes up the story. Abraham's journey with God had only just begun.

When Abraham was seventy-five years old, God addressed him, saying, "Go forth from your land, from your kindred, from your father's house, to the land that I will show you" (Gen 12:1). In obedient response, Abraham set off into the wilderness. His philosophical and spiritual roaming became a physical journey into unknown territory. God's charge—leave your land, kin, and father's house—highlights the radical severing that Abraham is called to do. Abraham had already broken with the religious culture of Mesopotamia. Now as an old man, he was called to break his physical ties as well.

One might imagine that Abraham's journey took him directly to the land that God would show him. This was not Abraham's experience. Years later, speaking to King Avimelech, Abraham reported, "God *hit'u* me from my father's house," meaning "God caused me to wander, to be lost, to go astray" (Gen 20:13). The twentieth-century Orthodox Jewish scholar Joseph Soloveitchik, commenting on this verse, emphasizes that God did not guide Abraham to his destination. Rather, "God willed Abraham to find out intuitively, to somehow smell the fragrance of the land, to feel the pull that the land exerts, to be attracted by the land spontaneously, so that the heart was Abraham's compass or lodestar."[5] Soloveitchik envisions Abraham wandering in devotion to God, guided by an intuitive attunement to his own heart, heading in the direction in which his heart was drawn.

The eleventh-century commentator Rashi (Rabbi Shlomo ben Isaac) brings a similar insight into the internal dynamics of Abraham's journey. Rashi observes that Abraham's passage through the wilderness was as much an inner as an outer journey. Reading the text closely, Rashi notes that God called to Abraham, "*Lech lecha*" (go to yourself).

---

4   *Genesis Rabbah* 39:14; Maimonides, *Mishna Torah*.
5   Joseph Soloveitchik, *Abraham's Journey* (New York: KTAV, 2008), 74.

Rashi interprets *lecha* (to yourself) to mean "for the sake of your own *tov*" (vitality).[6] Rashi's use of the word *tov* resonates with the feeling of delight God experienced upon seeing a work of creation: "*kee tov*" (it is vital), God exclaimed.[7] In Rashi's view, God called Abraham into deeper relationship with his *tov*, with the vital energy of creation that flowed into and through his being. Abraham answered the call. Standing at the edge of the great unknown, he gathered himself together and turned fully toward the *tov* of his life. Propelled by this vitality, Abraham set forth toward "the land that God will show you." He was now a free man, fully liberated from both the cultural and physical constraints of Chaldea. He had set sail on the prophetic stream.

God's Journey

From the beginning of creation, God has also been on a journey. God's delight with creation's bringing forth new things is evident in God's intention for humanity, as expressed in God's initial blessing for the man and the woman, "Be fruitful and flourish" (Gen 1:28). God wished humankind to flourish by bringing forth creative potential. Humanity, however, proved to be more challenging. Over the generations the Creator developed different strategies to support human flourishing, only to see each approach fall short. God's efforts were not fruitless, though. God learned from each failure and moved on to try a new way.

God's first attempt began in a paradisiacal garden. Everything the humans needed to thrive was provided. God also put in place one necessary limit so that the humans would know that they are finite, not gods. The humans must not eat of the fruit of the Tree of the Knowledge of Good and Evil.

We all know how that experiment turns out. Adam and Eve transgress the limitation and are unable to come clean when God asks, "Where are you?" (Gen 3:9). God then expels Adam and Eve from the garden, not to punish them, but because the garden failed in its purpose. God learned that the initial plan, situating human beings in paradise and imposing on them a single imposed limit, had failed to promote human flourishing. God turns to Plan B.

Plan B exposes the humans to a life of hard work and toil, subjecting them to a life in which the world itself will impose constraints—the limits of human energy and the limits of the earth to produce food. The humans, created in the image of the Creator, would meet the challenges

---

6   Rashi on Gen 12:1.
7   Gen 1.

of the world with creativity and imagination and thereby would flourish. Such was God's intention. Plan B did not develop well either. As humans began to multiply on earth, they began to use their "imaginations" to do violence.[8]

In response, God brought the great flood on the earth. After the flood, God develops Plan C. This plan has two parts: offer the humans moral guidance that proscribes murder and limits violence to animals, and make a global covenant that includes all living things and promises not to destroy all life on earth by flood.

The story of the rainbow covenant is so familiar that it is easy to ignore how startling it is. God, the Infinite, enters into a covenant with finite beings that limits God's use of power. Why did God choose to do so?

The Torah offers a clue. After the flood, God says, with regret for the violence of the deluge, "I will never again curse the ground on account of the human, for the formations of the human heart are evil from its youth, nor will I destroy every living thing, as I have done" (Gen 8:21[†]). God realizes that the violent flood was not really effective; it did not remove the evil inclination from the human heart.

There is a ray of hope, though. Before the deluge, God had observed, "Every thought formation of the human heart was only evil, continually" (Gen 6:5[†]). After the flood, God states that the evil imagination begins in one's youth, implying that people are not born with evil imagination. Evil is not intrinsic to human nature. God can then formulate a new plan based on the idea that humans might, with divine help, outgrow the inclination to do evil. The strategy that God arrives at to achieve this hope is to enter into a more mutual relationship with humans, a relationship with some clearly articulated terms—the rainbow covenant. God is learning that mutual trusting relationship, not violence or threats of punishment, creates the possibility of human flourishing.

Violence, in fact, hampers flourishing, as the postflood stories reveal. The damage done by God's violence is clear in the flood's aftermath. The trauma of the flood sets Noah to drink. Noah's descendants, also traumatized by God's use of overwhelming power, build a tower toward the heavens to challenge God's dominion. God notices this challenge and responds—but not with a flood, which would only perpetuate violence.

Instead, God takes a new tack, Plan D: God diversifies language. Diverse language, thought categories, and perceptions promote humility

---

[8] See Gen 6:5 and S. R. Hirsch commentary on that verse. Samson Raphael Hirsch, *The Pentateuch*, ed. Ephraim Oritz (New York: The Judaica Press, 1986).

and stimulate exploration. When people share a common language, they can imagine that their words capture reality; they can think that their understanding encompasses whole truth. Believing that they have apprehended the absolute, people can feel like little gods. Diverse languages, on the other hand, can make people aware that their perception of reality is limited, constrained by their use of certain words and phrases that emerge out of a specific cultural context. This experience of linguistic and cultural relativity can serve to humble a person and remind one that the perceptions of every finite being are inevitably partial and in need of further exploration.

The Torah does not record any particular outcomes from Plan D, merely naming the ten generations that followed Noah. We can infer from the Torah's silence that Plan D did not lead to disaster, but neither did it lead to human flourishing. God was on the right track with diversity, but something more was needed to nurture human growth.

The new plan involved Abraham. Abraham was a different man from Noah. Noah was a simple, obedient man who failed to stand up to God and argue for the lives of the people of his time. Abraham, by contrast, was not blindly obedient. He would stand up to God in the name of justice and compassion.[9] Abraham's philosophical and spiritual journeying, during which he broke with the culture around him, showed that Abraham was independently seeking to flourish, to unfurl his potential. In Abraham God found a person who shared God's goal for humanity.

As Abraham's covenanted journey partner, God's learning venture parallels Abraham's path through life. Like Abraham, God learns. Like Abraham and Sarah's journey, God's journey is not a straight and untroubled path. Along the way, God takes risks, falls short, and makes course corrections. This is the God whose name is "I will be what I shall be" (Exod 3:14)—a God who evolves.

The Journey of Abraham with God Brings Blessings

Abraham's departure from his father's house was a personal going forth with worldwide implications. God promised to create something radically new with Abraham, to "make [Abraham] a great nation" (Gen 12:2). Unlike all the surrounding nations, the grandeur of Abraham's descendants would not be measured by wealth or military might. Rather, the destiny of Abraham's children was to bring benefit to the whole world. God told Abraham, "through you all the families of the earth will be blessed" (Gen 12:3–4†).

---

[9] See Gen 18:17–18.

Abraham's journey with God is a blessing to the families of the earth both spiritually and practically. Spiritually, Abraham shows us all how to see behind creation to the power that moves it and provides an example of setting sail on the prophetic stream. Practically, Abraham's journey with God led him to the moral responsibility that flows from an understanding that all creation is one. The stories of how he lived out that moral responsibility are of practical value also because they show Abraham being, at times, troubled and uncertain about how to act. In that way, Abraham's journey is like our own.

Abraham's first deeds following God's charge to engrave the sign of the covenant into his flesh are acts of concern for people he does not know. These stories show that Abraham understood the covenant as binding him to care for the stranger and was not intended only for Abraham's family.

Immediately after marking the covenant on his body, Abraham hurried to provide hospitality for strangers. In this story Abraham was sitting in front of his tent communing with God when he saw three men approaching. He responded with urgency. He immediately turned from his spiritual meditation and "ran" toward the strangers to beg them to come to his tent to enjoy food and drink. When the strangers accepted his offer, Abraham hurried to Sarah to ask her to prepare fine meal for cakes, and then ran to the herd to slaughter a tender calf.

The very next narrative is the Sodom and Gomorrah story, in which Abraham was again concerned with the welfare of those outside his own family. It begins with an unusual passage in which God's inner thoughts are revealed to the reader:

Shall I cover up from Abraham what I am about to do? For Abraham will become a great and mighty nation, and all the nations of the earth will be blessed through him. For I have intimately known him so that he will charge his sons and his household after him to keep the way of the Living Presence to do what is right and just. (Gen 18:17–19†)

In this passage, God's private thoughts confirm Abraham's understanding of covenant. Both recognize that God's intimate relationship with Abraham naturally leads Abraham "to do what is right and just." Immediately after God told him what God was about to do, Abraham acted on his moral convictions. "While Abraham was still standing before the Living Presence, Abraham approached and said, 'Will you really wipe out the innocent with the guilty? . . . Will not the Judge of all the earth do justice?'" (Gen 18:23–25†).

Biblical scholar Jon Levenson emphasizes that the biblical phrase "to do what is right and just" (Gen 18:19) denotes far-ranging "acts of societal benevolence" toward one's fellow human beings.[10] As an example, Levenson cites a passage from the prophet Jeremiah: "Thus said the Living Presence: Do what is just and right; rescue from the oppressor him who is robbed; do not wrong the stranger, the orphan, or the widow, nor shed innocent blood in this place" (22:3).

The proximity of the two stories, one in which Abraham seeks justice for the residents of Sodom and the other in which he runs to provide hospitality for the stranger, communicate clearly the heart of the covenant to which Abraham and his descendants are called: to pursue the well-being of people who are not within one's family or clan. The stories clarify that the intent of the covenant is not to set the family of Abraham apart from other peoples but rather to bind them to concern for the welfare and blessing of "all the families of the earth" (Gen 12:3).

A commitment to care for the other does not guarantee moral certainty about how to enact this virtue. Throughout his life, Abraham struggled with moral ambiguity. For example, shortly after Abraham first set foot in Canaan, a famine forced Abraham and Sarah to flee to Egypt. As they approached Egypt, aware of Sarah's beauty and afraid for his life, Abraham sought to protect his life and the future that God had promised. He asked Sarah to say that she is his sister, putting Sarah at great risk. When they crossed into Egypt, Egyptian princes took her to Pharaoh's palace because of her beauty. Ultimately Pharaoh, of whom Abraham apparently thought the worst, upbraided Abraham, saying, "What is this that you have done to me? Why did you not tell me that she was your wife?" (Gen 12:18). Journeying with God does not mean that someone is never wrong or never afraid.

Again, just after Isaac was born, Sarah saw Ishmael, Hagar's son by Abraham, "Isaac-ing,"[11] that is, presuming to play the role of Isaac, the son promised by God. Sarah promptly ordered Abraham to cast out Hagar and her son, putting both of their lives in danger. Abraham was grieved. The act was clearly wrong in his eyes. But God told Abraham to

<hr/>

[10] Jon Levenson, *Creation and the Persistence of Evil* (Princeton, NJ: Princeton University Press, 1994), 104.

[11] Gen 20:9. The Hebrew *metsaheq* here is usually translated as "laughing" or "mocking." Robert Alter offers the translation "Isaac-ing." He comments, "Given the fact that she is concerned lest Ishmael encroach on her son's inheritance, and given the inscription of her son's name (Isaac, which means laughter) in this crucial verb (*metsaheq*), we may also be invited to construe it as 'Isaac-ing it' (above there was no 'it' —that is, Sarah sees Ishmael presuming to play the role of Isaac, child of laughter, presuming to be the legitimate heir" (Alter, *Genesis* [New York: W.W. Norton, 1996], 98).

listen to Sarah. The man who had been called to the path of righteousness must have been troubled and perplexed by God's instruction.

The crowning moral ambiguity of Abraham's life was the event that the Rabbis call "The Last Trial," the binding of Isaac. God charged Abraham to take Isaac to Mount Moriah to "raise him up there for an offering," or perhaps God meant "raise him up there as an offering" (Gen 22:2). The Hebrew text is terribly ambiguous. Is Isaac to accompany Abraham to an offering on Mount Moriah, or is Isaac to be the offering? The text is not clear. Abraham was left in the dark. Nevertheless, Abraham set out on the journey to Mount Moriah.

When an angel of God intervened and stayed Abraham's hand, Abraham and the reader are left to wonder whether it was right or not to be willing to sacrifice his son. The text is, again, ambiguous. God says, "Lay not your hand upon the lad," perhaps meaning that it is wrong to sacrifice your son, and then God adds, "for now I know that you fear God, seeing that you did not withhold your son, your only son from me" (Gen 22:12). This sounds, by contrast, as if God is pleased with Abraham. Is Abraham's deed laudable or abominable? Could this God of righteousness ask a man to sacrifice his son, or had Abraham misheard the charge?

The text does not tell us. And perhaps that is the point. The journey with God is a human passage. As such, the journey is a way rich in vulnerability, doubt, and uncertainty. The founder and patriarch Abraham did not find certainty as he wandered with God. Instead of certainty, he walked a path of human learning alongside a God who was learning. Abraham and God learned together how to create human flourishing through concern for all human beings and all creation. We are called to that mutual learning too. This unmapped path brings blessing to all the families of the earth.

CHAPTER 8

Rivalry and Resolution in Genesis

The life journeys of Abraham's immediate descendants are chronicled in the book of Genesis.[1] As in the Abraham narrative, the twin prophetic themes—journey and the challenge of mutual relationship—play decisive roles in the narrative of the lives of his progeny. We can read the entire book of Genesis as an extended study of personal relationships, or more specifically, an exploration of familial rivalry, beginning with Cain, who asks, "Am I my brother's keeper?" (Gen 4:9).

The focus in Genesis on familial relationships raises a question: is there a connection between the Bible's critique of imperial ways and the sustained attention given in Genesis to tensions among brothers and sisters? Why does a Scripture whose social and political vision extends to distant empires devote most of its first book to the internal dynamics of one family? These questions guide our exploration of Genesis.

The biblical story all but starts with family rivalry. The reader of Genesis cannot help but notice that the very first story in the post-Eden world involves fratricide:

> And in the process of time it came to pass, that Cain brought of the fruit of the ground an offering to the Living Presence. And Abel also brought of the firstlings of his flock and of the fat of it. And the Living Presence had respect for Abel and for his offering; But for Cain and his offering the Living Presence did not have respect. And Cain was very angry and his countenance fell. (Gen 4:3–5)

---

[1] The Bible, a series of texts that emerge from a patriarchal culture, unfortunately focuses more on the male personages. We do catch glimpses of women and hear some of their voices. All the matriarchs, including Moses's mother and sister, Yochebed and Miriam, respectively, play a significant role in the largely patriarchal drama, acting behind the scenes to shape the events that concern them.

Cain, terribly disheartened, swiftly resolves the sibling struggle. He murders his brother. Biblical readers have long judged God for favoring Abel, inciting Cain's fury. But we can appreciate the Scripture for giving us Cain's story to contemplate. Cain's suffering grabs our attention and focuses it sharply on an issue that is at the root of so much human suffering. We humans need to be valued by those around us, especially our parents, while all too often someone else appears to stand in the way.

Cain's fury also gives us insight into the complexity of the human condition. For even in the moment of rage, Cain must know that in murdering his brother, his own flesh and blood, something essential of himself will die as well. This is the painful dilemma that the people in Genesis repeatedly face: someone in the family appears to limit the favor or the blessing one receives. This dilemma arises from the perception that good things, including blessings from God, are scarce. Therefore, it appears that one must overcome another family member to receive those blessings. But displacing one's flesh and blood inevitably demeans oneself.

At the root of this quandary lies the perception of scarcity. The arc of the narrative in Genesis illustrates that this perception of scarcity, rather than one's family member, must be overcome on the journey toward mutual relationship.

In the first story of family rivalry in Genesis, Cain perceived God's favor to be limited. God offered Cain a way out of his dilemma, informing Cain that he, too, can receive God's blessing. God told Cain, "Why are you angry? and why is your countenance fallen? If you do well, shall you not be accepted?" (4:6–7).

But Cain does not respond to God; he cannot hear God's offering. For Cain, there is only enough favor for one son. He suffers a sense of God's disfavor and is understandably enraged.

Cain's pain and murderous rage cast a long, dark shadow over the book of Genesis. In each generation of Abraham's family, familial rivalry threatens to tear the family apart and bring to an end his family's journey with God. The dangerous simmering conflict within the family of Abraham drives much of the narrative until the familial conflict reaches a breaking point and then arrives at a resolution at the end of the book.

As with the prophets, the memes of outer and inner journey play a central role in the lives of Abraham and his descendants. Virtually all the patriarchs and matriarchs are on the move, often traveling vast distances. Abraham, Sarah, Rebecca, Jacob, Leah, and Rachel all make the long trek from Mesopotamia to Canaan. Even Isaac is repeatedly on the move until he ultimately settles in Beersheva. At the same time, these outer journeys in Genesis are paralleled by an inner journey, a struggle with the dynamics of mutual relationship. Each individual in these stories is challenged to pursue her or his unique destiny in the face of a family member who stands squarely in the way.

The strife begins with Abraham, who finds himself in conflict with his brother's son, Lot:

> And Abram was very rich in cattle, in silver, and in gold. . . . And Lot also, who went with Abram, had flocks, and herds, and tents. And the land was not able to bear them, that they might live together; for their possessions were great, so that they could not live together. And there was strife between the herdsmen of Abram's cattle and the herdsmen of Lot's cattle. . . . And Abram said to Lot, Let there be no strife, I beg you, between me and you, and between my herdsmen and your herdsmen; for we are brothers. Is not the whole land before you? Separate yourself, I beg you, from me; if you will take the left hand, then I will go to the right; or if you depart to the right hand, then I will go to the left. And Lot lifted up his eyes, and saw the valley of the Jordan, that it was well watered everywhere, before the Lord destroyed Sodom and Gomorrah, like the garden of the Lord, like the land of Egypt, as you come to Zoar. Then Lot chose for himself the valley of the Jordan; and Lot journeyed east, and they separated themselves, one from the other. (Gen 13:2, 5–11)

In this story Abraham embodies two noble qualities that lead to a peaceful resolution of a family conflict. First, Abraham sees abundance: "Is not the whole land before you?" he observes. Second, Abraham moderates his own ambition for prosperity to preserve his relationship with Lot. He emphasizes, "For we are brothers." Lot, on the other hand, places his own welfare above that of his uncle. By custom, Lot should have stepped back, giving his uncle the first choice of the land. Instead Lot was bedazzled by the fertility of the Jordan Valley and chose to settle in Sodom. The moral corruption of Sodom and its eventual destruction are a clear commentary on Lot's choice.[2]

The disharmony in Abraham's household comes closer to home in the conflict between Sarah and Hagar, the mothers of Abraham's two sons. Once again, the perception of scarcity is the root of the conflict. Concerned that Abraham's elder son Ishmael may be his heir, Sarah cajoles Abraham to banish Hagar and her son Ishmael from their camp. This

---

[2] See Gen 19.

banishment is "very grievous in Abraham's sight" (Gen 21:11), but he is unable to resolve it. A heavyhearted Abraham, listening to God's instruction, sends Hagar and Ishmael away. The issue of inheritance is clarified, but the conflict within the family of Abraham remains unsettled, foreshadowing the perilous struggles that are to come.

The exploration of familial rivalry continues in the generation of Abraham's grandsons, Esau and Jacob. Jacob and his mother, Rebecca, face a monumental dilemma. God has told Rebecca that Jacob, her younger son, will become master of his father's household and carry his lineage. But an aging Isaac asks his elder son Esau to prepare to receive his blessing. Rebecca and Jacob conspire to deceive Isaac so that Jacob can receive his father's blessing. Upon learning of the deceit, a profoundly hurt and furious Esau plans to kill his younger brother. The jealous rage of Cain now directly threatens the family of Abraham.

Esau is Cain's spiritual brother. Both are the oldest of twin sons, and they face the same brotherly dilemma.[3] The challenging sibling dynamic is most profound among twins. Intimate from the womb, born almost of the same flesh, each twin must distinguish himself from the other and find his own unique identity, all the time knowing in some primal way that he is of one body with his brother. Initially, this sibling struggle for identity finds its expression in a contest for the parents' attention. Esau and Jacob struggled to receive their father's blessing, as Cain and Abel had contested for God's favor. Is there enough blessing for all?

The Jacob story answers this question. Jacob did not need to deceive his father to receive Isaac's most consequential blessing, the benediction to carry the spiritual lineage of Abraham. Isaac gives this blessing to Jacob well after the masquerade has been exposed, when Jacob is about to depart for Haran:

> And God Almighty bless you, and make you fruitful, and multiply you, that you may be a multitude of people; And give the blessing of Abraham to you, and to your seed with you; that you may inherit the land where you are a stranger, which God gave to Abraham. (Gen 28:3–4)

Jacob flees from his brother, seeking refuge with his mother's brother Laban in distant Haran. Jacob did not escape the consequences

---

[3] The Torah does not identify Cain as a twin, but the midrash does. Noting that the description of Abel's birth lacks the familiar "conceived and bore" and only says that Eve "continued bearing his brother, Abel" (Gen 4:2), the Rabbis conclude that Cain and Abel were twins.

of deceiving his father and cheating his older brother. Upon his arrival in Haran, Jacob immediately meets and falls in love with Laban's younger daughter, Rachel. Jacob's love for Rachel is one of the great loves in the Bible. Jacob worked for Laban for seven years to earn the bride price for Rachel, and those years "seemed to him but a few days, for the love he had for her" (Gen 29:20). But when the time came to marry Rachel, Laban deceived Jacob and gave him the older daughter Leah as his bride.

Jacob meets his own shadow in Laban, a devious man.[4] For many years Jacob warily lived within Laban's household, within a culture of deception, at each turn conniving to outsmart his father-in-law. If he had stayed, the journey of Abraham's descendants would likely have come to an end. But ultimately, the resentment within Laban's household rose to such a level that Jacob needed to flee once again, this time along with his wives and children. To pursue his destiny, Jacob must ultimately turn himself around, separate himself from Laban, and finally face his brother Esau.

Once again the Torah speaks to us about the dynamics of family rivalry. Jacob becomes Israel, the father of a people, only after he puts his feet on the path that leads him toward his brother. Initially, the reunion does not look promising. As Jacob reenters Canaan, he learns that Esau is approaching him in the company of four hundred armed men. Jacob's initial moves are appeasement and manipulation. He sends a series of gift-laden messengers to mollify Esau. Then Jacob retreats to the far side of the river; he is not yet prepared to encounter his brother.

Before Jacob can meet Esau, he must encounter his own demon. In the dark of that night by the river, an angel jumps Jacob, and the two wrestle until dawn. The angel cannot prevail over Jacob and asks to be released. But Jacob says, "I will not let you go except you bless me" (Gen 32:27).[5] Jacob, who had received his initial blessing by guile, now honestly confronts the angel face-to-face and demands a blessing. This is the moment that confirms Jacob's transformation:

"He [the angel] said to him; What is your name? And he said: Jacob. Then he said: your name shall no longer be Jacob/Deceitful but rather Israel/God-wrestler for you have striven with God and men and have prevailed." (Gen 32:28–29†)[6]

---

[4]   The name Laban, "white" in Hebrew, hints at this shadow play. In the Torah, Laban is an archetypical dark character who carries the name "White."

[5]   Gen 32:26 in KJV.

[6]   Gen 32:27–28 in KJV.

The great manipulator has become a God-wrestler, and thereby the first to carry the name "Israel."

When Jacob finally encounters Esau, the context of their relationship has radically shifted from one of scarcity to one of abundance. The gifts he had sent in hopes of appeasing his aggrieved brother show how much the context had changed:

> He [Jacob] took of that which came to his hand a tribute for Esau his brother—two hundred female goats, and twenty male goats, two hundred ewes, and twenty rams, thirty milch camels with their colts, forty cows, and ten bulls, twenty female asses, and ten foals. (Gen 32:14–16)[7]

Esau also now lives with a sense of abundance. First, "Esau ran to meet him, and embraced him, and fell upon his neck, and kissed him; and they wept" (Gen 33:4). Then, in response to Jacob's gifts, Esau says, "I have enough, my brother; keep what you have to yourself" (Gen 33:9). Jacob replies, "Take, I beg you, my blessing that is brought to you, because God has dealt graciously with me, and because I have enough" (33:11). In attaching the word "blessing" to his gift offering, Jacob expresses his desire to make restitution for his earlier transgression. The two brothers who had wrestled from the womb, each striving to best the other, now reconcile in peace, each brother acknowledging that he has more than he needs.

The rivalry in the household of Abraham's grandchildren was not restricted to the men. The sisters Leah and Rachel are enmeshed in their own struggle, a contest for their husband Jacob's love and attention. Beginning with the birth of her first three sons, Leah named each child in the context of her rivalry with Rachel:

> Leah conceived, and bore a son, and she called his name Reuben . . . [for] the Living Presence has looked upon [*reu*] my affliction; now therefore my husband will love me. And she conceived again, and bore a son, and said, Because the Living Presence has heard [*shama*] that I was hated, he has therefore given me this son also; and she called his name Simeon. And she conceived again, and bore a son; and said, Now this time will my husband be joined [*lavah*] to me, because I have born him three sons; therefore was his name called Levi. (Gen 29:32–34)

---

7 Gen 32:13–15 in KJV.

But when Judah is born, Leah transcends her rivalry with Rachel. This is Leah's moment of liberation. She says, "This time I will give thanks to the Living Presence; therefore she called his name Judah (Giving-Thanks)" (Gen 29:35[†]). For Leah, gratitude for the gift of a son replaced sibling rivalry—for the moment. In naming Judah, Leah names the way forward for all of Jacob's descendants: gratitude. In place of rivalry, she felt gratitude. This shift, if only momentary for Leah, is nonetheless fundamental. The practice of gratitude opens a person to an awareness of abundance, and the awareness of abundance supports mutual relationship. Judah, at least in name, embodies the way forward for the children of Israel.

The family rivalry in the household of Abraham and Sarah, growing in intensity with each generation, reaches its denouement in the relations among Jacob's sons. Among his twelve sons, Judah and Joseph stand out as the most prominent. The descendants of Judah will become the core of the southern kingdom of Judah, while the Joseph tribes, Ephraim and Menasha, will form the core of the northern kingdom of Israel. In the tales of these sons, the usually concise narrative style of the Torah opens up into an extended account so that the reader can explore more carefully the danger of family rivalry and the path of family reconciliation.

The Judah and Joseph story plunges the reader deep in the midst of sibling conflict. In short order we learn that Joseph had brought "bad reports" about his brothers to his father, and that Jacob loved Joseph more than his siblings and had given Joseph an ornamented tunic as a sign of his love. The text tells us, "When his brothers saw that their father loved him more than all his brothers, they hated him, and could not speak peaceably to him" (Gen 37:4). Joseph then compounded the insult by relating two separate dreams in which, symbolically, the brothers all bowed down to Joseph. "Shall you indeed reign over us? or shall you have dominion over us?" the brothers ask. "And they hated him even more for his dreams, and for his words" (Gen 37:8). Upon hearing the dreams, the brothers' growing hatred toward Joseph reached a boiling point. After coming close to the violence of Cain, the brothers refrained from murdering Joseph. They sold him as a slave to a caravan heading down to Egypt.

The next chapter of the narrative begins on a dismal note: "And it came to pass at that time, that Judah went down from his brothers" (Gen 38:1). Judah, who had degraded himself by participating in the sale of Joseph, left his brothers and went down to live amid the Canaanites. Judah had given up on living in community with his brothers. As Judah leaves, the family of Abraham, the carriers of the covenant and God's promise, has apparently dissolved into mutual rivalry and hatred.

Judah leaves, but his misery continues. His first son, Ar, is wicked in the eyes of God.[8] God slays Ar, leaving his wife, Tamar, a widow. By tribal custom Ar's younger brother Onan was obligated to marry Tamar and raise his firstborn as his brother's heir. Onan, acting out of sibling rivalry, "spilled it [his seed] on the ground, lest he should give seed to his brother. And the thing which he did displeased the Living Presence, and He slew him also" (Gen 38:9–10).

Tamar enters the story as an active character after the death of her second husband. At this terribly low point in the narrative, this Canaan-ite woman will accomplish what none of the descendants of Abraham had managed to do. She will face down the impulse toward rivalry and will treat Judah, the man who betrayed her, with care and respect, thereby redeeming Judah and his heritage.

After Onan dies, Tamar is entitled to have a son through Shelah, Judah's third son, and so Judah has promised her. But fearing that Shelah will die as well, Judah withholds him from Tamar. In time, realizing that Judah will not allow her to marry Shelah, Tamar undertakes her own risky journey.

When Tamar was told that Judah was "going up" to Timnah to shear sheep, "she took off her widow's garments" (Gen 38:14). This is her exodus, her liberation on the journey away from hierarchy and toward mutual relationship. Desiring to bring forth progeny, she hides herself in veils and sits at "an Opening of the Eyes on the road to Timnah" (Gen 38:14[†]). Judah will not recognize the veiled Tamar, but his eyes will ulti-mately be opened by the encounter.

When Judah encounters the veiled woman alongside the road, think-ing her to be a harlot, "he turned to her by the way, and said, Come, I beg you, let me come in to you" (Gen 38:16). Tamar, possessed with both courage and vision, sees that she must not only conceive a child by Judah but she must also obtain proof of her child's lineage. So she asks for Judah's seal, cord, and staff in pledge. Judah "gave them to her, and came in to her, and she conceived by him" (Gen 38:18).

Three months later, Judah is told that Tamar "is with child by har-lotry" (Gen 38:24). In an act of righteous anger, Judah says, "bring her out and let her be burned" (38:24). As Tamar is brought out, she resists the temptation to expose her accuser. Instead she sends a message to her father-in-law, saying, "By the man whose these are am I pregnant. And she said, please recognize whose seal and cord and staff are these? Judah recognized them and said, she is in the right more than I, for I did not give her to Shelah my son" (Gen 38:25–26[†]).

---

[8]   Notice that his name, Ar, is the Hebrew word for "wicked," *ra*, spelled backward.

Tamar's words to "pray, recognize" this garment are the exact same words that the brothers spoke to Jacob when they held before him Joseph's blood-sodden cloak (Gen 37:32). The narrator's description of Judah's response also exactly parallels Jacob's response: "he recognized" (Gen 37:33; 38:26). Tamar, of course, is not aware of the dark resonance present in her words, "pray, recognize."

Judah knows the full story. He cannot fail to "recognize" the parallels between these two fateful encounters. He also notices the difference between them. While the brothers held the bloodied cloak before Jacob to deceive their father, Tamar presents Judah's cloak to expose the truth. And, more importantly, Tamar avoids rivalry with Judah. While she has in hand the means to humiliate the man who has betrayed her, she restrains herself. She does not directly accuse or implicate Judah. She invites him to recognize that she is in the right and that he has failed to keep his promise. In withholding her accusation and allowing Judah to come to his own reckoning, Tamar protects his dignity. After generations of unceasing rivalry, Tamar does not seek to vanquish her rival. She acts out of care and compassion. Her act opens the possibility for mutual respectful relationship.

Judah is clearly transformed by Tamar's concern for his welfare. He speaks a difficult truth: "She is more right than I. For after all, I did not give her to Shelah my son" (Gen 38:26).

This dramatic encounter with Tamar is the turning point for Judah. We next meet him united with his brothers in the presence of their father. When Judah rejoins his family, Canaan is suffering a severe famine, so the brothers must go down to Egypt to buy food. But Pharaoh's vizier (Joseph) will not receive them if they fail to bring Benjamin to him. Jacob resists. He cannot bear to put his beloved Benjamin at risk. Judah steps forward and says, "I will be surety for him; from my hand shall you require him" (Gen 43:9). In other words, Judah says, "I will be my brother's keeper." Ultimately, when Joseph contrives to take Benjamin and send his brothers back to Jacob without him, Judah again steps forward and says. "Let your servant [Judah] remain [in Egypt] instead of the lad" (Gen 44:33). Judah answers Cain's question in the affirmative: I am my brother's keeper.

With this courageous act, Judah breaks out of the pattern of family rivalry and begins the resolution of the multigenerational tension in Genesis. The Torah tells us that "Judah approached" Joseph (Gen 44:18); he steps forward toward his brother. As he steps forward, Judah offers the family a way forward, the only way forward, the way of brother and sister keeping.

Judah has lived into the meaning of the name Leah gave him at the moment she had transcended her rivalry with her sister. Judah (Giving

Thanks) carried in his name a sense of gratitude, a sensibility that opens to an expansive awareness of abundance. So named, and having learned from Tamar, Judah is aware that the apparently hopeless, dead-end confrontation with Pharaoh's vizier is open to alternative possibilities. There is a way forward to save his family. Filled with this awareness, Judah steps forward in place of his brother.

When an adult Judah "approaches" Joseph, the grand vizier of Egypt, he steps toward a brother who has also matured since their last encounter. The younger Joseph had reveled in sibling rivalry, bringing his father bad reports and relating rivalrous dreams. Like Judah, Joseph had to undergo a long journey and an internal transformation before he could truly meet his brother. Again, akin to Judah, Joseph's path toward transformation initially took him down to a dark place. First his brothers placed him in a pit, and later the captain of Pharaoh's guard consigned him to the dungeon.

Two years later, when Joseph is brought up from the dungeon to interpret Pharaoh's dreams, Joseph reveals that he has begun his journey of transformation. When Pharaoh asks him to interpret the dreams, the formerly arrogant lad answers, "It is not in me; God shall give Pharaoh a favorable answer" (Gen 41:16).

Judah's and Joseph's transformations both reach their climax at the same moment, the moment when Judah steps forward toward Joseph on behalf of their brother Benjamin. In response to Judah's plea to spare Benjamin and take Judah instead, Joseph can no longer restrain himself. He weeps aloud, uttering cries that were heard throughout the house of Pharaoh (Gen 45:1–2). Joseph cries not only for himself. In Joseph's tears, generations of familial pain and suffering find their expression, and a prime conflict in Genesis is resolved.

This reading of Genesis illustrates the prophetic stream flowing through the fertile human territory of family rivalry. Virtually all the patriarchs and matriarchs struggle with a familial rival. In these stories, the movement of the prophetic stream is expressed in the liberation of Jacob, Esau, Leah, Judah, and Joseph from the grip of rivalry, a liberation toward a more mutually respectful sibling relationship.

All these biblical persons traveled significant outer and inner journeys on their way to transformation. Each wrestled internally to arrive at a sense of self-worth and fulfillment that was independent of surpassing a family rival. Jacob, after a lifetime of guile and manipulation, finally encounters his adversary directly, wrestling face-to-face with the angel, fighting hand-to-hand for his blessing. Leah struggled through heart-rending disappointment when the birth of each of her first three sons did not wrest her husband's love away from her sister Rachel. Only with the birth of Judah did she transcend rivalry and see that her sense of worth could be found in being grateful for what she had received.

Judah and Joseph also wrestled for a nonrivalrous sense of self-worth. Both these brothers were thrown into a dark place where they were stripped naked of any false pretense before emerging with true caring for their siblings. In Judah's case, Tamar, the Canaanite woman, rescued him from imminent humiliation. Experiencing his personal vulnerability and Tamar's compassion in his moment of vulnerability, Judah comes into contact with his own compassion, with his own concern for his fellow human beings. Joseph, thrown into the pit and later into Pharaoh's dungeon, twice suffered the fall that came in the wake of his arrogance. He emerges from Pharaoh's prison humbled and more able to see the other, thereby more humane.

For all of these individuals, the liberation journey with God forces them to leave behind their metaphorical Egypt, to abandon a way of being that limited their ability to be in mutual relationship. Their journey then leads them through a wilderness, a place of risk and vulnerability, toward new possibilities in relationship.

In the lives of Jacob, Esau, Leah, and Joseph, we also see that the journey toward their brother or sister leads from a mind-set of scarcity to one of abundance. Following the model of Abraham, who generously offered his nephew Lot his choice of land, these descendants turned away from rivalry as they perceived the presence of enough sustenance, both spiritual and material, to nurture all involved.

We can now answer the question raised at the beginning of the chapter: what is the connection between the Bible's critique of imperial ways and sustained attention to family rivalries in the book of Genesis? The focus on family rivalry in Genesis serves to draw a direct line of causation between the dynamics of familial relationships and societal systems of domination. The Genesis narrative understands that the people Israel's quest to embody an alternative society based on mutual relationship necessarily must be based on mutual, respectful relationships within the family. In this view, oppressive structures of an imperial society ultimately grow out of how brothers and sisters treat each other.

The sequence of stories in Genesis, followed by the narrative in the beginning of Exodus, highlights the connection between family relations and oppressive social systems. Immediately after Jacob's children reconcile at the end of Genesis, the book of Exodus opens with the enslavement of the Israelites in Egypt. The contrast could not be starker—the flowering of family caring immediately interrupted by imperial oppression. This disparity between the emerging brotherly way of Israel and

Pharaoh's harsh domination is then immediately reinforced by Moses's very first act as recorded in Exodus. "And it came to pass in those days, when Moses was grown, that he went out to his brothers, and looked on their burdens; and he spied an Egyptian beating a Hebrew, one of his brothers" (2:11). At great risk to himself, Moses jumps to the defense of his Israelite brother. Like Judah, Moses is a brother-keeper.

The arc in Genesis is toward brother-keeping, but the Torah reveals the great challenges in this journey; the fruits of brother- and sister-caring are hard won. The troubling tale of family conflict within the family of Abraham exposes the roots of rivalry that lie deep in human nature. The implication of this scriptural insight is clear: if one seeks to address the roots of imperial, oppressive systems, one cannot focus solely on the discriminatory policies of political elites, but one must instead understand how every oppressive system is deeply rooted in human nature.

Sibling rivalry and political domination are grounded in the same fundamental dynamic of the human condition. Every human being must struggle with a core paradox. On the one hand, one needs to distinguish oneself as an individual with unique gifts to bring to the world. On the other hand, a person is aware, at least subconsciously, that his or her individuality is somewhat of an illusion, that all human beings are inextricably woven into one fabric of life. People, especially in Western cultures, may like to see themselves as independent, freestanding individuals. But in truth, at every moment, the content of a person's innermost experience, including one's will and one's very sense of self, is shaped by a myriad of external factors—past, present, and future—that includes an interdependence with one's brothers and sisters.

This is the psychic challenge of the human condition. Said another way, every human has an ego that desires to distinguish and define itself, and at the same time that independent ego is largely a mental artifice, an important part of the psyche but nonetheless a cultural and psychological construct. Each person is unique and at the same time deeply culturally conditioned and highly interdependent. How do we distinguish ourselves when we realize, at some level, that our focus on such distinctions obscures the reality that life is an undivided whole? Every human faces this crisis of identity.

Unfortunately, the easiest and most common way to distinguish oneself from an "other" is to ignore all the ways that one's life is interwoven with an other's existence and to believe that one is somehow better than that other. This mentality of hierarchy, expressed as superiority, exists at every level of human existence—in individuals, ethnic groups, religions, nations, and as a human species. Human beings and human societies all too commonly resolve challenges to identity and prove their self-worth by believing that they are superior to the other.

We witness this othering in discriminatory prejudices throughout every society. Within American society this kind of discrimination is evident in some white people's prejudice against people of color and immigrants or in the disdain expressed on both sides of the divide between liberals and conservatives. In relation to other nations, observers have long said that the United States needs an enemy to maintain a sense of American identity.

One effective and concrete means of proving one's superiority over an other is to have more: more power, wealth, or public attention; a larger house; or a fancier car. Whether pursued through discriminatory practices or through economic or political exploitation, the individual desire to distinguish oneself, or a certain group's need for distinction, all too easily find their expression in systems of domination and oppression. A person or a society seeks to demonstrate superiority by keeping an other down.

This psychic need to distinguish oneself is strongly enforced by the profound physical drive for survival. An individual's psychic and human survival needs to go hand in hand, especially if a person perceives a scarcity of resources. A person and a nation may feel more secure, psychically and physically, if the individual or the state can overwhelm the other.

Domination serves both the immediate psychological and survival needs of an individual and a group, but dominance comes at a great cost, to the oppressor as well as the oppressed. The cost to the oppressed is evident, but the oppressor is also diminished because oppressors inevitably become alienated from their humanity and from other human beings—indeed, from all of creation. Cut off and alienated, the oppressor can aggrandize, and in some ways even begin to flourish, but ultimately that flourishing is limited. Full flourishing, the gift of the prophetic stream, is a liberation journey into deeper mutual relationship. Full flourishing emerges in the journey *toward* the other. In dominating the other, the oppressor also limits him- or herself.

We can see this limitation in societies as well as in individuals. Imperial or rigidly hierarchic societies lack the capacity for mutual relationship that can support flourishing cultural differences. Inevitably, the ascendant segment in a society privileges the cultural norms of that group and attempts to impose those cultural norms on the rest of society. Differences between people and cultures—otherness—is managed through suppression. For example, even in twenty-first century America, people of color and women who wish to ascend within US society must learn how to talk and act in ways that are not too dissimilar to the ways of white males.

The narrative in Genesis offers an alternative vision: the long, hard learning journey toward mutual relationship. We can conceptually divide this journey in Genesis into three acts. At the outset of the journey, Abraham models the way forward in his relationship with Lot. Abraham, living with a sense of abundance and generosity, tempers his personal ambition and maintains his brotherly relationship with his nephew. In the second act of the Genesis journey, Esau and Jacob turn away from their deadly conflict and toward each other. They also speak in terms of abundance and generosity. In the same generation, Leah literally brings forth the seed of reconciliation when she embraces gratitude over jealousy and names her fourth son "Judah." Finally, at the end of the third act, the sibling drama in Genesis reaches its resolution. Judah, born in gratitude, approaches his brother Joseph, putting himself at risk to protect the life of his brother Benjamin. Cain's question has been decisively answered.

In this multigenerational sibling drama, Genesis reveals the internal terrain of the liberation journey toward mutual relationship. In this internal landscape, the powerful human inclination toward rivalry and jealousy blows like gale-force winds, buffeting the individual who journeys toward the other. The power of these winds can only be met by a clear and paramount commitment to brotherhood and sisterhood, a commitment to relationship, the kind of commitment witnessed in the deeds of Abraham and Tamar and, ultimately, in Judah. This commitment to relationship, in turn, must be buttressed by a sense of abundance, by an attitude of gratitude and generosity, as seen in Leah, Esau, and ultimately in Jacob. Commitment to relationship, awareness of abundance, and an attitude of gratitude and generosity are prime virtues of the liberation journey.

CHAPTER 9

Exodus

A Women's Liberation

The book of Exodus opens with vivid images of the people of Israel's precipitous fall from freedom into slavery. This devastating dehumanization is captured at the outset of Exodus by the loss of personal names. The first verses of the book detail the names of each of Jacob's sons who had descended to Egypt: "Now these are the names of the sons of Israel, who came into Egypt with Jacob; every man came with his household: Reuben, Simeon, Levi, and Judah, Issachar, Zebulun, and Benjamin, Dan and Naphtali, Gad and Asher" (1:1–4). Subsequently, in the generations after the death of Joseph, names are no longer mentioned. Even Moses's parents are not named: "And there went a man of the house of Levi, and took to wife a daughter of Levi" (2:1). This loss of names signals that the terribly oppressive Egyptian political order precipitated a process of degeneration: a de-Genesis. In the creation stories in Genesis, God names the heavens, the seas, and the earth. Then God brings "every beast of the field, and every bird of the air" to Adam "to see what he would call them" (2:19). Name-giving distinguishes one creature from another and signifies relationship. In the naming process of Genesis, an unfolding creation evolves toward greater differentiation and individuality. In Egypt, Pharaoh strips the Israelites of their individuality, reversing the process of increasing differentiation.

Egyptian oppression also dehumanizes the oppressor, Pharaoh. In Genesis, the ruler of Egypt is always referred to as "Pharaoh," an honorific title for the ruler of Egypt. In the opening of Exodus, Pharaoh is stripped of his title and referred to simply as "the king of Egypt" (1:17). The Hebrew midwives, Shifra and Puah, are the first people given names in Exodus. The Egyptian ruler is again called "Pharaoh" in his interaction with Shifra and Puah.

The dehumanization in Egypt is also expressed in the preternatural way in which the Israelites multiplied despite their oppression. Describing Israelite fertility, the exodus account uses the familiar terms, "they were fruitful and multiplied"—the same expression for fertility found in the creation story in Genesis. But the exodus narrative adds the word, "and they swarmed," a term applied to the insects in the story of Noah's ark and to fish fertility in the creation story. The exodus account places this word associated with animal fertility between "fruitful" and "multiplied": "the children of Israel were fruitful, and swarmed, and multiplied" (Exod 1:7[†]). The Israelites, stripped of their humanity, multiplied like insects and fish.

Threatened by the growing Israelite population, Pharaoh seeks to control Israelite fertility by imposing harsh labor upon them, forcing the Israelites to work on building store-cities.[1] This building project vividly symbolizes that Egypt had become the exact antithesis of God's intention for creation. In Genesis 1, God continually liberates, progressively empowering the potential within each form of life to bring forth a new, more differentiated form of life. Pharaoh, seeking to squelch the life force of the Israelites, moves in the opposite direction. He sets the Israelites to work building cities that will store up, encase, and tightly control the produce of nature. The term "store-cities" appears only a few times in the Bible. The most common reference is to King Solomon, who built store-cities for his chariots and horsemen.[2] Pharaoh's store-cities likely served a similar martial purpose. The Israelite men are not building houses in which people can live; they are building walls behind which goods are hoarded for war.

In the Genesis account, God works in partnership with creation to bring forth its potential. In Exodus, Pharaoh seeks to exert power over creation, to dominate creation for his purpose. While God empowers the transforming flow of life—the prophetic stream—Pharaoh seeks to suppress Israelite fertility and store away the fruits of the prophetic stream. The Rabbis capture Pharaoh's desire to entrap life in a most horrifying image. They imagined that "Pharaoh's police would strangle the Israelites in the walls of the buildings, between the bricks."[3] In this image, the hardening of clay into bricks and the construction of city walls become images for the endeavor to encase and "strangle" the life force, to block the flow of the prophetic stream.

---

[1] Exod 1:11.
[2] 1 Kgs 9:19.
[3] *Pirke d' Rabbi Eliezer* 48; quoted in Avivah Gottlieb Zornberg, *The Particulars of Rapture* (New York: Doubleday, 2001), 40.

God ultimately liberates the Israelite slaves from Egyptian bondage with "an outstretched arm and mighty judgments" (Exod 6:6). One might conclude that God's use of force, the ten plagues, was the decisive action that liberated the Israelites from Egypt. A careful reading of the text, however, leads to a more complex understanding.

The initial threat to Pharaoh was not a supernatural power from above, but a power from within the people. Israelite fertility, the life force within the enslaved people, was Pharaoh's prime concern. Expressing his fear, Pharaoh exclaims, "Behold this people, the Children of Israel, is many more and mightier [in number] than we!" (Exod 1:9).

The first resisters to Pharaoh are the midwives, Shifra and Puah, women who served the life force by saving the lives of Israelite male babies in the face of Pharaoh's decree to kill them. Standing up against Pharaoh, the midwives mirror the action of God in the Genesis creation story; they facilitate the life force, enabling the birth of new life. The midwives witness to the power of this life force when Pharaoh asks them, "Why have you done this thing, and have saved the male children alive?" (Exod 1:18). The midwives reply, "The Hebrew women . . . are lively, and deliver before the midwives come to them" (1:19).

The other key players in the initial stages of the liberation are also women: Moses's mother, Yochebed, his sister Miriam; and Pharaoh's daughter Batya.[4] All three women, including Batya, knowingly resist Pharaoh's decree to save the life of the infant Moses. The other feminine presence in this story of liberation is the River Nile, flowing water being an archetypical feminine image. Moses's mother, Yochebed, entrusted the life of her baby to the river, while his sister Miriam stood guard by the river. Pharaoh's daughter Batya came down to the river to bathe and saw the little ark bearing the child. The life of the first prophet, Moses, is preserved via the flow of the Nile, a physical manifestation of the prophetic stream moving in the world.

Contemporary biblical scholar Avivah Gottlieb Zornberg refers to women's role in the Bible as "the repressed narrative of the biblical text."[5] She goes on to observe that "*midrash* retains the traces of that narrative and brings it to consciousness, with marked effects on the manifest level of meaning."[6] A prime example of this midrashic consciousness of the repressed feminine may be found in the rabbinic midrashim exploring the leading role that women took in the early stages of the

---

[4] The Rabbis give Pharaoh's nameless daughter the name Batya, significantly meaning "daughter [not of Pharaoh but] of God."

[5] Zornberg, *Particulars of Rapture*, 9.

[6] Ibid.

liberation. The Rabbis expand on the courageous role taken by Shifra, Puah, Yochebed, Miriam, and Batya to include all the women of their generation in the acts of resistance and liberation:

> Miriam dared to reprove her father. Amram was at that time the head of the Sanhedrin, and when Pharaoh decreed that if it be a son, then ye shall kill him, Amram said that it was useless for the Israelites to beget children. Forthwith he ceased to have intercourse with his wife Yochebed and even divorced his wife, though she was already three months pregnant. Whereupon all the Israelites arose and divorced their wives. Then said his daughter to him: "Your decree is more severe than that of Pharaoh; for Pharaoh decreed only concerning the male children, and you decree upon males and females alike. Besides, Pharaoh being wicked, there is some doubt whether his decree will be fulfilled or not, but you are righteous and your decree will be fulfilled." So he took his wife back and was followed by all the Israelites, who also took their wives back.[7]

Miriam succeeded in reuniting husbands and wives, but her daring act was not enough to birth the next generation. Pharaoh's harsh decrees forced crushing labor upon the men to the point that they were too exhausted to mate with their wives. The key to Pharaoh's oppression was to exhaust the men's life force. The irony at the heart of the story is that Pharaoh thought that the men were the prime threat to his oppressive rule. He assumed that the reservoir of resistance lay with the men. In a parody of male dominance, to abort Israelite fertility, Pharaoh decreed that the midwives must kill all the male children and let the females live. In truth, females were the key to Israelite reproduction, both in their physical ability to give birth and in their psychological and spiritual dedication to continue to nurture life. Pharaoh, blind to the power of women, focused on the males and overlooked women's liberating power.[8]

Pharaoh succeeded in demoralizing and exhausting the men. They could not bear to see their children thrown into the Nile. They lacked the energy to mate with their wives. But the women were not deterred. As the Rabbis tell the story, "The women would go out with soup and hot water to the fields where the exhausted men worked. They would wash and massage them, eat and drink, and take them to the fringes of the fields to make love." The midrash sums up the role of the Hebrew

---

[7] *Exodus Rabbah* 1:12.
[8] See Matis Weinberg, *Frameworks Shemot* (Boston: Foundations for Jewish Publications, 1999), chap. 1.

women with these words: "Due to the merit of the righteous women of that generation Israel was redeemed from Egypt."[9]

Women played a defining role in subverting Pharaoh's regime because their activity embodied a particular kind of power. Pharaoh sought to dominate his subjects in order to compel them to surrender their creative power to his will. The women in the narrative tapped into a subversive, opposing force: the power of the prophetic stream. The women served and brought forth the indomitable power of giving birth and nurturing new life. In Exodus, the power of birthing and nurturing overcame a domineering power focused on building structures that impede the unfolding flow of God's creation.

The experience of women, specifically the experience of birth, shapes the entire Exodus story. As in human birth, the people go through a narrow passage amid the waters (the Sea of Reeds) and emerge on the other side of the waters into a great open space. The story describes the collective birth of a people. The family of Abraham becomes the Hebrew people, a new entity whose origin story is the liberation from slavery.

The activity of the women in the early chapters of Exodus is essential to subverting Egypt's dominance because Pharaoh's repressive building regime was in fact quite effective. The independent spirit of the Hebrew slaves was all too easily taken over by the pressure to keep building. As Zornberg writes, "The individual (all too easily) is built into the building. . . . All who are involved in building become the system, serve its automatism."[10] No external power could free these men until they reconnected to the creative life force. It fell to the Hebrew women to subvert oppressive "power-over" by tapping into a power within. Denied access to brute physical power and officially sanctioned power, the Hebrew women lived close to the hidden and subversive power within, the power of life itself. These women, including the midwives Shifra and Puah, knew the deep power of the life force from their own experiences; they understood that renewal comes from working with the life force. These women rebirth the people by mirroring God's work in creation, working in relationship, in partnership with life.

The Hebrew women, as well as Batya, resisted Pharaoh's power-over by bringing forth power from within. Moreover, they countered the brick-hard rigidity of Pharaoh's Egypt by practicing flexibility and adaptability as they worked with life and with each other. Witness the activity of Yochebed, Moses's mother. When she gave birth to Moses, she did not have a master plan for how to save her son's life; she could

---

[9]   B. *Talmud Sotah* 11b.
[10] Zornberg, *Particulars of Rapture*, 50.

not control the outcome. Undeterred, she devised a strategy one step at a time to preserve Moses's life. First, she hid him. When she was no longer able to hide him, she made an ark. Placing her trust in the waters of the river, she set the ark among the reeds on the Nile. When Batya discovered the baby, Yochebed became his wet nurse, and when Moses was weaned, Yochebed brought him to Batya to be raised as her son.

Women learn to be flexible because daily challenges to survival require oppressed people, which includes women, to be more flexible than people with power. Mary Catherine Bateson, in her study of women's lives, found this kind of flexibility to be common in the way women move forward. Bateson's work with diverse women found that each woman made multiple changes of direction and course corrections.[11]

Lacking the power to control events, the women in the exodus narrative also needed to muster great trust. Yochebed needed to trust that the River Nile would deliver her son into caring hands. Miriam needed to trust that Pharaoh's daughter would protect the infant Moses, and Batya needed to trust that her father would not punish her and kill the child.

All these women also demonstrated a willingness to act when the success of their efforts was well beyond their control. They possessed the courage to step out on an uncertain road and the vision to perceive that the uncertain path before them was nevertheless a promising way forward.

The qualities found in these women—adaptability, trust, willingness to act in the presence of uncertainty, and envisioning a promising way forward—taken together point to the shape of their faith. Shifra, Puah, Yochebed, Miriam, and Batya possessed an abiding trust or faith in life— a faith that life itself would find a way forward and a way to flourish, even in the face of great obstacles. Their deep connection to the life force gave these women the wisdom, courage, and vision to take bold and creative action.

These women's stories reflect the action of the prophetic stream refracted through an archetypal feminine lens. Unlike Abraham, who had to leave civilization behind to establish an alternative way, these women created an alternative culture right in Egypt's midst. Unlike Jacob, who wrestled alone, or Judah, who individually stood up for Benjamin, these women worked with each other, in relationship.

It is deeply problematic that the role of women has been too often overlooked in the exodus story and that the archetypal feminine aspect of the prophetic stream is not more evident in the biblical text. The

---

[11] See Mary Catherine Bateson, *Composing a Life* (New York: Grove Press, 2007).

feminine archetype contains an essential element of the prophetic stream—the act of consciously nurturing relationship. Nurturing is an essential process of the prophetic stream as exemplified by a God who nurtures forward the process of creation. The prophetic stream nurtures creation toward deeper, mutual relationship. In nature, including the human, mutual relations are not formed by an external power exerting force. Rather, mutual relations are nurtured from within and between life forms.

Christian feminist theologian Beverly Harrison highlights the power of nurture, placing the formidable effect of genuine nurturing at the center of the human journey:

> Women's lives literally have been shaped by the power not only to bear human life at the biological level but also to nurture life, which is a social and cultural power. Though our culture has come to disvalue women's role, which is to disvalue nurturance, *genuine nurturance is a formidable power.* Insofar as it has taken place in human history, it has been largely through women's action. For better or worse, women have had to face the reality that we have the power not only to create personal bonds between people but, more basically, to build up and deepen personhood itself. And to build up "the person" is to deepen relationship. . . . Because we do not understand love as the power to act-each-other-into-well-being, we also do not understand the depth of our power to thwart life and to maim each other. The fateful choice is ours, either to set free the power of God's love in the world or to deprive each other of the very basis of personhood and community.[12]

In recent millennia, nurture has been largely the work of women. However, the feminine archetype—in this context, the capacity to nurture—lives in men as well as women. Until recent times, the cultural distortions of patriarchal culture have dictated that men go out to explore and build while women stay home and nurture; men are strong, and women are sensitive. An alternative culture would encourage the builder and the nurturer, the archetypal masculine and the archetypal feminine, in every human being.

The prominent role of women in Exodus highlights the archetypal feminine, the power of "working with," as an expression of the prophetic

---

[12]   Beverly Wildung Harrison, *Making the Connections: Essays in Feminist Social Ethics* (Boston: Beacon Press, 1985), 11.

stream. Journeying out, an expression of the traditional masculine arche-type, is also an expression of the prophetic stream. The exodus from Egypt required the feminine as well as the masculine archetypes—the deeds of Miriam as well as those of Moses. To achieve freedom from bondage, the siblings Miriam and Moses had to go a step beyond the reconciliation that Judah and Joseph attained at the end of Genesis. In the exodus, these siblings joined to do the work of liberation. Each needed the other to leave Egypt and to cross the sea.

CHAPTER 10

Force and Transformation

The Israelite women nurtured personhood among the enslaved people, but their efforts, however essential, were not sufficient to bring about liberation. Nor were Moses's courageous confrontations with Pharaoh. In the end, God takes the people out of Egypt, "with a mighty hand, and with an outstretched arm, and with great awesomeness" (Deut 26:8). God's violent role in the emancipation process raises a question about the effectiveness of the prophetic stream working *with and within* people.

In Genesis, the God of creation models a power that *works with* rather than dominates over, a power that acts *in relation to* a given order so as to release the potential of the status quo. In acting to free the Israelite slaves, by contrast, God states that the liberation process cannot go forward in the absence of overwhelming force: "I [God] am sure that the king of Egypt will not give you leave to go, if not by a mighty hand. And I will stretch out my hand and will strike Egypt with all my wonders which I will do in its midst, and after that, he will let you go" (Exod 3:19–20).

The exodus narrative raises the difficult question concerning the role of physical force in the liberation process. According to sixteenth-century Italian commentator Sforno, God acted because of "their [the Israelites] debilitating and destructive oppression."[1] God acted because the liberation movement initiated by the midwives and Miriam was being crushed by Pharaoh's oppression. The liberating power working from within had to be aided by an external overwhelming force.

God's use of force to take the Israelites out of Egypt suggests that sometimes overwhelming violence is necessary for the liberation journey. Is there a positive role for violence in the liberation process, and if so, what is that role?

---

[1] Sforno commentary on Exod 2:23, found in Mikraot Gedolot author's translation.

During the Holocaust, Martin Buber and Mahatma Gandhi famously engaged the conversation about the role of force to relieve oppression. Gandhi advised the Jews to employ *satyagraha*, "nonviolence" or "soul power," against the Nazis in Germany. Buber argued that the situation in Germany could not be compared to the regimes that Gandhi faced in South Africa and India. Buber wrote,

It does not seem to me convincing when you base your advice to us to observe satyagraha in Germany on these similarities of circumstance. In the five years I myself spent under the present regime, I observed many instances of genuine satyagraha among the Jews, instances showing a strength of spirit in which there was no question of bartering their rights or of being bowed down, and where neither force nor cunning was used to escape the consequences of their behavior. Such actions, however, exerted apparently not the slightest influence on their opponents. . . . An effective stand in the form of nonviolence may be taken against unfeeling human beings in the hope of gradually bringing them to their senses; but a diabolic universal steamroller cannot thus be withstood.[2]

Buber's view reflects the perspective of the exodus story. There are times when only violence can save a group from destruction. The many acts of genocide in the twentieth century serve as powerful examples. As Samantha Powers details in her carefully researched book on genocide, the world stood by during repeated acts of genocide during the century: Turkey's murder of the Armenians, the Holocaust, Pol Pot's reign of terror in Cambodia, Iraq's slaughter of the Kurds, Bosnian Serbs' mass murder of Muslims, and the Hutu violence against the Tutsi in Rwanda. Powers argues that force should not be the first response to potential genocide; diplomatic and economic pressure can quickly be brought to bear. However, as in Pharaoh's Egypt, the window of time to save a people is limited, and violent force may be necessary to stop the killing.[3] It takes time to nurture internal resistance or to ratchet up diplomatic and economic pressure, so force may be necessary to save human lives.

The exodus narrative alerts us to also be aware of the limits of violence. The use of force comes at a terrible cost, not only to the oppressor, but also to the oppressed. With overwhelming force, God took the peo-

---

[2] Martin Buber, "Open Letter to Gandhi Regarding Palestine," February 24, 1939, www.jewishvirtuallibrary.org.

[3] Samantha Powers, *A Problem from Hell: America in the Age of Genocide* (New York: Basic Books, 2013).

ple out from under Egyptian oppression, but that external force could not take the internal effects of oppression out of the people. The use of force, which inevitably mirrors the violence of the oppressor, has the negative effect of reinforcing the grip of the "internalized oppressor" in the thinking of the oppressed. As Paulo Freire famously observed, oppression from without naturally creates such an "internalized oppressor" within the psyche of the oppressed:

> During the initial stage of the struggle [for liberation], the oppressed, instead of striving for liberation, tend themselves to become oppressors, or "sub-oppressors." . . . Their ideal is to be men; but for them, to be men is to be oppressors. This is their model of humanity. The phenomenon derives from the fact that the oppressed, at a certain moment of their existential experience, adopt an attitude of "adhesion" to the oppressor. Under these circumstances they cannot "consider" him sufficiently clearly to objectivize him—to discover him outside themselves.[4]

While physical force can sometimes remove external oppression and save lives, such force cannot liberate the oppressed from the "internalized oppressor," cannot educate the oppressed to find within themselves a power that is totally unlike the violence of the oppressor. Force can temporarily remove some of the barriers to transformation, but external force does not create inner transformation or social transformation. This kind of liberating transformation only grows out of human nurture and the deepening of mutual relationship. The cultivation of relationships is the work of the prophetic stream within a person and within a society.

The thickening of the bonds of mutual relationship can only take place over time, during which the suffering of oppression continues. Herein lies the great temptation and therefore the terrible danger of violence. External force can effect rapid external change. Consequently, in the face of oppression, people are often tempted to resort to violence in many situations in which violence is not called for and will only be counterproductive. The world witnessed the tragic temptation of violence in the 2003 U.S. invasion of Iraq, which illustrated the idolatrous or false worship of violence, the mistaken belief that violence is reliably effective. In 2003 President George W. Bush informed the nation that he had exhausted all diplomatic efforts to address the problem of supposed weapons of mass destruction in Iraq. Therefore, he was turning to a

---

[4] Paulo Freire, *Pedagogy of the Oppressed*, trans. Myra Bergman Ramos (New York: Continuum, 2003), 25.

strategy that, while terrible, would certainly be effective: brute military force. I call this trust in violence "idolatrous worship" because, as in service to an idol, it is based on an ignorant misattribution of effectiveness. Like invoking the power of a god, the assumption behind the turn to violence is that enough force will accomplish the desired goal. In the war in Iraq, faith in violence offered false assurances that military might would prove successful.

The exodus story, in which God forcibly takes the people out of Egypt, therefore adds a new level of complexity to our understanding of the prophetic stream. The prophetic stream is that force within creation, within people, and within a society that leads a people to undertake the risky journey toward flourishing, toward more freedom to enter mutual relationship. In some cases, however, the stream meets a deadly and immovable obstacle, such as Pharaoh. In those cases, external force, a power that cannot nurture transformation, must be employed against the oppression. Nevertheless, the great harm done by violence, to the oppressor and the oppressed, makes the use of force a very serious and risk-laden matter.

The biblical account itself portrays a God who later recognizes the negative consequences of using overwhelming force against Pharaoh. In the testimony of the prophet Jeremiah, who lived many centuries after the exodus, God reflects on the exodus and acknowledges that the application of external force had not nurtured a covenantal relationship with the people. Speaking through Jeremiah, God takes responsibility for failing to prepare the people to keep the covenant. God promises to make a "new covenant" with the people, a covenant that will be active inside the people, a teaching placed in their hearts:

> Behold, the days come, says the Living Presence, that I will make a new covenant with the house of Israel, and with the house of Judah. Not according to the covenant that I made with their fathers in the day that I took them by the hand to bring them out of the land of Egypt; my covenant which they broke, although I was their master, says the Living Presence. But this shall be the covenant that I will make with the house of Israel; after those days, says the Living Presence, I will give my Torah in their inward parts, and I will be writing it in their hearts; and I will be their God, and they shall be my people. (31:30–32)[5]

---

[5] Jer 31:31–33 in KJV.

Similarly, in the prophecy of Second Isaiah, a prophet who lived in Babylonian exile a generation after Jeremiah, God envisions the people's departure from Babylon as what we might call exodus 2.0, a nonviolent exodus. In direct contrast to the mighty and powerful deeds of the original exodus, Isaiah envisions a liberation that totally lacks the loud cries and massive destruction of violent intervention:

> He [Israel] shall not cry, nor lift up, nor cause his voice to be heard in the street. A bruised reed shall he not break, and the dimly burning flax shall he not quench; he shall bring forth judgment to truth. . . . Behold, the former things have come to pass, and new things do I declare; before they spring forth I tell you of them. Sing to the Living Presence a new song. (Isa 42:2–3, 9–10)

God learned from the people's waywardness, from their lack of mental and spiritual preparedness, at the time of the exodus. External force does not nurture internal growth. Awe in the presence of God's power alone cannot create ongoing devotion. Such devotion is a relationship that must be nurtured over time. For the exiles in Babylonia, God will do "new things." God will nurture the people from within, placing the Torah in their hearts. In this process of nurture, God will build relationship: "I will be their God and they shall be my people" (Jer 31:32). In turn, Israel will be able to sing "a new song." Israel will possess more of the relational consciousness that will enable them to sing the song of freedom.

In these prophetic testimonies, God learns the limitations of violence. This divine learning reinforces the irreplaceable role of women in the exodus process and the essential role of the feminine archetype in the liberation journey. Liberation may appear to come in a moment, when a revolutionary war is won or a wall is torn down, but these dramatic events obscure the nature of true liberation. Actual liberation—increased capacity to enter freely into more conscious and mutual relationships—is a process to carefully and lovingly nurture over time.

CHAPTER 11

The Reluctant Prophet and the Unprepared People

God chose Moses to lead the people out of Egypt. Moses profoundly embodied the moral outrage, daring, and vision that typify a prophet. He was angry when he witnessed the terrible oppression of his people, and he showed bravery and leadership as he led the people out of bondage. Yet Moses tried remarkably hard to reject God's call. Given his clarity, compassion, and courage, why did Moses so vigorously resist God's direction to confront Pharaoh and mobilize the people? This chapter explores Moses's qualifications to lead the people out of Egypt, the roots of Moses's prolonged resistance to undertaking his mission, and the condition of the people that made his task so challenging. An investigation into Moses's character and the mental state of the enslaved, unprepared people offers a deep look into the dynamics of the prophetic stream.

The Torah records nothing about Moses's early life, with the exception of the miraculous circumstances of his birth. Scripture's account of the details of Moses's life begins when Moses is an adult: "And it came to pass in those days, when Moses was grown, that he went out to his brothers, and looked on their burdens" (Exod 2:11).

The defining act in Moses's life was to move toward his brothers, much like Judah's defining act three generations earlier. Moses's venture out to his brothers was not a casual visit. When Moses departed Pharaoh's palace, he left behind the security and familiar comfort of his former life, in much the same way that his ancestor Abraham left behind the comfort of his life to undertake his journey. His journey toward "his brothers" crossed a significant boundary. Moses left behind his privileged life as an Egyptian prince to become the "brother" of an enslaved people. The Torah uses the word "*v'yetze*" (and he was going out) to describe his departure. This same word is used for the people's exodus from Egypt. Moses's journey out of Pharaoh's palace foreshadowed the people's exodus from Egypt forty years later.

Israeli biblical scholar Nechama Leibowitz captures the significance of Moses's departure:

> Moses, the adopted son of Pharaoh's daughter, came to the resolve to ruin his chances of following a "brilliant career" as a member of the Egyptian royal house, and throw[s] in his lot with his persecuted brethren, whose very customs and habits were foreign to him.[1]

Moses, the future prophet, refused to stand idle while the Hebrew slaves suffered terrible bondage. Putting his life at risk, the Egyptian prince transformed himself into a champion of his stricken people.

When Moses left the palace, he witnessed the burden of his brothers; in particular, he saw an Egyptian beating a Hebrew. Here Leibowitz points out that Moses's seeing went far beyond the visual perception of the eyes:

> For to which Egyptian was the spectacle of Jewish slaves being maltreated by their taskmasters not a familiar sight? But we must understand the "looking" as Rashi interprets it, "he directed his eyes and heart to share their distress."[2]

Moses saw into the suffering of the Hebrews and refused to look away.

Moses not only saw the oppression, he intervened. In fact, in quick succession Moses intervened three times to save the victim from the aggressor. First, he struck an Egyptian taskmaster who was beating a Hebrew slave. The next day he defended a slave who was being bullied by another Hebrew slave. Finally, after fleeing Egypt for his life, Moses arrived in Midyan and immediately stood up for a group of Midyanite women who were being driven from the well by male shepherds.[3] As Leibowitz points out,

> Each of these [three interventions] represents an archetype. First he intervenes in a clash between a Hebrew and a non-Hebrew, second between two Hebrews, and third between two non-Hebrews. In

---

[1]   Nechama Leibowitz, *Studies in Shemot: Exodus* (Jerusalem: World Zionist Organization, 1976), 39.

[2]   Ibid.

[3]   See Exod 2:11–17.

all three cases Moses championed the just cause. Any further clash must belong to one of these three categories. . . . The Bible abounds in examples of repeated trials, particularly the third one successfully withstood, that prove the mettle of the personality involved.[4]

The pattern of Moses's interventions demonstrates a significant moral progression from a strictly tribal impulse to defend his own to a broader concern for the welfare of all. In the third case, Moses defended people who were as unlike him as possible: Midyanite women.

The narrative demonstrates that Moses possessed the character and courage to put himself at risk in order to intervene on behalf of the oppressed. This alone might qualify him to partner with God in leading the Hebrews out of slavery, but there is more. In Midyan, Moses married the daughter of the priest of Midyan and took up shepherding his father-in-law's sheep. As a shepherd, Moses "led the flock to the farthest reach of the wilderness" (Exod 3:1[†]). Searching for pasture, Moses crossed a cultural boundary; he went far more deeply into the wilderness than most shepherds would go. It is here, at the far end of the wilderness, that Moses met God at the burning bush, and another critical aspect of his character emerged.

The Torah tells us that the angel of God appeared to Moses from out of the bush. Then the text gives us Moses's inner dialogue. Catching sight of the bush out of the corner of his eye, Moses says to himself, "I will please turn to the side to see this great sight, why the bush is not burnt up" (Exod 3:3). The added word "please" signals a boundary crossing within Moses's psyche. For Moses, as for any human being, the normal course of action is to stay on the trodden path. In Moses's case, he had a job to do: looking after his father-in-law's sheep. He did not need to turn aside to observe a burning bush, especially because bushes struck by lightning are a common sight for a shepherd in the wilderness. Moses felt the tug of the familiar inclination to keep moving forward, to stay on the predetermined path, but he resisted the pull of habitual behavior. Addressing himself, he said, "I will please. . . ." The word "please" indicates that Moses was making a request, asking permission of the habitual part of his nature to release him so that he might turn aside and see the sight. Moses was not path-determined. He was open to the unexpected, to the new. Moses's ability to respond flexibly to the call of the moment enabled him to perceive the angel of God.

The text tells us what happens next: "When the Living Presence saw that he turned aside to see, God called to him out of the midst of the

---

[4] Leibowitz, *Studies in Shemot*, 40–41.

bush" (Exod 3:4). Moses's ability to turn aside was a form of exodus, a leaving of the planned in response to the needs of a moment. God was looking for such a one to lead the people out of Egypt.

Moses possessed the courage to stand up for the oppressed and the willingness to go off the beaten path. Nevertheless, he resisted God's call to lead the people out of bondage. He felt inadequate to the task. "Who am I, that I should go to Pharaoh, and that I should bring forth the people of Israel out of Egypt?" (Exod 3:11). After God attempts to assure him, Moses says, "O, my Lord, I am not eloquent, neither yesterday nor the day before, or since you have spoken to your servant; but I am slow of speech, and of a slow tongue" (Exod 4:10). Moses is in good company in expressing feelings of inadequacy. The great prophets Isaiah and Jeremiah uttered similar responses when God first addressed them.[5] But Moses did not stop with his initial resistance to God's call. In the face of God's reassurance, "I will be with you" (Exod 3:12)—the same reassurance that God offered Jeremiah—Moses was not reassured. Rather, he dug in his heels and put up a prolonged opposition to God's call.

According to the midrash, the testy conversation between God and Moses lasted seven days.[6] Given Moses's history as a man who intervened on the side of the disadvantaged, Moses's protracted resistance to God's charge is striking. What was Moses thinking? What caused Moses to stand in such fervent opposition to God's will?

Moses was concerned that neither he nor the people were prepared for the liberation journey. He doubted his ability to motivate the people, and he doubted the people's ability to hear the promise of liberation. "They will not believe me, nor listen to my voice" (Exod 4:1), he exclaimed.

For Moses, the people's inability to listen presented more than the immediate practical problem of receiving the people's assent to undertake the exodus. Moses understood that listening is the essential, irreplaceable practice for the liberation journey itself. In his view, listening to God and God's prophet was the only way out of bondage. Deep listening would connect the people to the movement of the prophetic stream. Moses believed that a people who could not listen could not be liberated.

God responded to Moses's concern about his heavy tongue, informing Moses that Aaron, his more eloquent older brother, would speak for Moses. But despite prolonged effort, God did not address to Moses's satisfaction his second concern: the inability of the people to listen.

---

[5] Isaiah proclaims, "I am a man of unclean lips" (6:5). Jeremiah protests, "I don't know how to speak for I am still a boy" (1:6).

[6] *Exodus Rabbah* 3:14.

Moses ultimately gave up his resistance, but only after God spoke to him in anger. As Moses returned to Egypt to rally the people and confront Pharaoh, he certainly had questions on his mind: Would the people listen? Were the people mentally prepared to hear the promise of liberation?

Moses's concern turned out to be well founded. When Pharaoh responded to Moses's initial entreaty by forcing the people to make bricks without straw, the people stopped listening to Moses. Instead, they turned on him, accusing Moses of inciting Pharaoh's punishing wrath. The Torah says that the people lacked the capacity to listen because of "*kotzer ruach*" (shortness of spirit).[7] The physical and emotional anguish of slavery had crushed the people's spirits and stripped them of the capacity to hear the promise of liberation. As Moses had feared, the people, unable to listen, were unprepared to take part in their own liberation.

Moses was also limited in his abilities, but his weakness was not that he was heavy of tongue. His shortcoming was in his relationship with God. He did not trust fully in the sustained nature of God's liberating power. Over time, this lack of trust led Moses to take his eye off God's active involvement in the journey and to feel increasingly isolated in his leadership role. Cut off from the power of the prophetic stream, Moses became ever more frustrated by the people's grumbling. The Torah text records Moses's growing impatience as, with each new hardship, the people demanded, "Why have you brought us up out of Egypt?" (Exod 17:3).[8] Early on Moses cried out to God, "What shall I do with this people?" (Exod 17:4). Finally, Moses lost all self-restraint. In a fit of anger, he failed to speak to the rock to bring forth water as God had instructed. Instead, "He struck the rock twice, and water came out abundantly" (Num 20:11).

God's response was swift and terrible: "Because you did not believe me to sanctify me in the eyes of the people of Israel, therefore you shall not bring this congregation into the land which I have given them" (Num 20:12). God saw Moses's mounting frustration and anger as a sign that Moses still carried the same doubt that had plagued him at the burning bush. He did not trust fully that God could liberate the former slaves. While Moses's doubts are understandable and his fate is heartbreaking, God's position was clear. Moses's lack of trust and his consequent impatience and anger made Moses unfit to lead the people into the promised land.

---

7   Exod 6:9.
8   See also Exod 14:11; Num 11:20; 14:2; 20:5; 21:5.

Moses may have underestimated God's sustained commitment to the liberation journey, but he was correct in his assessment of the people's lack of preparedness. When God took the people out of physical bondage, they were still not liberated from their slave mentality. Physical freedom did not automatically bring societal liberation. The people still had a long journey ahead toward the promised land of a society that nurtures the flourishing of all its members.

Moses doubted his abilities and the people's preparedness. His shortcoming, however, was not the doubt itself. Moses allowed his doubts to distance him from the support of the prophetic stream and to contort his relationship with the people. That was his limitation.

Doubt is a common experience for the social activist. As was the case with Moses, the forces of oppression often seem to be too strong to overcome. The exodus story speaks to that doubt, suggesting that no person or society is ever entirely prepared to overcome the obstacles along the liberation journey. Indeed, we are each called to a liberating passage for which we are not prepared. In response, we need to face our doubts, accept that we will make mistakes, and carry on. Along the liberation journey, we need to be willing to fall short, take risks, and go astray.

In taking on the risks of the liberation journey, we are not alone. The God of creation and the exodus walks with us. The power of the prophetic stream supports our journey. When Abraham began the great liberation passage, he buoyed himself for the journey ahead by turning toward this same energetic stream. Lifted by waters that activate ever unfolding potential, he left the fixed and known world behind and set off to create an alternative future. Moses, despite the depth of his doubt, confronted Pharaoh and led the people toward freedom. In his journey he was certainly strengthened by God's promise, "I will be with you" (Exod 3:12). In our day, we also are called by the liberating God to turn toward the prophetic stream and take up the path that the patriarch Abraham blazed and Moses walked.

CHAPTER 12

Head for the Hills

ORIGINS OF THE LIBERATION JOURNEY

The exodus from Egypt is the most formative event in the biblical narrative. At the same time, the exodus is the embodied archetype for the liberation journey that is the preeminent theme of the entire Hebrew Bible. The patriarchal and matriarchal stories, the entire prophetic testimony, and the laws in Deuteronomy all develop aspects of the liberation journey.[1] The great themes of liberation—breaking free from oppressive sociopolitical structures, caring for the most marginal, and seeking more mutual relationships—run through all these texts.

Given the Bible's radical critique of dominating hierarchic power, including criticism of the kingship and the priesthood in Deuteronomy and the Prophets, we need to ask this question: how did a persistent, subversive critique of established institutions find its way into the biblical text? After all, sacred texts in the Ancient Near East primarily justified and glorified the power of kings.[2] What historical circumstances led the Israelites to compose and preserve stories, statutes, and prophetic testimony that challenged royal power?

The answer to this question lies deep in the history of the clans and families that became Israel. Their story is explored in this chapter. The exploration begins over three millennia ago in Canaan.

In the thirteenth century BCE, Canaan was not unified by a single ruler. Shaped by the rugged topography of the land, Canaanite society consisted of a number of discrete and independent small cities, each ruled

---

[1] We could also find this liberation theme in Numbers, many of the psalms, Ruth, and the Song of Songs.

[2] Joshua Berman, *Created Equal* (New York: Oxford University Press, 2008), 16–27.

by a king. Early in the twelfth century BCE, these petty kingships collapsed. Afflicted by decreased trade and agricultural production, plagued by overcentralized and corrupt bureaucracy, and threatened by invaders, the Canaanite city-state system disintegrated. The petty Canaanite kings of such cities as Acco, Megiddo, Shechem, and Gezer lost social control. They could no longer protect their people nor demand their allegiance. Political chaos ensued.[3] This great social upheaval was both a disaster and an opportunity. Disadvantaged and impoverished families throughout Canaan precipitously abandoned the populated valleys and coastal areas of the region and fled to the relatively unsettled and more arid central highlands. These refugees left behind the highly stratified societies in which the king had owned all the land and headed to the unsettled high country to build a new life. In the isolation of the forbidding hills of Canaan, they were free to establish a more egalitarian society, to foster small communities in which a farmer's family could own the land, where farmers and herdsmen alike would be free of heavy tribute exacted by the king.[4]

This pursuit of social equality was not modern egalitarianism with its emphasis on the individual. Instead, this ancient pursuit of equity focused on households and envisioned an association of free farmers and herdsmen in which extended kinship groups owned the land and other means of production.

Over time, impoverished peoples from outside of Canaan, including very possibly those fleeing slavery in a weakened Egypt, joined these refugees.[5] This loose confederation of diverse peoples, whom some scholars call "proto-Israel," was bound by a common purpose rather than

---

[3]   Archaeologists have uncovered ample evidence for the Late Bronze Age decline from 1500 BCE onward, and the collapse early in the twelfth century BCE. Evidence for this collapse is well documented in the entire eastern Mediterranean world, including the famous Amarna letters, an archival collection of clay tablets primarily consisting of diplomatic correspondence between the Egyptian administration and its representatives in Canaan. Scholars have analyzed the Canaanite conditions reflected in the Amarna letters and found in them the factors that in other historical situations led to a "social revolt." The type and distribution of settlements in Canaan provide local documentation for radical changes in that region, including the rise of "family-centered" housing structures that were particular to proto-Israelite clans and remained a feature of Israelite housing well into the monarchic period. See William G. Dever, *Who Were the Early Israelites and Where Did They Come From?* (Grand Rapids: Eerdmans, 2003), 174–76.

[4]   Ibid.

[5]   Ibid., 176–82, and Richard Elliot Friedman, *The Exodus* (New York: HarperCollins, 2017).

by common kinship.[6] They sought to establish a less stratified society, a polity governed by an association of extended families rather than by a king. They were also bound by the challenges and hardships of farming on the less arable highlands. Together they needed to dig cisterns for water and build elaborate terraces to farm the sloping hillsides— relatively new technologies that enabled them to survive in a dry and forbidding environment.

The ruins these communities left behind testify to the nonhierarchical, family-centered society they developed. Archaeologists found that the high-country settlements of the ancient proto-Israelites lack the elaborate shrines and temple complexes found in the Canaanite city-states. Also, the size of the houses uncovered varied less than those in Canaanite cities. More specifically, the predominant housing discovered in these highland settlements was "four-room houses" that are considered "type-fossils of Ancient Israel—that is uniquely characteristic and thus a reliable ethnic indicator" of Israelite or proto-Israelite settlement.[7] Archaeologist William G. Dever continues, "This distinctive house-form has no real predecessors in the long settlement history of Canaan and appears suddenly on the 13th/12th century BCE horizon. . . . It reflects the typical Israelite ideal of the 'good life,' based on close-knit families and communal values."[8]

Archaeologists have found scant direct evidence for the religious beliefs of those early proto-Israelite communities, but these scholars assert that the proto-Israelite settlements must have developed beliefs different from those their neighbors held, for the highly stratified religious systems of nearby cultures would have ill suited the proto-Israelites' more egalitarian religious needs. The religious epics and beliefs of the Canaanite, Egyptian, and Mesopotamian societies sanctioned strict social hierarchy. In those societies, the hierarchic structure of human society was legitimized by the sociopolitical order of the heavens. In ancient Mesopotamia, epic texts depicted entire hierarchies of gods. The role of the gods at the bottom of the hierarchy was to serve the pleasure of the gods at the top. Mesopotamian human social order mirrored the heavens; people at lower strata in the society served the people who enjoyed a higher social ranking. In ancient Egypt the social hierarchy received divine sanction in a different way. In Egypt the king was a demigod. Only the king had direct access to the world of the gods,

---

6   The term "proto-Israel" refers to the ancestors of the tribes that would become Israel. Israel did not become a unified people until the rule of King David at the beginning of the tenth century BCE.

7   Dever, *Who Were the Early Israelites?*, 103.

8   Ibid., 105.

and only the king could rule with divine authority. The rest of Egyptian society served the king.[9] The religious texts and practices of these societies would not have served the more egalitarian social order of the proto-Israelite settlements. The proto-Israelites needed stories, statutes, and practices that supported the alternative society these families sought to nurture.

The refugees who built those small settlements in the central Canaanite highlands were likely the ancestors of the ancient Israelites, the people whose stories, statutes, and religious practices are preserved in the Hebrew Bible. While the earliest written texts within the Hebrew Bible date from the tenth century BCE, two hundred years after the great exodus to the hills of Canaan, scholars find a strong cultural connection between those proto-Israelite peoples and early biblical texts. Unlike any other Ancient Near Eastern text, the biblical text is replete with teachings and statutes that protect the commoner and limit the power of the elites. Equally powerfully, the biblical God does not address the king or the elites. Rather, God speaks to the entire people, including "your little ones, your wives, and your stranger who is in your camp, from the hewer of wood to the drawer of water" (Deut 29:10).[10] The God of the Hebrew Scriptures limited the power of kings and repeatedly warned against the oppression of the widow, the orphan, and the stranger. The Hebrew Bible also includes extensive statutes that protect a family's land tenure, limit taxation, secure ownership rights, and provide debt easement and poverty relief—all rulings that would preserve the holdings of farming families against the encroachment of more powerful elites. These religious teachings and statutes that elevated the common person very likely began their evolution among the proto-Israelite communities in the Canaanite highlands.[11]

The people who became Israel needed to develop new social, political, and economic institutions as well as new religious understandings. Stable times generally don't lend themselves well to significant social innovation. Israel's inventive journey would not have been possible if dramatic historical events had not created an unusual opening—an extended period of unprecedented social and political volatility. The political chaos that enabled the proto-Israelite clans to flee from the Canaanite cities extended far past Canaan. The twelfth century BCE, toward the end of the Late Bronze Age, was a time when a perfect storm of drought, famine, earthquakes, invasions, and internal rebellions caused the breakdown of the great empires as well as the small Canaanite kingdoms.

---

[9]   Berman, *Created Equal*, 9, 16–27.
[10]   Deut 29:11 in KJV.
[11]   Ibid., 29, 41, 64–67, 88–107.

The collapse of the Egyptian Empire to the south, the Mesopotamian to the east, and the Hittite to the north, alongside the disintegration of the Canaanite city-states, created a power vacuum throughout the Eastern Mediterranean world. This vacuum drew a number of invading peoples from the west, the so-called Sea Peoples. Political instability also created an opportunity for the incipient proto-Israelite tribes to establish and develop their unique culture in Canaan.

This period of imperial weakness lasted from the Late Bronze Age collapse in the late twelfth century BCE to the Assyrian ascension in the middle of the eighth century BCE. During this time, Israel was relatively free to develop from a loose confederation of highland settlements to an independent kingdom and ultimately to two independent kingdoms, Israel in the north and Judah in the south. For five hundred years, the military power of the great empires of the region receded enough to create an opening, in time and space, for a radically new political and cultural entity to emerge. Israel was that new entity.

This historical window of opportunity ended abruptly with the rapid rise of the Assyrian Empire. In 722 BCE the Assyrian Army destroyed the northern kingdom of Israel. The surviving people were scattered throughout the Assyrian Empire and lost to history. The southern kingdom of Judah was overrun a century and a half later by the Babylonian Empire.

Fortunately, the exiles from Judah met a different fate than their northern kinsman. The Judean exiles were brought en masse to one place: Babylon. The destruction of the Temple and the exile that followed served to increase the influence of those among the exiles who sought alternatives to the power of the king and the priesthood.

After fifty years in Babylon, historical events once again favored these social and religious pioneers. In 539 BCE the Persians defeated the Babylonians, and King Cyrus freed the Judeans to return to their homeland. Following the return of some of the exiles to Judah, the Jewish communities in both Babylon and Judah continued to develop institutions and practices that would eventually replace the king and the Temple in Jewish life.

Over these formative centuries, external enemies were not the only threats to the people Israel's liberation journey. The effort to create a more egalitarian society faced internal threats as well. A society in which all can flourish required dramatic shifts in political and economic structures and in interpersonal relations. In all these areas—political, economic, and relational—Israel both sought and resisted change. As in any challenging and innovative venture, Israel repeatedly lost its way and struggled to learn from its mistakes. The Hebrew Bible presents the transcendent inspiration and the massive challenges of Israel's unprecedented journey—the efforts of a people who had experienced oppression to create a society that would not oppress.

A prime example of the people's resistance to political innovation was their desire to have a king like all other nations. The very raison d'être for Israel was to escape royal oppression. During the entire period of the Judges, the twelfth to the eleventh centuries BCE, "there was no king in Israel."[12] God was their king. Nevertheless, the people cried out for a human king.

The people felt most strongly in times of war the need for a king to unite them.[13] The conflict within Israel over kingship reached its peak in the face of the Philistine attacks in the late eleventh century BCE, when Samuel, the leader at the time, was nearing the end of his life. In the face of the mounting Philistine threat, the people wanted to be unified by a king. At God's behest, Samuel warned the people,

> [A king] will take your sons, and appoint them for himself, for his chariots, and to be his horsemen . . . and will set them to plow his ground, and to reap his harvest, and to make his instruments of war, and instruments of his chariots. And he will take your daughters to be perfumers, and to be cooks, and to be bakers. And he will take your fields, and your vineyards, and your olive trees, the best of them, and give them to his servants. And he will take the tenth of your seed, and of your vineyards. . . . He will take the tenth of your sheep; and you shall be his servants. (1 Sam 8:11–17)

The people's inability to heed Samuel's warning testifies to the challenge of creating a society in which political authority resides in the people. Despite the threat of servitude and high taxation, the people still wanted a king.

The people, most especially the privileged, were also resistant to maintaining an economically equitable society. Soon after the founding of the monarchy, the egalitarian nature of Israelite society began to erode. By the eighth century BCE, a time of relative prosperity in Israel and Judah, the disparity between the rich and the poor had become extreme.

For the people Israel, the growing economic inequality was both a moral and an existential crisis; the journey toward establishing an equi-

---

[12] Judg 9:6, 8, 15–16; 17:6; 18:1; 19:1; 21:25.

[13] In biblical times, as in our own, a society organizing around war naturally regresses to more oppressive political forms.

table society had gone off track. As we discussed in chapter 1, the depth of the existential crisis in Israel gave rise to an extraordinary phenomenon—the Hebrew prophets. Unfortunately, the elites in Israel and Judah were unwilling to heed the prophets' warning.

In addition to chronicling the resistance to political and economic equity, the biblical narrative also explores the interpersonal challenge of an egalitarian social order. Hierarchic societies are ordered by power; the overwhelming power of those at the top of the hierarchy enforces societal stratification. In contrast, equitable societies are ordered by relationship; equity in a society is grounded by mutual relationships and caring for one's neighbor. As highlighted in our exploration of the Genesis narrative, the Bible repeatedly presents people who struggle with the tension between fulfilling their own desires and caring for their neighbor. All the patriarchs and matriarchs are courageous people who respond to God's call and appear as flawed human beings who mistreat other people as they pursue their own needs. In narrative form, the Bible thus reveals and explores essential relational challenges for people who aspire to live in an equitable society.

Israel's resistance to transformation is painful to behold. Taken out of context, major sections of the Bible appear to present the unredeemed chronicle of a stiff-necked people. In the context of an inspired and challenging journey, however, the setbacks recounted in Scripture take their place as hard-earned wisdom. They are teachings that serve to edify later generations about the obstacles to transformation and about the way forward in the face of those obstacles.

These teachings took their place alongside other cultural elements—legal statutes, religious rituals, ancient songs, and prophetic testimony—that Israel needed to support the challenging journey toward a more egalitarian society. Over the generations these cultural creations were gathered, edited, and woven together into sacred Scriptures. The Hebrew Bible we read today is the complex, multigenerational testimony that grew out of Israel's liberation journey with God.

CHAPTER 13

A Scribal Tradition

In the last chapter, we explored the early history that led the Israelites to collect and preserve subversive stories and prophetic testimonies. At this point we need to ask an additional historical question: how did subversive texts that critique royal rule survive the many centuries of Israelite and Judean monarchy? Scholars agree that most of the Torah narratives in Genesis and Exodus, as well as the core of the legislation in Deuteronomy, were written and edited during Israel's monarchic era. These written texts are necessarily the work of scribes employed by elites—kings, priests, and wealthy merchants. Why would scribes who worked for privileged elites preserve traditions that are subversive to their employers' power?[1]

While it is difficult to offer a definitive answer to this question, we can explore some likely motivations. First, the scribes who did the final redacting of the Torah needed to account for the destruction of Judah and envision a way forward. Scribes included subversive materials and prophetic testimonies because these texts uniquely fulfilled that need. They critiqued hierarchic domination and offered the covenant relationship with God as an alternative to the suzerainty bond to a king.

Second, the people's attachment to some stories gave the scribes no choice but to include them. Two prime examples are the stories of how David acquired two of his wives, Abigail and Bathsheba. Neither story reflects well on King David. In both narratives David marries a woman immediately after her husband dies suddenly. Working with the reality

---

[1] The biblical text itself suggests that some scribes allied with the prophets in their critique of the monarchy. In three passages in Jeremiah, a prominent scribal family takes measures to protect Jeremiah from the elites who are threatened by his prophecy. The son and grandson of Shaphan, King Josiah's scribe, defended the prophet. See Jer 26:24; 39:14; 40:6.

that Israelite folklore certainly would have preserved stories about these women, a Davidic scribe constructed narratives that put David in the most favorable light. David emerges from the Abigail story without any responsibility for her husband's death. In the Bathsheba story, David is a fully repentant man who listened to the stern admonition of his prophet Nathan.[2]

Third, and most important for our thesis, the very nature of the scribal craft nurtured awareness in some scribes that led them to value subversive and prophetic texts. The scribal art embodied a revolution in human technology and thereby in human consciousness. When the spoken word became written, human beings obtained a capacity that had not before existed. They could consciously shape a people's stories. All storytellers shape their stories, but not with the consciousness and the precision of writers. Writers bring a self-consciousness to their craft that storytellers don't necessarily have.

This self-consciousness appears abundantly in the work of the final scribes of Deuteronomy, who also redacted the historical books of Joshua, Judges, Samuel, and Kings.[3] These scribes had access to archives containing many texts. Perhaps they maintained these archives themselves. The archived texts likely included the chronicles of the kings of Israel and Judah alongside ancestral stories, legal statutes, epic poetry, and isolated historical reports. With these materials in hand, the scribe could do something the storyteller could not do—take a variety of diverse sources and weave them together into a single extended history. The scribe could, and did, shape a particular history—a historical account that met the needs of a people to define themselves, both in terms of where they came from and how they sought to live. The final scribes of Deuteronomy and the books of Joshua through Kings, living a century and more before the Greek historian Herodotus, were the first historians in what became the Western world.

These scribes thus gave to humankind both the beginnings of historical consciousness and the notion of God working in historical time. Hearing the work of these scribes, the listener could conceive of God acting not only in the cycles of nature but also in human history. These

---

[2] See 1 Sam 25 and 2 Sam 11. For a rich analysis of how the Davidic scribes shaped the biblical text to cast David in the most favorable light, see Joel Baden, *The Historical David: The Real Life of an Invented Hero* (New York: HarperOne, 2013).

[3] Richard Elliott Friedman describes in some detail the work of the Deuteronomic scribe; Friedman believes the history was written by one man. See Friedman, *Who Wrote the Bible?* (New York: Harper Collins, 1997), 129–32.

historically conscious scribes created the idea that a people's communal life is an extended journey with God.[4]

This profound change in human consciousness—an awareness of the process of historical change—is inherently subversive of royal consciousness. As Walter Brueggemann points out in *The Prophetic Imagination*, royal consciousness is static. For the king, the present moment and the current social order are immutable. Anarchy is the only alternative to the order the king maintains. *Après moi, le déluge!* Here is Brueggemann's description of royal consciousness as exhibited by the prime biblical example of such consciousness, King Solomon:

> Solomon was able to create a situation in which everything was already given, in which no more futures could be envisioned because everything was already present a hundredfold. The tension between a criticized present and an energized future is overcome. There is only an uncriticized and unenergizing present.[5]

The ability to read varied historical accounts and to shape a written history gave the scribe an awareness of historical evolution, an awareness that would be threatening to most kings.

In addition to an awareness of historical change, the task of writing history shaped scribal consciousness in an even more subversive way. The scribes living in Jerusalem after the destruction of the northern kingdom and before the fall of Jerusalem, between 722 and 587 BCE, had in hand two different collections of the people's formative stories. These scribes possessed both the text written in the northern kingdom (Israel) and the text developed in the southern kingdom (Judah). Scholars have named these two texts E (Northern) and J (Southern) in keeping with the name of God used in these texts.[6] Immersed in the perspectives offered in E and J, these scribes had the opportunity to develop a quality of consciousness that seems quite modern: the understanding that the "reality"

---

[4] Several biblical passages emphasize the importance of the written word and its promulgation among the people. Deuteronomy prescribes the septennial reading of the Torah to all the people. Several other biblical narratives describe public Torah readings. See Deut 31:11–12, 19; Josh 8:32–35; 2 Kgs 23:1–3; Neh 7:72–8:18. See also discussion in Joshua Berman, *Created Equal* (New York: Oxford University Press, 2008), 114–15.

[5] Walter Brueggemann, *The Prophetic Imagination*, 2nd ed. (Minneapolis: Fortress Press, 2001), 25.

[6] Scholars call the Israelite text "E" for the text's use of the word "Elohim" for God. Scholars name "J," for the use of the word "Yahweh" (or among Christian scholars, "Jehovah") for God's Name.

of any event depends on the perspective of the observer. This awareness of different perspectives created a radically new possibility for the scribe: a text could present more than one point of view and include many voices. In other words, a text could embody a conversation.

Clearly the Jerusalem scribes who worked with these two sources, J and E, valued conversation between diverse perspectives. They valued conversation so much that they did something remarkable. In an effort to create a common text for both the people of Judah and the survivors of Israel who had fled south, these scribes wove together two different texts—J and E. They included conflicting stories and the contradictions between them, not attempting to cover up or smooth over these differences. As a result, the Bible includes two separate creation stories, as well as two variant narrative strands that run through the patriarchal/matriarchal and Joseph stories, the exodus story, and the account of the events at Mount Sinai.[7]

The same appreciation of difference is present in the work of the later postexilic scribe(s) who edited Deuteronomy. These scribes had in hand the earlier version of Deuteronomy, the scroll found in the Temple at the time of King Josiah. This scroll, likely written at the time of the great king, a time of relative strength and security, presents a rosy framing of the history of Judah, culminating in the reign of King Josiah. The postexilic scribe needed to tell a darker story, a narrative that ended with the capture of the Judean king, the destruction of the kingdom, and the beginning of the exile. Yet the postexilic scribe left the earlier text in place, including God's unconditional promise that the throne of David would be established forever. Rather than editing out that perspective, the scribe added in the understanding that the covenant was conditioned on the faithfulness of the people and that the people's abrogation of the covenant had brought on the fall of the kingdom.

This art of inclusion is also apparent in the work of the even later postexilic scribe who brought all the sources together—J, E, P (priestly), and D (Deuteronomy)—into one text: the Torah. This postexilic Torah scribe did not attempt to cover up the many marked differences in these four sources. The scribe let the differences be, weaving together a text that is itself a conversation of many voices, presenting many points of view.

Many voices are also included as the people returned from Babylon when Ezra the scribe read the completed Torah to the reconstituted community in Judah. The account of that event specifically names thirteen individuals who "read in the book in the Torah of God clearly, and gave

---

[7] For specific examples, see Friedman, *Who Wrote the Bible?*, chaps. 2 and 3.

the interpretation, so that they understood the reading" (Neh 8:8). Ezra needed this assistance to reach a large assembly and to translate for the people who spoke Aramaic and would not have understood the Hebrew text. But Scripture explicitly says that these individuals did more than translate; they "gave the interpretation," adding their commentary to the text. Naturally, each person's commentary was unique to that individual. Hence, from the first reading of the Torah, thirteen distinct commentaries circulated through the community.

This first reading of the Torah demonstrates a pattern of discourse that would develop over the next six hundred years through scribal tradition until it emerges in the Pharisees in the second century BCE and ultimately as the rabbinic tradition late in the first century CE. The heart of this scribal tradition is the inclusion of many voices and the embrace of conflicting points of view. This tradition was already old by Ezra's time. The seeds of rabbinic discourse were already present in preexilic Jerusalem when scribes chose to weave together the disparate J and E texts.

This style of discourse, a many-voiced conversation across differences, is inherently self-critical. No single point of view is the absolute truth. The limits of each perspective are challenged and thereby critiqued by other points of view. For example, Genesis contains two interwoven flood stories, one from J and one from P. The P version presents the flood as an overwhelmingly supernatural event brought about by a transcendent God. In P, "All the fountains of the deep were broken up and the windows of the heavens were opened" (Gen 7:11). The flood in J arises from natural causes, forty days and nights of rain. Similarly, the God in the J version is starkly anthropomorphic and thereby less transcendent than the God in P. Biblical scholar Richard Elliot Friedman succinctly sets out the difference:

> J pictures a deity who can regret things that he has done (6:6, 7), which raises interesting theological questions, such as whether an all-powerful, all-knowing being would ever regret past actions. It pictures a deity who can be "grieved to his heart" (6:6), who personally closes the ark (7:16) and smells Noah's sacrifice (8:21). This anthropomorphic quality of J is virtually entirely lacking in P. There God is regarded more as a transcendent controller of the universe.[8]

The transcendent God of P challenges the anthropomorphic God of J, silently asking how an all-knowing God can regret. Similarly,

---

8   Ibid., 59–60.

the anthropomorphic God of J challenges the transcendent God of P, silently asking how a people can be in a covenant relationship with such a distant God. A rich conversation about the nature of God's relation to creation arises from the creative tension between P and J.

The multivocal nature of the Torah text naturally subverts royal authority by undermining imperial speech. An emperor issues edicts; an imperial society is characterized by a uniformity of speech. The scribes of J/E, Deuteronomy, and the Torah present the Bible in a nonimperial form, as a conversation inclusive of many voices. Reading the Bible involves opening oneself up to diverse points of view. While processing the contradictions and inconsistencies created by the inclusion of multiple perspectives, the discerning reader is challenged to come to her own understanding of the text.

In this way, the multivocal text promotes dialogue within the reader and, as a consequence, within the learning community. Hannah Arendt famously observed that an individual or a society that cannot entertain an inner dialogue among conflicting voices cannot truly think critically.[9] The multivocal conversation woven into the biblical text animates critical thinking.

This spirit of critique is an essential aspect of the Bible's prophetic stream. The first move of the prophet is an incisive critique of the accepted institutions of a society. At each new stage, the liberation journey is propelled by clear-eyed critique.

Valuing diverse worldviews, the scribes also placed subversive narratives right alongside texts that reflected the worldview of kings and priests. As a result, two distinct traditions, the prophetic and the royal, run alongside each other throughout Hebrew Scripture. The prophetic narrative places prime importance on the people's journey with God toward a more egalitarian, relational society. The royal narrative values the maintenance of the central institutions of the society: the kingship and the Temple. A dynamic society requires both narratives, one that values the stability of established institutions and one that articulates the oppression inherent in those structures and envisions an alternative future.

The two worldviews are not of equal importance, however. A careful reading of the biblical texts reveals that the prophetic strain in the Bible is more fundamental than the royal because the Bible's central concern is the process of evolution—inside the person as well as in the community—toward an equitable society.

---

[9] Hannah Arendt, *The Origins of Totalitarianism* (New York: Harvest Book Harcourt, 1968), 476, and Arendt, *Eichmann in Jerusalem* (New York: Viking, 1963).

The biblical scribes highlighted the centrality of prophetic tradition by placing the exodus story at the heart of the biblical narrative. In the scribal telling, the exodus narrative became *the* core story for the Israelite people and the essential vehicle for their continuity. The exodus story was retold at virtually every important transition point in the people's historical experience. When communal survival and continuity were at stake, the leader of the people at that time retold the exodus story. At a liminal time when the future was in question, the exodus story recalled to the people the essential meaning of their communal existence. Significantly, the great exception to this pattern occurs when King Solomon built the Temple, a moment of asserting static imperial rule.

The first instance of retelling the exodus story occurs when Moses learned that he will die in the wilderness. He responded to the communal crisis that will happen with his death by retelling the people's journey with God, beginning with the exodus from Egypt. The book of Deuteronomy is essentially Moses's extended review of this journey.

In the next generation, when Joshua was about to die, he also recounted the exodus: "Jacob and his children went down to Egypt. I sent Moses also and Aaron, and I plagued Egypt, according to that which I did among them; and afterwards I brought you out" (Josh 24:4).

Next, during the period of the Judges when the people's will faltered, God sent messengers to retell the story of the exodus (Judg 6:8; 1 Sam 2:27–29). When the prophet Samuel began his ministry, he summoned the people together and retold the exodus story (1 Sam 10:17–18). At the end of Samuel's ministry, he said to all Israel, "When Jacob came to Egypt, your fathers cried out to the Living Presence, and the Living Presence sent Moses and Aaron, who brought your fathers out of Egypt and made them live in this place" (1 Sam 12:8).

Six centuries later, in the mid-sixth century BCE, when the prophet Isaiah addressed the people in Babylonian exile and sought to inspire their return to Judah, he envisioned the return of the people to Judah as a second exodus:

A voice cries, Prepare in the wilderness the way of the Living Presence, make straight in the desert a highway for our God. . . . O Israel, Fear not; for I have redeemed you. I have called you by your name; you are mine. When you pass through the waters, I will be with you. . . . I gave Egypt for your ransom. (Isa 40:3; 43:1–3)

This central role of the exodus story in the life of the people continues to our own day. The Passover Seder is the most widely observed

Jewish ritual and is essentially a reenactment of the exodus story. Every participant is to consider as if she herself had gone out of Egypt. The Passover Haggadah sets forth, "And when a child asks the meaning of the Seder rituals, you shall tell your child on that day: 'This is done because of what the Living Presence did for me when I came forth out of Egypt'" (Exod 13:8).

The continual retelling of the exodus story is intended to shape Israelite identity as a people on a liberation journey. In particular, the Bible presents the retelling of this story as a means to cultivate empathic concern for the welfare of the most marginal in society—the widow, the orphan, and the immigrant. On five separate occasions, the Torah adjures the Israelites to attend to the welfare of those most in need because "you were strangers in the land of Egypt."[10] In a passage from the Holiness Code, located literally as the central text of the central book in the Torah, the book of Leviticus proclaims, "The stranger who dwells with you shall be to you as one born among you, and you shall love him as yourself; for you were strangers in the land of Egypt; I am the Living Presence your God" (19:34).

Scriptures repeatedly retell the exodus story to inspire and guide the people. With this practice, the ancient story and the age-old journey are continually made new. In each generation the people are called to bring a new understanding to the exodus story in the light of contemporary challenges.

I have written this book in that tradition. This exploration of the movement of the prophetic stream through Scriptures is my reading of the exodus journey into our day. In this exploration I have retold the exodus story, now identifying the story with a prophetic stream that moves through the Scriptures, inspiring people to leave behind oppressive social structures and to create more relational ways of being in society. In this retelling I have highlighted the revolutionary and subversive qualities that are at the heart of the Scriptures.

Many people don't see this revolutionary and subversive core in the Bible. In fact, many people think of the Hebrew Bible as a conservative document that honors time-bound traditions. This view, preached from many pulpits and taught in many religious schools, misses the Bible's true nature.

Why are the more subversive and transformative aspects of the Scriptures often obscured from view? The sociopolitical and religious elites of every society in which the Bible is held sacred have a stake in how the Scriptures are read and interpreted. These communal leaders recognize

---

[10] Exod 22:20; 23:9; Lev 19:34; 25:23; Deut 10:19.

that the Bible is a powerful cultural medium. The Hebrew Scriptures address the fundamental issues at the core of a society's identity: its origin, goals, core beliefs, fundamental values, and guiding principles. The Scriptures can provide legitimacy to a sociopolitical order or powerfully challenge the status quo. As we might expect, the political and economic leaders want to read the Scriptures in a way that supports the current regime. These leaders often ally with religious elites to promulgate a conservative understanding of Scriptures.

We witness this dynamic in our contemporary society. Conservative religious leaders are likely to look past the lengthy sections of Scripture that mandate wealth redistribution and care for the immigrant and the poor and to focus on a single verse concerning same-sex relations. Similarly, many right-wing Christians in the United States and fundamentalist Jews in Israel cite God's land promises to justify the expropriation of Palestinian land and the oppressive occupation of the West Bank while ignoring the entire prophetic testimony against land expropriation and systematic oppression.

On a subtler level, ruling elites and their religious allies favor those aspects of the Bible that mirror society's hierarchal order. The image of God ruling from the heavens supports the authoritarian rule of human leaders in high places. Belief in a commanding God who issues edicts from afar serves to normalize the overwhelming power of earthly elites. At the same time, leaders of a highly stratified society relate to scriptural passages that present a sinful people and a harsh God. The wayward nature of the people and God's severe judgments justify the punitive and often oppressive legal structure of such a stratified society.

Certainly one meets a harsh God and an errant people in the Scriptures. But portrayals of a severe God and the sinful people represent the inherent challenge in the liberation journey, not its trajectory. An emphasis solely on the wayward aspect of the people and God's harsh judgment obscures the Scriptures' transformational intent. In the Bible God and human beings are both on the move; they are evolving. People grow in their ability to enter mutual relationship; witness Jacob, Judah, and Joseph. They evolve in their awareness of a liberating God; witness Miriam and Moses. They advance in their ability to recognize and call out injustice; witness the prophets. God evolves as well. Over many generations God deepens the divine relationship with human beings as God seeks to nurture a more relational consciousness and a more egalitarian society. The Bible is the account of God's working with the people to give birth to a more evolved human being and a new society.

Part Two

Contemporary Reflections on Prophetic Wisdom

CHAPTER 14

A Mighty Stream

CONTEMPORARY PROPHETIC CRITIQUE

Prophets speak to us even now.

The liberating power of the prophetic testimony is often dismissed by the observation that people did not heed the prophets' words in their day. Despite repeated and dire prophetic warnings, the northern and southern kingdoms both failed to reform and were ultimately destroyed. Nevertheless, this dismissive perspective on the prophetic word is shortsighted. Influential scribes valued the prophetic testimony and preserved these texts through the years of the Babylonian Exile and after. These scribes believed that those texts would help a devastated people come to grips with the destruction of Judah and offer the surviving community a way forward.

The scribal expectation was fulfilled. Prophetic witness had a significant impact long after active prophecy ceased. In the late sixth century BCE, when some of the people returned to Judah following the end of Babylonian captivity, the prophetic texts became a foundation for communal rebuilding.[1] The words of the prophets helped the people grapple with the meaning of the devastation that they had experienced. The prophetic testimony also articulated the terms of a renewed covenant with God. The prophetic writings together with the Torah gave the Judean community a new way of participating in the covenant. The people could now hear and discuss the word of God as expressed in these texts.

Over the succeeding centuries, the scribes' many-voiced conversation about the Scriptures shaped the discourse of the Pharisees and then the Rabbis. In turn, the tradition of the Rabbis, embodied in multiple Torah

---

[1]   Scholars agree that only a portion of the people returned to Judah from Babylon, beginning in the year 538 BCE.

commentaries and Talmudic conversation, carried the scribal tradition of dialogue, critique, and iterative learning across two millennia and into modern times.

In the last two centuries, the words and the worldview of the Hebrew prophets have inspired multiple liberation movements, including the Unitarian-inspired abolitionist movement and the Latin American liberation theology movement, as well as the US civil rights movement that emerged from the black churches in the South.

This same prophetic stream has also activated contemporary prophets who have articulated their testimony for the current day. Just as the biblical prophets courageously decried the injustices of their day and dramatically pronounced the unsustainability of the reigning order, in our time contemporary prophets have articulated a clear-eyed diagnosis of the roots of current societal problems.

A careful study of these contemporary prophets reveals that, despite significantly different cultural backgrounds, all these modern-day prophets uncover the same roots from which injustice grows: a lack of mutual relationship, a lack of community, and ultimately a lack of human solidarity.

Martin Luther King Jr. placed mutual responsibility and community at the center of his social critique. He wrote that the central challenge facing humanity is

the adventure of community . . . the mutually cooperative and voluntary venture of man to assume a semblance of responsibility for his brother. . . . The universe is so structured that things do not quite work out rightly if men are not diligent in their concern for others.[2]

King saw that the plague of segregation was ultimately rooted in a lack of genuine relationship, a lack of human affinity:

[Segregation involves] physical proximity without spiritual affinity. It gives us a society where men are physically desegregated and spiritually segregated, where elbows are together and hearts are apart. It gives us special togetherness and spiritual apartness. It leaves us with a stagnant equality of sameness rather than a constructive equality of oneness.[3]

---

[2] In Martin Luther King Jr., *A Testament of Hope: The Essential Writings and Speeches of Martin Luther King Jr.*, ed. James Washington (New York: Harper Collins, 1991), 122.

[3] Ibid., 118.

In assessing the scourge of segregation in the United States and oppressive colonization in the developing world, King said,

> What is needed is a restless determination to make the ideal of brotherhood a reality in this nation and all over the world. . . . In a real sense, we must all learn to live together as brothers, or we will all perish together as fools. We must come to see that no individual can live alone; no nation can live alone. We must all live together; we must all be concerned about each other.[4]

Gustavo Gutiérrez, the Peruvian priest and father of liberation theology, echoed King's focus on the need for more robust "brotherhood" or, in Gutiérrez's terms, "neighborliness." Strikingly, Gutiérrez identified "sin" as the disruption of friendship with God and with other human beings. For Gutiérrez, a breach in care for one's neighbor implied a lack of friendship with God, a condition that he considered to be the "ultimate root" of injustice:

> Sin is the breaking of friendship with God and with other human beings. . . . To sin is to refuse to love one's neighbors and, therefore, the Lord himself. Sin—a breach of friendship with God and others—is according to the Bible the ultimate cause of poverty, injustice, and the oppression in which persons live. In describing sin as the ultimate cause we do not in any way negate the structural reasons and the objective determinants leading to this situation. It does, however, emphasize the fact that things do not happen by chance and that behind an unjust structure there is a personal or collective will responsible—a willingness to reject God and neighbor.[5]

Friendship with God. This is a powerfully intimate, embracing, and expansive sensibility!

Feminist and Christian social ethicist Beverly Harrison also placed mutual, heartfelt relationship at the center of her societal critique. In her teaching, Harrison held that the patriarchy concentrated its attention on the power of conquest and overlooked the essential power of love to "create one another":

> We do not yet have a moral theology that teaches us the awe-ful, awe-some truth that we have the power through acts of love or

---

4   Ibid., 89, 209.

5   Gustavo Gutiérrez, *A Theology of Liberation* (Maryknoll, NY: Orbis Books, 1973), xxxviii, 24.

lovelessness literally to create one another. . . . Because we do not understand love as the power to act-each-other-into-well-being we also do not understand the depth of our power to thwart life and to maim each other. . . . I believe that our world is on the verge of self-destruction and death because the society as a whole has so deeply neglected that which is most human and most valuable and the most basic of all the works of love—the work of human communication, of caring and nurturance, of tending the personal bonds of community. This activity has been seen as women's work and discounted as too mundane and undramatic, too distracting from the serious business of world rule. . . . This urgent work of love is subtle but powerful. Through acts of love . . . we literally build up the power of personhood in one another.[6]

Rabbi Abraham Joshua Heschel, writing in the wake of the Holocaust, saw the lack of reciprocal human responsibility, and a consequent lack of human solidarity, as the root of the catastrophe that unfolded before his eyes. Contemplating the horror and unimaginable devastation that Germany, the most advanced culture in the West, had perpetrated, Heschel wrote, "I was slowly led to the realization that some of the terms, motivations, and concerns which dominate our thinking may prove destructive of the roots of human responsibility and treasonable to the ultimate ground of human solidarity."[7]

Heschel turned to the Hebrew prophets in search of new, but also very old, ways of thinking: fresh but timeless premises that would guide human thought toward mutual responsibility and human solidarity. In his groundbreaking study, Heschel found that the prophets root their passion for social justice and human responsibility in God's avid concern for the world. In prophetic understanding, the initial break in relationship is not between one person and another but between people and God. The prophets attributed the injustices they witnessed, and the inevitable disaster that would come in its wake, to a loss of solidarity with God's concern and care for creation:

This, then, is the ultimate category of prophetic theology: [God's] involvement, attentiveness, concern. Prophetic religion may be defined, not as what man does with his ultimate concern, but rather what man does with God's concern. . . . The theme of

---

6 Beverly Wildung Harrison, *Making the Connections: Essays in Feminist Social Ethics*, ed. Carol Robb (Boston: Beacon Press, 1985), 11–12.

7 Abraham Joshua Heschel, *The Prophets* (New York: Perennial Classics, 1962), xxviii.

prophetic understanding is not the mystery of God's essence, but rather the mystery of His relation to man. . . . What the prophet knows about God is His *pathos*, His relation to Israel and to mankind. . . . The ground of the relation is moral.[8]

For Heschel and the Hebrew prophets, relationship must be the starting place for all thought. "In the light of prophetic insights, we are faced not merely with a relationship to God, but also with a living reality which is a relationship, having its origin in God."[9]

In other words, relationship is the essence of God's creation. The difference between prophetic insight and the modern thought, according to Heschel's critique, is, "There [in modern thought] existence is experiencing being; here [in prophetic thought], existence is experiencing concern."[10]

For Heschel, "existence is experiencing concern." Gutiérrez taught that friendship characterizes the proper relationship with God, among people and between people and the world. Harrison proclaimed that people create one another through love. King repeatedly exhorted people to recognize the "brotherhood" of all humankind. All these modern prophets call upon their readers to view the world through a different lens. While Western civilization has trained people to perceive entities such as dogs, trees, or people as independent and freestanding, Heschel, Gutiérrez, Harrison, and King challenge their audiences to perceive the relationship among objects and people, to see "a living reality that is a relationship."[11]

These modern prophets view caring, mutual relationship as the fundamental reality "having its origin in God."[12] By divine intent, being is for the sake of relationship; creation is the place of relationship. Therefore, relationship and one's responsibilities within relationship need to be the premise of all thought and the first principle of all social, economic, and political structures that humans bring forth. As in the days of the prophets and scribes, this is how we recover our community.

Perhaps the most illuminating exploration of the dynamics of mutual relationship can be found in Martin Buber's work *I and Thou*. Like Heschel, Buber witnessed firsthand the rise of the Nazi regime and attempted to grasp the widespread dehumanization that engulfed his homeland. Like Heschel, Buber attributed the disaster to a breakdown in genuine

---

8   Ibid., 619–21.
9   Ibid., 622.
10   Ibid., 619.
11   Ibid.
12   Ibid.

relationship. In Buber's language, the root of the problem was the accelerating societal tendency to treat people as an objectified "It."

In *I and Thou*, Buber famously distinguished between "experiencing" people—and indeed the world itself—as an objectified It as distinct from "relating" to a person, or a tree, as a Thou. Buber referred to this distinction as the "twofold attitude":

> The attitude of man is twofold, in accordance with the twofold nature of the primary words which he speaks. The primary words are not isolated words, but combined words. The one primary word is the combination I-Thou. The other primary word is the combination I-It.[13]

Buber's conception of combined words, I-Thou and I-It, implies that there is no separate freestanding individual; there is no discrete person. "There is no I taken in itself, but only the I of the primary word I-Thou and the I of the primary word I-It."[14] Human life is always hyphenated, composed by a tandem, either I-Thou or I-It.

The I-It relationship arises when a person experiences some "thing," be that thing an object or a living being. By contrast, "When the Thou is spoken, the speaker has no thing; he has indeed nothing. But he takes his stand in relation."[15]

> If I face a human being as my Thou, and say the primary word I-Thou to him, he is not a thing among things, and does not consist of things . . . nor is he a nature able to be experienced and described, a loose bundle of qualities. . . . Rather I stand in relation to him, in the sanctity of the primary word [I-Thou].[16] . . . The relation to the Thou is direct. No system of ideas, no foreknowledge and no fancy intervene between I and Thou.[17]

Buber distinguished between "experiencing" something as an It, and the nonobjectified "meeting" the Thou in "relationship." For Buber, all real living is meeting.[18] But he also realized that human life cannot consist only of such sacred meetings. "Every Thou in our world must

---

[13] Martin Buber, *I and Thou*, trans. Ronald Gregor Smith (New York: Charles Scribner's Sons, 1958), 12.

[14] Ibid., 4.

[15] Ibid.

[16] Ibid., 8.

[17] Ibid., 11.

[18] Ibid.

become an It. . . . Every Thou in the world by its nature is fated to become a thing, or continually to re-enter into the condition of things."[19] For human beings, the world is necessarily "twofold."

The I-It "attitude" is a necessary and inevitable aspect of human life. The problems that Buber saw were the "progressive augmentation of the world of It" and "the decrease of man's power to enter into relation."[20]

The I-It "attitude" is not inherently bad, but the I-It attitude becomes "evil" when it presents itself as the fullness of life:

> If a man lets It have the mastery, the continually growing world of It overruns him and robs him of the reality of his own I. . . .[21] Man's will to profit and to be powerful have their natural and proper effect so long as they are linked with, and upheld by, his will to enter into relation. There is no evil impulse till the impulse has been separated from the being.[22]

Buber, the modern prophet, raised the alarm because he witnessed in his society just such a separation from being, from the I-Thou relationship:

> In this moment . . . you can hear, as I do, that the levers of economics are beginning to sound in an unusual way; the masters smile at you with superior assurance, but death is in their hearts. They tell you they suited the apparatus [modern industrial society] to the circumstances. But you notice that from now on they can only suit themselves to the apparatus—so long, that is to say, as it permits them. Their speakers teach you that economics is entering on the State's inheritance, but you know that there is nothing to inherit except the tyranny of the exuberantly growing It, under which the I, less and less able to master, dreams on that it is the ruler.[23]

For Buber, a vital life and a healthy society must be centered on relationship. Like the Hebrew prophets, Buber witnessed the people of his day practicing a form of idolatry, betraying the sacred I-Thou relationship to treat people and the world as things.

Emmanuel Levinas, twentieth-century French Jewish philosopher, was also seared by the Holocaust, and he was influenced by Martin

---

19 Ibid., 17.
20 Ibid., 37, 39.
21 Ibid., 46.
22 Ibid., 48.
23 Ibid.

Buber. Like Buber, Levinas criticized any school of thought that presented the independent self as the fundamental reference point for perceiving the world. For Levinas, relationship—what he calls "facing the other"—must be the first perception and the basis for all later inquiry. Levinas was critical of the entire stream of Western philosophy that lays primary emphasis on the exploration of the nature of Being, on an independent existence that precedes relationship. Descartes's first premise, "I think therefore I am," is a prime example.

For Levinas, no being precedes relationship. Every being is constituted by relationship. In his critique, this error in Western philosophy—conceiving of an independent self who defines itself by thinking about the world—has profound implications. By beginning with an independent self that attempts to know the world, Western tradition inevitably relegates the other to the *object* of one's knowing. The other, perceived as an object of thought, can never be encountered as an equal cosubject. This ego-centered philosophy leads naturally to a self that sees itself as the center of the world, regal and sovereign. The other and one's obligations to the other take on secondary importance, forever in the shadow of establishing the primacy of the self. By contrast, Levinas placed the encounter with the "face of the other" at the center of philosophical exploration. In this way, one's existential dependence on the other and one's obligations to the other take center stage.

In considering Levinas's other-oriented ethic, we should keep in mind that human beings have an ambivalent relationship with an other. On the one hand, humans need to be in relationship with others in order to thrive. A human being cannot find meaning and well-being in isolation. Any break in the web of human connection hurts the human soul.

On the other hand, others can be fundamentally threatening to human beings on at least three levels. On the physical level, humans sometimes compete with one another, or one tribe competes with another tribe, for the resources to survive and flourish. On a psychological level, the worldview or the needs of the other can threaten our values and beliefs or challenge the justice of honored societal institutions. On a sociological level, demonization of the other is the easiest way for a society to export internal tensions and to thereby strengthen communal solidarity.

This ambivalence toward the other or the strange extends to our neurology, to human consciousness. One aspect of human awareness fears the strange and the unknown. Human awareness constantly sifts through the infinite amount of data that pours in at every moment to construct a finite, settled, comprehensible world. For the sake of survival, it craves order and predictability and recoils from the unexpected.

At the same time, human consciousness is drawn to the incomprehensible. This quality of mind intuits the presence of a relational reality that is larger than its immediate knowing. It feels the vibrations of the great web along fibers it cannot measure and whose ends it cannot see. It perceives the presence of a Mystery it cannot understand. This second aspect of mind is animated by the divine word that set Abraham on his journey: "Get yourself out, leave your land, your kin and your family" (Gen 12:1†). This is the mind that continually seeks to transcend itself, to connect to the larger life of which it is a part. This is the aspect of consciousness that experiences the relationship that constitutes all being.

In Martin Buber's terms, the first aspect of mind constitutes the I of the "I-It attitude," and the second aspect of mind emerges in the "I-Thou attitude."

Jewish mysticism calls the first aspect of consciousness *moach d'katnut* (small mind). The second aspect is called *moach d'gadlut* (big mind). Both *moach d'katnut* and *moach d'gadlut* are important aspects of human consciousness. Human life is impossible without *moach d'katnut*. Human life is debased without *moach d'gadlut*. The beauty and the challenge of human consciousness is holding these two aspects of mind in a dynamic balance.

An oppressive society by its very nature disrupts the balance between *moach d'katnut* and *moach d'gadlut*; it reinforces the fear of the other and the I-It attitude, the human inclination to treat another person as an object to be used. The Brazilian educator and activist Paulo Freire discussed this objectifying aspect of oppression. In his pivotal work, *Pedagogy of the Oppressed*, he described the objectifying "possessive consciousness" that grips both the privileged and the oppressed:

> Once a situation of violence and oppression has been established, it engenders an entire way of life and behavior for those caught up in it—oppressors and oppressed alike. Both are submerged in this situation. . . . This climate creates in the oppressor a strongly possessive consciousness—possessive of the world and of men and women. Apart from direct, concrete, material possession of the world and of people, the oppressor consciousness could not understand itself—could not even exist. [Erich] Fromm said of this consciousness that, without such possessions, "it would lose contact with the world." The oppressor consciousness tends to transform everything surrounding it into an object of its domination. The earth, property, production, the creation of people, people themselves, time—everything is reduced to the status of

objects at its disposal. . . . For them, *to be is to have.* . . . Any restriction on this way of life, in the name of the rights of the community, appears to the former oppressors as a profound violation of their individual right.[24]

In this passage, Freire is writing in distinctly prophetic terms. He sees that economic oppression naturally leads to an obsessive need to control everything that the oppressor encounters, including people as well as property. For Freire, oppression and an insatiable need to control are co-occurring phenomenon. Similarly, the Hebrew prophets perceived that injustice and idolatry are co-occurring phenomenon. They saw that controlling people through oppressive systems and attempting to control God through idolatrous practice go hand in hand. Both idolatry and oppression attempt to seize undue control rather than venturing into the risky territory of friendship, of mutual relationship with people and with God.

The contemporary thinkers I have cited all point to a common cause of suffering—a lack of mutual relationship. Contemporary ecology provides a similar vision about the importance of mutual relationship for living beings. While ecologists do not use terms like "love" and "friendship," these life scientists recognize that mutually beneficial cooperation is essential to the development and maintenance of life. This is not to suggest that living forms do not compete for limited resources; they do. Competition culls those life forms that are less successfully adapted. But cooperation, the profoundly complex interrelationship among species, enables life to thrive and evolve. Cooperative interrelationship enables new possibilities. Over the eons, cooperation has empowered the evolving of more conscious, and more mutually related life forms.[25]

Similarly, anthropologists have identified cooperation within small clans of humans as the distinctive quality that enabled our earliest ances-

---

24   Paulo Freire, *Pedagogy of the Oppressed*, trans. Myra Bergman Ramos (New York: Continuum, 2003), 57–58, 143.

25   Robin Wall Kimmerer, *Braiding Sweetgrass: Indigenous Wisdom, Scientific Knowledge, and the Teaching of Plants* (Minneapolis: Milkweed Editions, 2013), 128–40; Robert Axelrod and William Hamilton, "The Evolution of Cooperation," *Science* 211 (March 27, 1981): 1390–96; Mark Bertness and Ragan Callaway, "Positive Interactions in Community," *Tree* 9, no. 5 (May 1994): 191–93; John F. Bruno, John Stachowicz, and Mark Bertness, "Inclusion of Facilitation into Ecological Theory," *Trends in Ecology and Evolution* 18, no. 3 (March 2003): 121–25; Rob Brooker et al., "Facilitation in Plant Communities: The Past, the Present, and the Future," *Journal of Ecology* 96 (2008): 18–34; E. Toby Kiers et al., "Mutualisms in a Changing World: An Evolutionary Perspective," *Ecology Letters* 13 (December 2010): 1459–74.

tors to feed, clothe, and shelter themselves. Competition among clans took place, but on a relatively small scale. For nearly two hundred thousand years, close cooperation within small groups of people enabled our species to survive and ultimately to thrive. Significant competition within a community only arrived on the human scene relatively recently, around ten thousand years ago, with the advent of agriculture. As Sebastian Junger wrote in his book *Tribe*, "Agriculture . . . changed the human experience. The accumulation of personal property allowed people to make more and more individualistic choices about their lives, and those choices unavoidably diminished group efforts toward a common good."[26]

Even in agricultural and industrial societies, communal cooperation in the form of civic groups and volunteer associations has played a key role in nurturing the well-being of the society. In recent years, however, these associations have diminished in American communal life. In the last thirty years a number of sociological studies have expressed grave concern about the fraying of mutual caring relationships and the consequent growing loneliness in contemporary society.[27] Sebastian Junger also focuses on the loneliness of modern life:

A person living in a modern city or suburb can, for the first time in history, go through an entire day—or an entire life—mostly encountering complete strangers. They can be surrounded by others and yet feel deeply, dangerously alone. . . . Numerous cross-cultural studies have shown that modern society—despite its nearly miraculous advances in medicine, science and technology—is afflicted with some of the highest rates of depression, schizophrenia, poor health, anxiety, and chronic loneliness in human history.[28]

Junger's analysis is strongly critical of the growing penchant toward "individualistic choices" in agricultural and industrial societies. The deleterious effects of excessive individualism in contemporary life are certainly clear. At the same time, individualism has also brought profound advances. We must acknowledge the tension between the benefits and the

---

[26] Sebastian Junger, *Tribe: On Homecoming and Belonging* (New York: Twelve, 2016), 18.

[27] Robert Bellah, *Habits of the Heart: Individualism and Commitment in American Life* (Berkeley: University of California Press, 2007); Robert Putnam, *Bowling Alone: The Collapse and Revival of American Community* (New York: Touchstone, 2001); Sherry Turkle, *Alone Together: Why We Expect More from Technology and Less from Each Other* (New York: Basic Books, 2017).

[28] Junger, *Tribe*, 18–19.

adverse effects of individualism to appreciate fully the daunting cultural challenge of creating a more communal and less individualistic society. The development of the individual is the glory of the West. Western civilization gave humankind a hard-earned respect for individual human reason and also propagated the honoring of universal human rights. The rise of the individual and the empowerment of ordinary individual human beings is truly a great accomplishment.

In the modern era, however, the ever-increasing emphasis on individual achievement and individual rights has become extreme and has facilitated widespread suffering and oppression. Western individualism, despite its benefits, has become destructive because it rests on a flawed assumption. Since the eighteenth century, forward-thinking people have assumed that the accumulated achievement of free individuals pursuing their destiny would naturally create a society that benefited most of its members. Societal leaders assumed that all boats would rise on the tide of individual success. This assumption has not been born out.

In its enthusiasm for individual rights, Western culture, particularly in the United States, has failed to hold the creative tension between individual freedom and communal obligation. While glorifying individual initiative and marketplace competition, Western societies have undervalued cooperative efforts devoted to the common good. The Western focus on the individual has excluded an understanding of the essential importance of relationship, community, and communion. As a result, many apparently successfully people in our society have arrived at the end of the rainbow only to find that the pot of gold lacks real worth.

Virtually everybody I know is insanely busy, attempting to hold down a job while also caring for little children and perhaps aging parents as well. Our lives have become full of doings and impoverished in genuine relating. In Buber's terms, we live in a culture of the "exuberantly expanding It," a culture that values production and consumption at the expense of relationship.

Personally, I recognize that Western culture has significantly shaped the way I perceive the world. I was raised and nurtured on the presuppositions of twentieth-century America. I was taught to do good in the world, to care about other people, especially the needs of the poor. But beyond the circumscribed world of family and friends, I was not raised to value relationship itself, to seek continually to deepen and broaden the scope of my relations. I was raised to love certain people, but not to place loving at the center of my life.

This isolating worldview in which I was acculturated was not primarily the work of my parents. These values were in the cultural soil from which I grew. Instrumental and objectifying premises about life were in the air I breathed. Like oxygen, the profound implications of these premises were invisible to me. The only inner dissent I experienced was a subtle ache deep inside my body, the feeling of hollowness and thinness that my heart increasingly sensed, the growing awareness that something fundamental was missing in the picture of life I had been given.

The full dimensions of this empty feeling became clear to me in my early adulthood when I was a graduate student in American history. Friends and colleagues shared my days. Nevertheless, our lives did not seem to touch each others' in meaningful ways. I often felt isolated and hungered for heartfelt conversation. When I first read Buber, he gave me language for what I was feeling. The "I" of most of my day was indeed the I of the I-It attitude. I felt as if I treated myself like an object, like a piece on the Monopoly board, doing what I could to land on places that brought me pleasure and to avoid places that brought me pain. I was good at the game, but I lacked a felt sense of real connection either to my own inner life or to the inner life of those around me. I was succeeding in the outer world and dying inside.

The loneliness and isolation that I felt is an all too common feature of contemporary life, most certainly among the privileged in Western industrialized countries. The advantaged few in these societies are rich in things and impoverished in human solidarity. Meanwhile, much of the rest of the world suffers a lack of the necessities of life. The lives of billions of people are scarred by deprivation and degradation.

As in prophetic times, this social-economic order cannot stand. The growing economic and political instability around the world as well as the destabilizing changes in the global climate signal that the current order is imminently unsustainable. In the words of the contemporary prophet Walter Brueggemann, the current regime is "doomed."[29]

The current order is doomed, but the people who live under this order are not. The life-giving dynamism of the prophetic stream, the energy that created and continually creates the world, the torrent that freed the Israelites from Egypt, is fully alive and well. King, Heschel, Buber, Levinas, Gutiérrez, and Harrison all drank from this stream and proclaimed its goodness and vitality. They found in the Hebrew prophets an alternative vision: fundamental ways of thinking and valuing that would lead to a more relational world, to a world and society that would be good for all.

Creating that world is the imperative task.

---

[29] Brueggemann pronounced the doom of the current order in a talk delivered at Temple Beth Shalom in Santa Fe in October 2014.

CHAPTER 15

A Listening Lineage

At its heart, the prophetic witness was a way of listening, listening beyond the social norms of the day, listening to the word of the liberating God. The prophets urged the people to listen to God's word because the discourse of the king, princes, and wealthy landowners was too narrow and was limited to the interests of these elites. This conversation did not include the voices of suffering people. The prophets, in God's name, offered a much broader discourse, a conversation that listened to and addressed the needs of the poor and the disadvantaged.

Listening for a more expansive word is an important aspect of the people's liberation journey from the very outset. While the Israelites were still in Egypt, Moses's primary concern was that the people could not hear and would not listen to God's liberating word. Moses understood that the people's discourse had been so dominated by generations of slavery that they could not imagine freedom from bondage. He saw that the people needed to listen to God's promise of liberation in order to break through their mental constraints. If the people could not listen, they could not go free. For Moses, listening was an essential practice for the liberation journey.

Later prophets also perceived that listening connected the people to God's life-giving and liberating word, as in this passage from Isaiah:

Hear now, Jacob my servant; and Israel, whom I have chosen. Thus says the Living Presence who made you, and formed you from the womb, who will help you. Fear not, Jacob, my servant; and you, Jeshurun, whom I have chosen. For I will pour water upon the thirsty land, and floods upon the dry ground; I will pour my spirit upon your seed, and my blessing upon your offspring. And they shall spring up as among the grass, as willows by the watercourses. (44:1–4)

In the midrash, the Rabbis extol the liberating power of listening:

Man has two hundred and forty-eight limbs, and the ear is but one of them; yet even *though* his whole body be stained with transgressions, as long as his ear hearkens [to the Torah], the whole body is vivified, for it says, "Hear, and your soul shall live." (Isa 55:3)[1]

The biblical scribes and the Rabbis preserved the prophetic testimony so that future generations would have the benefit of the prophets' expansive listening. Contemporary prophets—Gutiérrez, King, Heschel, Harrison, Brueggemann—received the prophetic word from the scribal texts and used it to expand their listening, and ultimately to challenge the listening of their society.

Thanks to all these generations of listening, the prophetic listening tradition is alive today to inspire people to listen beyond the established conversation. The prophetic tradition challenges us to listen especially to the cries of those who suffer and to listen to the voice of alternative possibility, to the voice of God.

The prophets call upon us to listen to *both* God's word as articulated by the prophets themselves and to God speaking through the world. God's speaking in the world takes the form not only of spoken words but as a Presence in the physical world. The divine word is the ever-flowing source of the creative power of creation. The word of this Living Presence includes the *tov* of Genesis, the vitality and dynamism of all that is.

The Living Presence also speaks within our lives, wordlessly calling us out into life, encouraging us to grow beyond our current limitations. This Presence breathes into us desires and visions of whom we might become. Listening to the word of God is opening to the often-wordless speech of this Presence, allowing the transcendent to touch us, to inspire us, to beckon us across boundaries, to take the next step in our lives. Listening well to our inner lives—to the thoughts, inclinations, images, and emotions that arise within us—is an important practice along the liberation journey.

Listening is essential in relationship to the Living Presence and in mutual relationship with people. The intimacy of hearing and listening animates the relational quality of the liberation journey. Hearing is the physical sensation of receiving vibrations inside us. When we hear something, the physical world has permeated us. Closely related to hearing,

---

[1] *Exodus Rabbah* 27:9.

listening is also receptive. Listening involves consciously attending to the vibrations that have come inside. When we attend to these sensations with a quiet mind, our sense of a separate self evaporates. We become, for the moment, informed by what we hear. In this way, listening fosters connection and relationship.

A mutual relationship with another person happens only through such attentive listening. An I-Thou meeting can take place when the mind is quiet and the heart is open to take in the other person, attending to her experiences, desires, sufferings, and dreams.

Listening to another person also makes our own liberation possible. In any particular moment, each of us is limited by the categories of thought and perception we habitually impose on what is happening. We become liberated from these limitations when we receive the perceptions and experiences of another person, especially a person whose culture, background, and experience are very different from our own. The act of deeply listening to an other is a primary way that our limiting categories of thought and perception are punctured so that we might transcend them and grow beyond them.

Listening to another person and listening to the Living Presence are of one piece. The Living Presence speaks to us through our encounters with other people as well as through events in the world, through Scripture, and through our personal inner life. We are called to listen, widely and deeply.

Societies must listen too. They are also called to be on a liberation journey toward ever more mutual relationship, toward policies and programs that support the well-being of all. Here, too, attentive listening is the essential practice. A community can recognize how societal structures constrict human flourishing only through listening beyond privileged society's comfort zone, especially hearing the voices of those who suffer the most.

Listening also reveals unrecognized possibilities. The world is full of potential, possibilities that emerge out of the suffering, yearning, and dreaming of people worldwide. Courageous listening animates the societal liberation process.

In my life, listening is a prime spiritual practice. Throughout the day, I seek to listen. I find that I sometimes hear the words but do not bring my full attention to listening. A friend is speaking to me; am I listening with a quiet mind? I see the beauty of the roses in my garden. Am I listening internally, taking a moment to notice the effect that the beauty of the roses has on me? I hear an undocumented immigrant in my community describe how her family lives in fear. Am I listening with a responsive heart? I read a story in the newspaper about heroin addiction in our state. Am I listening? I study a passage in Scripture. Am I paying attention to the details in the passage? Am I providing the time and attention to notice what the text might be stirring up in me?

I cannot listen to everything. There is also a listening for what I am called to be listening for. This, too, is listening.

Over the years I have witnessed the tremendous power of listening. At the beginning of each year of Beit Midrash, the learning circles whose work is the basis for this book, I always say, "The most powerful thing we do in Beit Midrash is to practice deep listening." In Beit Midrash, our first listening is to the biblical text itself, allowing Scripture to speak to us before we bring our thoughts and judgments to the text. Our second listening is to our fellow classmates. We listen carefully, taking in the words and the full presence of the person behind the words. To facilitate respectful listening, we often slow down the conversation, sometimes pausing after a person speaks to allow time for that person's thoughts to be absorbed. I like to say that my mind can move at light speed, but my heart and soul move at water speed, so I need us to pause for a moment to take in what was just said. Whenever I make a comment of that nature I sense everybody relax a little bit, glad for the chance to listen more carefully to what is being said. Inspired learning virtually always emerges from our study because the circle is really listening. When people sense they are being truly heard, they feel more empowered to speak something of significance.

Similarly, as a longtime spiritual director, I have spent years listening with people for the movement of the Living Presence in their lives. I don't do much beyond listening. Yet, over time, I have witnessed awe-inspiring growth in the people with whom I have sat.

Listening is an essential practice along the liberation journey. Deep listening challenges our internal status quo and exposes us to new possibilities. The world is full of possibilities for healing and wholeness, for well-being and joy. Like the biblical prophets and contemporary people who live in their lineage, all those of us on a liberation journey are called to listen, to learn, and then to act to bring a more fruitful future into the world.

CHAPTER 16

We Make the Road by Walking
LIFE AS JOURNEY

When we listen to the world—to people, to our fellow creatures, and to plant life—we hear great suffering. Multiple living systems of our planet are under serious threat. The political, economic, and social institutions of our day are not serving the flourishing of life. We stand today where the Hebrew prophets stood over two and a half millennia ago. Like the prophets, we can now see clearly that some of the foundational assumptions and values of our society have led us astray, and therefore the social, political, and economic order built on those assumptions cannot stand.

In this place of shattering crisis, the prophets rooted themselves in the animating word of the Living Presence, in the energy at the core of creation that continually brings forth new possibilities. Immersed in that creative stream, the prophets perceived a way forward; they articulated an alternative way of coming together into community. In our day, we are called to be such prophets. We are called to draw from the dynamic stream that animates our lives in order to bring forth vision and action that renews the fabric of relationship and community.

The cultural transformation we are called to pursue is monumental, so much so that we can feel overwhelmed by the task. In the face of our fear that the task is too great, the prophetic testimony offers important perspective. Prophetic vision would have us see our contemporary challenge in the context of expansive time and deep time. Expansive time suggests that the transformation we seek does not come in a year or in a generation. As the prophets saw, the transformation to a more relational society involves a multigenerational liberation process—an extended learning journey. To convey their sense of extended time, the prophets located their contemporary moment in the epic stream of the exodus journey. Speaking within the grand context of that multigenerational learning journey, the prophets were able to envision and invoke a reality that was wholly different from the historical context in which the people found themselves. This understanding of history, of a prolonged journey with God, empowered the prophets to stand up to the king and the high priest and proclaim that a radically new day was coming.

Deep time suggests that profound and powerful forces of creation, the waters of the prophetic stream, energize and support our transformation journey. The involvement of these deep forces suggests that we cannot ever know the ultimate outcome of our actions.

Taken together, expansive and deep time suggest that we urgently need to apply ourselves now to take meaningful steps toward an inclusive, flourishing society, while recognizing that we are playing a small part in a journey whose depth and expanse are far beyond our understanding. This expansive and deep perspective on time offers present-day people the opportunity to perceive themselves—ourselves—as participants in the exodus journey, a multigenerational liberation process supported by the energies at the heart of creation. In the remainder of this book, I bring in the work of twentieth-century prophets to explore the powerful resource this prophetic perspective offers to contemporary activists. This exploration will set forth the contemporary significance of the twin prophetic assertions; the people are on a liberation journey with God, a journey toward ever-greater mutual relationship. Let us turn then to the first prophetic assertion: the people are on a liberation journey with God.

When I was a child, I thought that one day I would be all "grown up." I did not imagine that adults needed to continue to evolve in the quality of their consciousness, to develop in their ability to embrace the world—to leave behind earlier, less loving, and less compassionate ways of being.

Modern psychology, by contrast, offers models of human growth that delineate stages of human development spanning a lifetime. Inspired by the work of Piaget, Erik Erikson described eight stages of human development. Following Erikson's lead, Lawrence Kohlberg delineated stages of moral development, and James Fowler described discrete stages of faith development. Many subsequent psychologists and sociologists built on this work to describe ever more refined stages of human growth.[1] These scholars conceive human life as a process of evolution, a learning journey.

---

[1]   See the work of Loevinger, Cook-Greuter, Kegan, Sullivan, and Wilbur.

Contemporary American popular culture presents an understanding of human life that reflects my childhood conception; it lacks an evolutionary perspective. In this worldview, the goal of life is to get somewhere, to achieve some high status, rather than continually to undertake a journey of discovery. Significantly shaped by a supercharged advertising industry, the contemporary ethos extols attaining a certain station in life by producing and consuming, placing little value on the development of consciousness and relationships through learning and growing. The emphasis in our culture is on external achievement and success, not on internal development in awareness, compassion, and wisdom.

Prophetic insight offers a worldview close to the human growth model of modern developmental psychology. This prophetic worldview, that life is a learning journey, is inherently liberating. I can illustrate this liberation by relating a brief encounter that changed my life. When I was in my early thirties, I was telling an older friend about some of the foolish things I had done in my early twenties. My friend smiled at me and said, "If you don't look back on yourself ten years from now and ask yourself how you could have been so foolish, you will not have grown."

My friend's observation gave me the freedom to make mistakes, to blunder forward, and to learn. The freedom to fail and not feel like a failure has enabled me to devote myself to tasks in which success was far from guaranteed. It has enabled me to take risks, to fail and try again. I am not suggesting that I don't suffer when I fail. In truth, sometimes I judge myself harshly when I fall short. My inner voice can condemn me with unkind words like, "What a stupid thing to do." But I usually catch myself in those judgments. I remind myself that I am committed to taking risks in order to grow, that failing at something is an opportunity to learn. With these thoughts my heart softens, my backbone straightens, and I am ready to take responsibility for my mistake. I am ready to learn something new and to do my best to bring healing to any hurt I might have caused.

One of my teachers, Brother Joseph Schmidt, once told me that his constant prayer is, "Father, forgive me, for I have sinned." I initially heard this prayer as too sin-soaked for me. But I have great respect for Br. Joe, so I pondered his prayer until I found its wisdom. I came to see that his prayer for forgiveness was the natural prayer at the center of a creative and adventurous life. If I want to cross beyond familiar boundaries and take risks in the hope of connecting more deeply to people and to life itself, I need to be prepared to see clearly my current limitations. I need to see where I have fallen short in the past, and in the face of my shortcomings I need to risk venturing forward into new ways of being.

Such a journey of exploration requires that I travel light. It requires me to take responsibility for my mistakes and then forgive myself.

In the prophetic worldview, God supports falling forward, mistake-ridden risk-taking, and boundary crossing for the sake of growth in consciousness and relationship. The prophets perceive God as energizing this journey, animating all life forms to bring forth new ways, to explore new relationships. The prophets also teach that God offers forgiveness to the people when their adventure goes off track, when they behave in ways that betray their friendship with their fellow humans and with God. The God of the prophets continually calls a wayward people to return to right relationship that they might be healed of the consequences of their mistakes: "Assuredly, thus says the Living Presence: If you return, then I will bring you back, and you shall stand before me, and if you take out the precious from the vile, you shall be as my mouth" (Jer 15:19).

The prophetic stream supports learning, the evolution of life toward greater consciousness, and every movement toward justice and communal well-being. At the same time, the prophetic stream offers healing waters when we become aware of our mistakes, cleansing waters that enable us to learn from our mistakes and to move forward.

A prophetic perspective is particularly important in our day because we have some serious learning ahead of us, individually and communally. Uprooting multiple oppressive systems requires more than good policy. We need to transform abiding societal values and ways of thinking. These deep cultural changes don't come easily or quickly; they will require the sacrifice of cherished ways and treasured possessions.

In the face of these monumental challenges, the prophetic testimony encourages us to be undaunted by the enormity of the transformation we need to pursue. When we assume a prophetic stance and see our challenges from the perspective of an extended journey, we do not need to envision the final form of an alternative society. All we need to perceive is the direction of the journey—toward mutual relationship—and the next step in that direction. Along this journey we will take risks and make mistakes.

Contemporary liberation thinkers and activists articulate the same wisdom, the understanding that liberation is not a single act but rather an ongoing journey, an extended multistage learning process. Paulo Freire wrote,

> The rightist sectarian differs from his or her leftist [i.e., Marxist] counterpart in that the former attempts to domesticate the present . . . while the latter considers the future pre-established. For the rightist sectarian, "today," linked to the past, is something given

and immutable; for the leftist sectarian, "tomorrow" is decreed beforehand. . . . Closing themselves into "circles of certainty" from which they cannot escape, these individuals "make" their own truth. It is not the truth of men and women who struggle to build the future, running the risks involved in this very construction. Nor is it the truth of men and women who fight side by side and learn together how to build this future—which is not something given to be received by people, but rather something to be created by them.[2]

Freire understands that oppressive systems shape the consciousness of those who live within them so that these systems appear to be inevitable and immutable. Liberation requires deep reflection, learning, and action. In Freire's words,

One of the gravest obstacles to the achievement of liberation is that oppressive reality absorbs those within it and thereby acts to submerge human beings' consciousness. Functionally, oppression is domesticating. To no longer be prey to its force, one must emerge from it and turn upon it. This can be done only by means of the praxis: reflection and action upon the world in order to transform it.[3]

Freire encapsulated his understanding of the dynamics of the liberation process with his famous saying, "We make the road by walking."[4] I like the word "walking" because it captures the sense of a skillful falling forward. For Freire, "walking" is a powerful kinesthetic metaphor for learning, a metaphor that highlights that learning includes both inner reflection and outer action. As an educator, Freire understands that liberating learning is an iterative process—reflection followed by action followed by reflection followed by action, step by step. Freire's two-beat, iterative understanding of the learning path holds great wisdom for contemporary change agents. We may not know how to journey from the present-day Egypt to the promise of a more freely relational society, but we can reflect on the present moment to discern the next step in the direction of freedom and then reflect on the outcome of that step.

---

[2] Paulo Freire, *Pedagogy of the Oppressed*, trans. Myra Bergman Ramos (New York Continuum, 2003), 38–39 (bracketed phrase added).

[3] Ibid., 51.

[4] Freire adapted the quote from a line in the poem "Proverbs and Song-Verse" by Spanish poet Antonio Machado: "se hace camino al andar" [you make the way as you go].

The human rights activists James and Grace Lee Boggs also placed learning at the center of a liberation movement. In their study of twentieth-century revolutionary movements in Africa, China, and Vietnam, the Boggses distinguished between political independence and national liberation. Examining the historical record, they pointed out that independence from colonial powers did not necessarily lead to liberation, to a society in which people are free to flourish relationally. A national liberation movement must engage people in a process of learning to think differently:

> Revolution must have as its goal and its modus operandi not only the elimination of the oppressor but the most rapid development and transformation of the oppressed as well. It must involve the people both in struggle against their oppressors and in a cultural revolution against their own weakness, their own traditional attitudes. The people must be mobilized to fight *mental battles* as well as physical ones, so that not only their physical courage but also their *intelligence*, their daily participation, their capacity for confronting new problems in new ways, their ability to think for themselves can be expanded.[5]

The Boggses articulate how the pain of oppression energizes the oppressed to learn. In the concluding chapters of their study, the Boggses observe that in contemporary America, middle- and working-class Americans also experience the pain and suffering that spurs radical learning:

> Today in the United States [the 1970s] the Vietnam War has come home to Americans in ways that they never suspected. . . . Blacks, Chicanos, Puerto Ricans, Asian-Americans, Indians, Appalachian whites, young people—all are in a state of rebellion, inspired or accelerated by their realization that the citadel of world capitalism can be breached by a tiny nation lacking in the technological might. . . . They continue to live in accordance with their philosophy that the pursuit of economic benefits will solve all their problems and the problems of this society. But they are not so sure that this is still true. . . . Usually the search for a new philosophy begins with the break-up of old values and old standards. . . . Such a situation exists in the United States today.[6]

---

[5] James and Grace Lee Boggs, *Revolution and Evolution in the Twentieth Century* (New York: Monthly Review Press, 2008), 90–91 (emphasis added).
[6] Ibid., 199, 198.

Paulo Freire and the Boggses teach that liberation is necessarily a learning process. True freedom requires that people learn a new way of thinking—new first premises and priorities—and embody a new way of being in the world. This pedagogic approach to social transformation empowers people and communities to act even when the way forward is far from clear. An emphasis on learning places the focus on the best next step, even when the entire way forward is impossible to see.

Frances Moore Lappé, the contemporary writer and change agent, expressed the spirit of the liberation journey when she said, "If you expect to see the ultimate result of your work you simply have not asked a big enough question."[7]

In prophetic understanding, such liberating learning is not an exceptional activity that people undertake only at certain historical moments, only when the community is experiencing severe oppression. Rather, the prophets saw life itself as a learning journey, an exodus process being brought forth from the core of creation itself. With this unifying insight into the human story and the universe story, the prophets placed the people's learning in the grand context of a learning creation. In this prophetic perspective, the people are accompanied and buoyed, as they learn, by profound physical and spiritual forces, by all of creation. Creation itself is a liberation process, a learning journey of transformation. The divinely animated, creative prophetic stream runs through all that is.

This insight into reality, understanding the transforming nature of creation itself, enabled the prophet to stand up against the apparently insurmountable power of the king and the priest. A static rule will inevitably fall in the process of change. Similarly, in our day, perceiving the upwelling of transforming forces within all of life can empower people to work on behalf of transformation in the face of powerful forces of resistance and reaction.

Czech leader Vaclav Havel placed this insight—the liberating quality of the life force itself—at the center of his resistance to Soviet totalitarianism. He wrote, "Life, in its essence, moves towards plurality, diversity, independent self-constituting and self-organization, in short toward the fulfillment of its own freedom."[8]

The prophet Isaiah expressed the same insight in classical biblical terms: "Behold, I [the Living Presence] will do a new thing. Now shall it spring forth; shall ye not know it? I will make a way in the wilderness, and rivers in the desert" (43:19).

---

[7] Francis Moore Lappé, interviewed on National Public Radio, September 22, 2016.

[8] Vaclav Havel, "The Power of the Powerless," in *Vaclav Havel: Living in Truth*, ed. Jan Vladislav (London: Faber and Faber, 1986), 43–44.

The prophets, both ancient and modern, have helped me to learn to walk toward liberation. Even with their help my stride is challenged and unsure. Their example, though, has given me, and can give all of us, the courage to take risks and honor mistakes as we struggle to learn our way forward. With this learning we can take the next step on the liberating path.

CHAPTER 17

Dialogue Is the Way

In the Bible, people learn and grow through dialogue, by listening and responding to one another. Biblical scholar Robert Alter observes the extraordinary role that dialogue plays in the Scriptures. He distinguishes biblical narrative from Homeric poems in which the characters deliver grand monologues and also from more modern narrative strategies in which the narrator describes the action as an observer. Beginning with the call-and-response of creation itself, biblical narrative sets a scene, delineates the characters involved, and moves the action forward through dialogue.[1] Alter writes, "In Biblical literature . . . dialogue is made to carry a large part of the freight of meaning. . . . Spoken language is the substratum of everything human and divine that transpires in the Bible."[2]

Dialogue is the "substratum," the elemental material, out of which biblical stories are formed. Biblical characters learn, repent, and heal through dialogue.[3]

This central role of dialogue communicates the biblical awareness that reality itself is dialogical. That is to say, reality is fundamentally relational. Reality is not atomized or static but is constituted by give-and-take, by conversation. In the midrash, the Rabbis found an etymological basis for teaching that all of creation is a conversation. The creation story refers to "שיח השדה" (plants of the field) (Gen 2:5). The word for "plant" in this term, "שיח," also means "conversation." Making a wordplay, the Rabbis teach that "all the trees of the field converse with each

---

[1]   Robert Alter, *The Art of Biblical Narrative* (New York: Basic Books, 1983), Kindle loc 1522.

[2]   Ibid., Kindle loc 801, 1510.

[3]   Alter's *Art of Biblical Narrative* contains many examples. See chap. 4, "Between Narration and Dialogue."

other and with humankind."[4] Creation converses with itself. Creation is a conversation!

The spiritual implications of this insight cannot be overstated. If all creation is a conversation initiated by the Creator, then the pathway to God is to join the conversation, to listen diligently, and to respond. This insight suggests that God does not seek thoughtless obedience. Rather, the Living Presence desires humans to engage in ongoing conversation, with God and with all of God's creation. In the Bible, dialogue is the way of faithfulness.

Martin Buber and Paulo Freire also present dialogue as an essential dynamic at the heart of the learning journey. In his essay "Education," Buber explores how learning emerges from encounters, from a person's dialogical relationship with the world:

> The world, that is the whole environment, nature and society, "educates" the human being: it draws out his powers and makes him grasp and penetrate its objections. . . . He is educated by the elements, by air and light and the life of plants and animals, and *he is educated by relationships.*[5]

According to Buber, "the relation in education is one of pure dialogue."[6] He describes a nonverbal dialogue between a learner and the world. In this kind of dialogue, the world draws out a learner's powers; the learner in response seeks understanding by grasping and penetrating the reality she has encountered. This interchange—encounter and response—is repeated as long as the learner is open to being met, to receiving the world.

The educator facilitates this exchange by structuring an engagement with a "selection of the effective world"[7] that draws the student into relationship. The purpose of the teacher's efforts is to nurture the student's ability to meet the world, to enter into dialogue with the environment.[8] Through the teacher's "delicate approach, the raising of a finger, perhaps, or a questioning glance,"[9] the student's "heart is drawn to reverence for the form, and educated."[10]

---

[4] *Genesis Rabbah* 13:2.

[5] Martin Buber, "Education," in *Between Man and Man*, trans. Ronald Gregor Smith (Mansfield Centre, CT: Martino Publishing, 2014), 89–90 (emphasis added).

[6] Ibid., 98.

[7] Ibid.

[8] Ibid.

[9] Ibid., 88.

[10] Ibid.

Buber presented dialogue as the method of education because dialogue should be the goal of education. Only through dialogue will a human being lead a fulfilling and responsible life:

> This fragile life between birth and death can nevertheless be a fulfillment—if it is a dialogue. In our life and experience we are addressed; by thought and speech and action, by producing and by influencing we are able to answer. For the most part we do not listen to the address, or we break into it with chatter. But if the world comes to us and the answer proceeds from us, then human life exists, though brokenly, in the world.[11]

Paulo Freire's thought is clearly influenced by Martin Buber.[12] Like Buber, he taught that authentic learning brings a person into dialogical relationship with a dynamic world. He contrasts real learning with what he calls "banking education," a kind of teaching that presents an unchanging world and thereby supports the static worldview of oppressive power. In banking education, "The teacher talks about reality as if it were motionless, static, compartmentalized, and predictable. . . . His task is to fill the students with the contents of his narration—contents which are detached from reality."[13]

Freire argues that this static portrayal of reality directly serves the interests of the oppressors:

> This is the "banking" concept of education in which the scope of action allowed to the students extends only as far as receiving, filing, and storing the deposits. They do, it is true, have the opportunity to become collectors or cataloguers of the things they store. But in the last analysis, it is the people themselves who are filed away through the lack of creativity, transformation and knowledge. . . . The capability of banking education to minimize or annul the students' creative power and to stimulate their credulity serves the interests of the oppressors, who care neither to have the world revealed nor to see it transformed.[14]

The static reality presented in banking education assumes that the world is an object, an inert object that humans dwell on. This nondynamic

---

[11]   Ibid., 92.
[12]   See Paulo Freire, *Pedagogy of the Oppressed*, trans. Myra Bergman Ramos (New York: Continuum, 2003), 167.
[13]   Ibid., 71.
[14]   Ibid., 72, 73.

perspective denies human beings any possibility of dialogical, cocreative relationship with the world. "Implicit in the banking concept is the assumption of a dichotomy between human beings and the world: a person is merely *in* the world, and not *with* the world and with others; the individual is spectator, not re-creator."[15]

By contrast, Freire offers "education as the practice of freedom," which he calls "problem-posing education." This way of teaching is based on an understanding that reality is dynamic, "reality is really a process, undergoing constant transformation."[16] Here Freire echoes a biblical perspective: reality is not an object, but a process, a journey.

Approaching the world as a process rather than as an object has profound implications for the educator. Since there is no fixed reality that the teacher can deposit in the student, the teacher "does not regard cognizable objects as his private property, but as the object of reflection by himself and the students. . . . The students—no longer docile listeners—are now critical co-investigators in dialogue with the teacher."[17]

This process-oriented pedagogy locates people "with the world and with others."[18] In dialogue with other people and with the world, humans create reality at the same time that reality shapes human consciousness:

> Education as the practice of freedom—as opposed to education as the practice of domination—denies that man is abstract, isolated, independent, and unattached to the world; it also denies that the world exists as a reality apart from people. Authentic reflection considers . . . people in their relations with the world. In these relations [human] consciousness and world are simultaneous: consciousness neither precedes the world nor follows it.[19]

Human consciousness and reality coemerge from a dialogue among people and between human beings and the world. This philosophical understanding makes dialogue essential. In problem-posing education, the learner constantly reforms her reflections in critical dialogue with the world and with other people:

> Problem-posing education regards dialogue as indispensable to the act of cognition which unveils reality. . . . Authentic thinking, thinking that is concerned about reality, does not take place in

---

15 Ibid., 75.
16 Ibid.
17 Ibid., 80–81, 83.
18 Ibid., 75.
19 Ibid., 81.

ivory tower isolation, but only in communication. . . . Without dialogue there is no communication, and without communication there can be no true education.[20]

For Freire, dialogue is much more than a cognitive activity. Rather, dialogue includes both reflection and action:

As we attempt to analyze dialogue as a human phenomenon, we discover something which is the essence of dialogue itself: *the word*. . . . Within the word we find two dimensions, reflection and action, in such radical interaction that if one is sacrificed—even in part—the other immediately suffers. There is no true word that is not at the same time a praxis. Thus, to speak a true word is to transform the world. . . . When a word is deprived of its dimension of action . . . the word is changed into idle chatter, into verbalism, into an alienated and alienating "blah." It becomes an empty word. . . . On the other hand, if action is emphasized exclusively, to the detriment of reflection, the word is converted into activism. The latter—action for action's sake—negates the true praxis and makes dialogue impossible.[21]

Freire articulates a crucial prophetic understanding: a true word includes action. In the creation story, God's words activate the creative process. In like fashion, the prophets speak words that have transformational power. For example, when God initially commissions Jeremiah, God says, "Behold, I have put my words in your mouth . . . to destroy and to throw down and to build and to plant" (Jer 1:9–10). In the Bible, these words have power because they come from God. For Freire, human nature is the source of the transforming power of a true word:

Human existence cannot be silent, nor can it be nourished by false words, but only by true words, with which men and women transform the world. To exist, humanly, is to *name* the world, to change it. . . . To say the true word—which is work, which is praxis (reflection and action)—is to transform the world. . . . Dialogue is the encounter between men, mediated by the world, in order to name the world. . . . If it is in speaking their word that people, by naming the world, transform it, dialogue imposes itself

20   Ibid., 83, 77, 92–93.
21   Ibid., 87–88.

as the way by which they achieve significance as human beings. Dialogue is thus an existential necessity.[22]

For Freire, people fulfill their humanity through transforming the world. Therefore, an authentic human word includes transformative action. This assertion brings to mind the biblical creation story in which human beings are created in the image and likeness of the Creator, who is at work transforming the world.

Freire's understanding merits pondering. In contrast to a capitalist culture that holds that the human purpose is to enjoy the pleasures of consumption, Freire asserts that humans are created to transform the world. To fulfill this purpose, human words must name the world. This naming includes the awareness of what the named reality might become and a solid commitment to enact that transformation. Humans undertake their essential transformative work through dialogue, "the encounter between men, mediated by the world, in order to name the world."[23] Dialogue, then, includes both reflection and action.

Given the devastation that human ingenuity has brought upon the world, one might be concerned that Freire's perspective might be used to support destructive human activity. Freire himself seemed to be aware of this danger. He was quick to add that one can truly transform the world only through profound love for the world and for people:

> Dialogue cannot exist, however, in the absence of a profound love for the world and for people. The naming of the world, which is an act of creation and re-creation, is not possible if it is not infused with love. Love is at the same time the foundation of dialogue and dialogue itself. . . . Love is commitment to others. . . . If I do not love the world—if I do not love life—if I do not love people—I cannot enter into dialogue.[24]

The work of transformation is to release the potential of the beloved, to enable something to become what it can be. Freire viewed both people and the world as unfinished; creation is an ongoing process of becoming:

> Problem-posing education affirms men and women as beings in the process of *becoming*—as unfinished, uncompleted beings in and with a likewise unfinished reality. Indeed, in contrast to other animals who are unfinished, but not historical, peo-

---

22 Ibid., 88–89.
23 Ibid.
24 Ibid., 88–90.

ple know themselves to be unfinished; they are aware of their incompletion.[25]

Freire understands the unfinished nature of human beings in relational terms. He asserts that human "consciousness is in essence a '*way toward*' something apart from itself, outside itself."[26] In other words, it is in the nature of human consciousness to be aware of something apart from itself, and to seek to move toward that something, to move into deeper relationship.[27]

Freire's writings on the human journey parallel prophetic insight. Like the prophets, Freire teaches that the work of liberation is the human vocation. Along the path of liberation, people transform their relationships with other people and with the world. The prophets and Freire also both assert that dialogue moves the liberation journey forward.[28]

Dialogue, by its very nature, is well suited to propel the process of liberation. Every real dialogue is a journey away from the settled and familiar toward the unsettled and unknown. The partners engaged in dialogue don't know where the conversation is going. In the Bible, the journey of discovery commences with creation. At the beginning of each day God calls out, "Let there be," and creation responds by further unfolding its potential. At the end of each day, God exclaims in surprised delight, "*Kee tov!*" (it is vital). The vitality of creation emerges out of this kind of back-and-forth dialogue. When dialogue is curtailed, the journey of transformation is thwarted.

Genuine dialogue is rare in our society. All too often, people wall themselves off from engaging with people who hold different perspectives. Our civic life often feels like a shouting match; our public spaces lack the civility of genuine conversation. Deficient in dialogue, the ongoing process of societal development and transformation grinds to a halt.

Dialogue, or lack thereof, is not an accident. A society, through social norms, can either nurture or discourage dialogue. Imperial societies squelch

---

[25] Ibid., 84.

[26] Ibid., 69 (emphasis added). Freire is fully aware of the human tendency to demonize the other. He attributes that tendency to the internalization of oppressor consciousness and the effects of propaganda, management, and manipulation.

[27] There is also an elemental aspect of human nature that is threatened by the other or the unknown. Freire attributes some of this fear to a false consciousness imposed by the oppressor.

[28] Freire himself placed his pedagogy in the prophetic tradition. "Problem-posing education is revolutionary futurity. Hence, it is prophetic. Hence, it corresponds to the historical nature of humankind. Hence, it affirms women and men as beings who transcend themselves, who move forward and look ahead" (*Pedagogy of the Oppressed*, 84).

dialogue. Our contemporary American society, still in the midst of throwing off imperial cultural patterns, has not yet affirmed the essential value of dialogue, has not yet made dialogue a central civic virtue. In our educational system, for example, dialogue is not highly valued. If we look at high schools through a Freiren lens, in a few classrooms students are dialogically engaged in problem-solving learning, while most classrooms are focused on teaching to the test, a form of "banking education."

A robust democratic society thrives on dialogue. Open and searching conversation is the only way that people with disparate values and needs can work together across differences to arrive at inclusive programs and policies. In the absence of such dialogue, a society is reduced to warring factions of citizens that seek to dominate each other rather than entering into relationships that serve the flourishing of all.

In the face of the political gridlock of American contemporary society, we need consciously to lift up dialogue as an essential civic virtue. Dialogue and the open-minded listening essential to dialogue are not innate skills; they must be cultivated. We can best cultivate dialogue by holding it up as an essential civic virtue and by recognizing, valuing, and cultivating a number of related virtues that support dialogue. These related virtues are curiosity, courage, vulnerability, respect, and empathy.

Dialogue requires *curiosity*. A person only enters into dialogue if she has genuine interest in learning more about another person's point of view. Valuing curiosity as I do, I loved reading the Curious George stories to my daughter when she was small. George was a brown monkey whose curiosity repeatedly led him into trouble. I loved the irony of those stories: the wayward George was the hero of the tale. The man in the yellow hat always patched things up, but the reader knew that George's curiosity was untamable and George would soon be wandering off again. As we laughed with George, my daughter was learning a liberating lesson: indulge your curiosity even in the face of societal disapproval. Some aspects of our educational system and our society seek to discourage curiosity, rather than rewarding it. An appreciation for dialogue would have us do just the opposite: reward curiosity in our schools and in our public life.

Robust dialogue calls for *courage*. Open-minded listening is a courageous act in which one must put at risk one's settled and comfortable worldview. Our society would do well to honor and reinforce the courage of the bold listener.

Genuine dialogue calls upon *vulnerability*. To hear a different perspective, a person must be willing to have his mental structures pierced, her worldview disrupted. Hence, dialogue requires that a person willingly embrace the risk of naked exposure to a verbal challenge. In our contemporary society we have overvalued safety, we have settled for settling in. We must instead remember God's call to Abraham: go forth into unknown territory so that your life might be a blessing.

We must avoid the kind of vulnerability in which we expect people with less power and privilege to be vulnerable in the presence of people with greater power and privilege. The more marginalized person is already vulnerable to the power structures that favor the privileged person. In all cases, a conversational partner must avoid telling another person to be vulnerable. Vulnerability can only be freely undertaken, without coercion.

Dialogue requires *respect*. Respect, from the Latin root *respicere* (to look at anew), means to see a person clearly, unclouded by prior judgment, to be aware of a person's intrinsic worth and unique individuality. In dialogue, one must momentarily drop one's own perspective in order to see and value how another person views an issue. Respect leads one to value and see the other.

Dialogue requires and results in *empathy*. A person needs to listen between and behind the words so as to feel what another person is feeling. Contemporary neuroscience reveals that "mirror neurons" in the brain give humans an innate ability to experience the pain and happiness of others. Human beings are born to be empathic because survival requires that one can feel beyond one's personal situation and identify with what another person is feeling. Beyond mere survival, the human capacity for empathy enriches life. In support of dialogue, a culture needs to cultivate empathy among its members.

Every society nurtures some virtues and not others. The members of a society are often unconscious of the virtue training that they imbibe. In our day of extreme societal challenge, we cannot afford to be unaware of the virtues that are taught in our schools, promulgated in diverse media outlets, and embraced as normative in social and civic behavior. We need to think carefully about the virtues our society needs for the benefit of all. Hebrew and contemporary prophets alike urge us to lift up and cultivate the virtues that support dialogue.

We can witness an example of the liberating power of dialogue in Washington State's Initiative 1631. In Washington, dozens of environmental, labor, and tribal leaders, as well as representatives from organizations working in communities of color, came together to create a ballot measure that would significantly reduce carbon emissions and at the same time meet the employment needs of unions and the equity needs of disadvantaged communities. Through extensive dialogue among people from very diverse groups, an initiative was crafted that would reduce carbon emissions by over 40 percent by 2035. Initiative 1631 would also direct funds raised by the initiative to create high-wage jobs, revitalize impoverished communities, provide job retraining and wage protection for workers in the fossil-fuel industries, and help low-income families pay for energy. The coalition behind the initiative easily gathered the 260,000 signatures needed to put the initiative on the ballot. Thanks to the hard dialogical work of building community through engaging people from diverse backgrounds, the initiative gained broad support.[29] Initiative 1631 is just one example among many of the transformative powers that flow from bringing people together to dialogue about oppressive conditions and to envision a more fruitful future.

---

[29] Sasha Abramsky, "This Washington State Ballot Measure Fights for Both Jobs and Climate Justice," *The Nation*, August 13–20, 2018, 20–23.

CHAPTER 18

Dialogue against Oppression

Freire thought that people seeking liberation must confront and investigate the reality in which they live to see clearly all the limiting conditions in "the concrete, present situation" that thwart their flourishing as human beings.[1] He further asserted that this "act of cognition which unveils reality" could not be pursued in isolation. Only dialogue can produce this liberating learning.[2]

Freiren dialogue is rooted in critical thinking about reality:

> True dialogue cannot exist unless the dialoguers engage in critical thinking . . . thinking which perceives reality as a process, as transformation, rather than as a static entity—thinking which does not separate itself from action. . . . Critical thinking contrasts with naïve thinking, which sees historical time as a weight, a stratification of the acquisitions and experiences of the past.[3]

For Freire, this liberating critical dialogue takes place specifically among people who desire to "name" the world, among people who intend to recognize and uproot oppression:

> Hence, dialogue cannot occur between those who want to name the world and those who do not wish this naming—between those who deny others the right to speak their world and those whose right to speak has been denied them. Those who have

---

[1] Paulo Freire, *Pedagogy of the Oppressed* (New York: Continuum, 2003), 95.

[2] Ibid., 83.

[3] Ibid., 92.

been denied their primordial right to speak their word must first reclaim this right and prevent the continuation of this dehumanizing aggression.[4]

Freire further stipulates that liberating dialogue must be free from the dynamics of domination and dogmatic arguments that sometimes appear in political discussion: "This dialogue cannot be reduced to the act of one person's depositing ideas in another. . . . Nor yet is it a hostile, polemical argument. . . . It is an act of [collaborative] creation; it must not serve as a crafty instrument for the domination of one person by another."[5]

This collaborative and creative dialogue requires humility among its participants. There is no room for elitism in Freiren dialogue:

Dialogue, as the encounter of those addressed to the common task of learning and acting, is broken if the parties (or one of them) lack humility. . . . How can I dialogue if I consider myself a member of the in-group of "pure" men, the owners of truth and knowledge, for whom all non-members are "these people" or "the great unwashed"? How can I dialogue if I start from the premise that naming the world is the task of an elite? . . . At the point of encounter there are neither utter ignoramuses nor perfect sages; there are only people who are attempting, together, to learn more than they now know.[6]

Finally, for Freire, dialogue "requires faith in humankind":

Faith in their power to make and remake, to create and re-create, faith in their vocation to be more fully human . . . Faith in people is an *a priori* requirement for dialogue: the "dialogical man" believes in others. . . . His faith, however, is not naive. The "dialogical man" is critical and knows that although it is within the power of humans to create and transform, in a concrete situation of alienation individuals may be impaired in the use of that power. Far from destroying his faith in the people, however, this possibility strikes him as a challenge to which he must respond. He is convinced that the power to create and transform, even when thwarted in concrete situations, tends to be reborn. And that rebirth can occur—not gratuitously, but in and through the

---

4   Ibid., 88.
5   Ibid.
6   Ibid., 90.

struggle for liberation—in the supersedence of slave labor by emancipated labor which gives zest to life. Without this faith in people, dialogue is a farce which inevitably degenerates into paternalistic manipulation.[7]

The Boggses also thought deeply about the role dialogue plays in the liberation process:

[Liberating insights] come from creative, thoughtful individuals, reflecting upon a specific historical reality which they recognize must be changed. . . . Out of that reflection, and in a close and continuing dialogue . . . they must create a new conception of the new social tasks.[8]

Grace Lee Boggs's thoughts on dialogue first emerged out of her interactions with people in the black community in Chicago in the early 1940s.[9] Immersed in rich conversations about the effects of racial oppression and in large-scale grassroots organizing to demand racial desegregation, Boggs learned the value of including many voices in the analysis of a problem and in the planning of an action—in this case the black community's March on Washington. She was critical of leaders who limited internal debate. Later, in New York, Boggs participated in the struggles within the Socialist Workers' Party over the party's relationship with the Soviet Union. Through these struggles Boggs saw that individuals naturally perceived the world through the lens of their own particular interests. Only a dialogue that involved diverse groups of people and included a broad spectrum of ideas could produce an analysis and program that addressed the interests of the entire society. Boggs concluded that all serious contributions to "a new civilization" needed to be "collective." In New York and later in Detroit, Boggs organized intergenerational conversations to reflect on a given historical situation, recognized what must be changed, and organized action to produce that change. Like Freire, Boggs thought that liberating dialogue needed to be inclusive of the spectrum of people who want to act to change a given condition.[10]

---

[7] Ibid., 90–91.
[8] Boggs, *Evolution and Revolution* (New York: Monthly Review Press, 2008), 83.
[9] Boggs herself was of Chinese descent. Her husband, James, was an African American man.
[10] Stephen Ward, *In Love and Struggle: The Revolutionary Lives of James and Grace Lee Boggs* (Chapel Hill: University of North Carolina Press, 2016), chap. 4.

People with privilege have a moral responsibility to join in the liberation dialogue and struggle. As the African American liberation theologian James Cone articulated in prophetic terms, the God of the Bible is a liberating God, seeking the freedom and flourishing of all people. The God we meet in the Scriptures calls all people to the moral responsibility to seek justice. Justice requires active participation in the liberation struggle. People who benefit from privilege and don't actively seek to dismantle oppressive societal structures are not merely bystanders to oppression; they are giving their life energies to support oppressive structures.

In addition to moral responsibility, people with privilege have reason to engage in liberating dialogue and struggle for the sake of their own humanization. The privilege that advantages some people also harms them by tightly tying their self-worth and security to unending material accumulation. Privilege also diminishes people's lives by isolating them and depriving them of meaningful interactions with the vast majority of humanity.

The extreme racial and class divides in our society present formidable barriers to honest dialogue among people from different socioeconomic and racial groups. Imperial systems intentionally separate and insulate privileged elites from those people who lack privilege. Hence, most American neighborhoods, schools, and social clubs are de facto segregated according to class. In addition to barriers created by imposed societal divisions, dialogue across class and racial lines is inherently difficult. People are generally more comfortable being in conversation with people who appear to be most like them. Inclusive conversations need to be carefully planned and skillfully facilitated to allow people to find common ground and build human bonds.

Another obstacle to dialogue across lines of difference is the reality that these conversations can bring forward the anger that oppressed people feel about their situation and the guilt that privileged people feel in response to that anger. In the absence of skillful facilitation, these uncomfortable feelings of anger and guilt are real obstacles to meaningful encounter across socioeconomic lines.

In spite of all the obstacles, these uncomfortable and unsettling aspects of inclusive conversations about social change are exactly why dialogue across socioeconomic, racial, and ethnic differences is so important. In the absence of these dialogues, advantaged people in our society rarely confront the harmful effects of privileging the few. People with privilege can avoid making the connection between the security and comfort of their lives and the oppression experienced by others.

James Cone observed that even socially conscious people with privilege rarely enter significant conversation with less privileged people and therefore lack real understanding of the conditions under which less privileged people live.[11] He asserted that only extended dialogue enables a person who is not African American to begin to understand the extent of the suffering caused by racism. Cone later in his career applied this same analysis to other oppressed communities.

Courtney Martin, a white journalist who has written extensively about race, focuses on the power of inclusive dialogue in the liberation struggle. She understands that "the beloved community"[12] can only emerge when people with privilege leave their comfort zone and form relationships across class and racial divides. Martin also appreciates the significant challenge that these relationships pose. She observes that emotional fragility keeps people with privilege from engaging in dialogue with people who experience oppression. She calls upon white people like herself to exercise courageous imperfection:

If white people want to belong to the beloved community . . . then we have to show up as bold and genuine and imperfect. We have to be weary of our fragility. We have to be intolerant of our own forgetfulness. If it feels difficult, and it does to me, you're probably on the right track. Dismantling centuries of dehumanizing institutions and practices—both in the world and within ourselves—can't be a simple process. The good news is that transforming your fragility into courageous imperfection is the beginning of a lot more joy. It's the beginning of a lot more connection. It's the beginning of the end of racism.[13]

In my experience as a person with many privileges, I have discovered how important it is for people with privilege to begin the dialogue across difference by listening—for a long time. If we listen, we will hear voices like Claudia Rankine, an African American poet, essayist, and playwright, who wrote an article titled "The Condition of Black Life Is Mourning":

---

[11]   James Cone, *The Cross and the Lynching Tree* (Maryknoll, NY: Orbis Books, 2013), Kindle loc 1530.

[12]   "Beloved community" was a term often used by Martin Luther King Jr. for the gathering of people and ultimately a society shaped by love for one's fellow human being.

[13]   Courtney E. Martin, "Transforming White Fragility into Courageous Imperfection," On Being blog, June 26, 2015.

Though the white liberal imagination likes to feel temporarily bad about black suffering, there really is no mode of empathy that can replicate the daily strain of knowing that as a black person you can be killed for simply being black: no hands in your pockets, no playing music, no sudden movements, no driving your car, no walking at night, no walking in the day, no turning onto this street, no entering this building, no standing your ground, no standing here, no standing there, no talking back, no playing with toy guns, no living while black.[14]

Listening to people who have suffered oppression inevitably leads to mourning—mourning the many lives lost, scarred, traumatized, and continually thwarted. Uprooting oppression in our society requires a process of truth and reconciliation that begins with acknowledging the enormity of the loss suffered by oppressed people, an acknowledgment that starts with listening and mourning.

Acknowledgment must be followed by sustained action. If dialogue is not followed by action, people who experience oppression are wasting their time talking with people with privilege. The action needs to be in response to the limiting conditions experienced by people experiencing oppression, and the action needs to be led by them. The liberation journey calls people with privilege to stand with oppressed people to dismantle systems of oppression and provide reparations for some of what has been lost. As Freire taught, dialogue must include reflection and action or it is mere verbalism.

Freire called people into dialogue in order to investigate and transform the conditions that limit human flourishing. A full exploration of these limiting conditions requires people with privilege to be in conversation with each other about the many unearned benefits of their privilege. Eula Biss, award-winning white author of *Notes from No Man's Land*, an exploration of race and identity in America, uses the term "forgotten debt" to illuminate how people can become unaware of the way in which society has been constructed to benefit them at the expense of others. She explains "forgotten debt" with the example of a home purchase:

Once you've been living in a house for a while, you tend to begin to believe that it's yours, even though you don't own it yet. When those of us who are convinced of our own whiteness deny our debt, this may be an inevitable result of having lived for so long

---

[14]   Claudia Rankine, "The Condition of Black Life Is Mourning," *New York Times*, June 22, 2015.

in a house bought on credit but never paid off. We ourselves have never owned slaves, we insist, and we never say the n-word. "It is as though we have run up a credit-card bill," [Ta-Nehisi] Coates writes of Americans, "and, having pledged to charge no more, remain befuddled that the balance does not disappear." The illusion of ownership . . . depends on forgetting the redlining, block busting, racial covenants, contract buying, loan discrimination, housing projects, mass incarceration, predatory lending and deed thefts that have prevented so many black Americans from building wealth the way so many white Americans have, through homeownership.[15]

People generally avoid thinking about or discussing forgotten debt or unearned privilege. These conversations are sensitive and need to be engaged in small group gatherings among people who know, respect, and trust each other. But people with privilege should not let the sensitivity of these conversations deter them from having the conversations. People with privilege, like myself, cannot participate in the liberation journey, meaning they cannot participate in the essential human vocation to grow in mutual relationship, if they isolate themselves from people who are less privileged and remain in denial of the societal structures that benefit the few at the expense of the many. The prophetic tradition calls upon people with privilege to acknowledge forgotten debt and stand alongside disadvantaged people in the struggle to bring down oppressive structures and to promote human flourishing.

The historian Walter Scheidel has studied extensively the historical circumstances that have brought an end to oppressive regimes and produced social "leveling." He found that during the last ten thousand years of human history only violent events have led to significant redistribution of wealth. In his study, Scheidel identified four types of destruction—massive warfare, revolution, state failure, and lethal pandemics—that brought periods of significant inequality to an end.[16]

The Hebrew prophets saw that imperial and entrenched power will likely end in violence. Amos envisioned God holding a plumb line to a wall, proclaiming that an unjust society is like a severely leaning wall; both will inevitably fall. However, the prophets also imagined an alternative to the violent end of empire. They envisioned the possibility of a peaceful transformation to a society whose benefits extend to the most vulnerable—to the widow, the orphan, and the stranger.

---

[15] Eula Biss, "White Debt," *New York Times Magazine*, December 2, 2015.

[16] Walter Scheidel, *The Great Leveler* (Princeton, NJ: Princeton University Press, 2017), 6, 392–94.

In our day, we face the challenge and the opportunity to work for that nonviolent transition to a society that thrives because all the members of the society can flourish. Such a peaceful transformation can only take place if people with privilege stand alongside people lacking privilege to name the oppressive aspects of the current order and work together to bring about a social order in which all can flourish.

Freire, Boggs, and Cone argue that inclusive dialogue is the only way that diverse voices can be brought together to articulate the aspects of reality that thwart human flourishing and strategize a liberating way forward. Inclusive critical dialogue is the ambitious, humble, and faithful way forward to an alternative future.

CHAPTER 19

The World Is Built with Love (Ps 89:3)

> *Simon the Just was one of the last survivors of the Great Assembly. He used to say: the world stands on three things: On Torah, on Divine Service and upon Love*
>
> —*Talmud Bavli Tractate Avot 1:2*

Dialogue—reflection and action—is the way forward on the liberation journey. Loving concern for people and for the world is the ground on which dialogue can take place. Greater love—deeper mutual relationship—is the direction of the liberation journey. Love, then, is both the ground and the destination of the journey.

The movement away from oppressive structures and toward a more loving society has been slower than we might wish, in part, because we have not articulated clearly enough the psychic cost of oppression, even to the privileged, and the psychic cost of loving.

Erich Fromm's discussion of faith provides insight into the psychic costs of oppression and loving. Fromm distinguishes between two kinds of faith, "faith in power" and "faith in life." Faith in power values control, the ability to dominate. People who practice this faith seek to vanquish all vulnerability and uncertainty through exercising strict control in their lives. Fromm calls faith in power "irrational" because it is an "unstable achievement," giving a person only a temporary sense of control.[1]

Faith in power is at the root of every oppressive regime. Elites in these regimes seek meaning and security through domination, through controlling people and the natural world. The psychic cost of faith in power to

---

[1]   Erich Fromm, *The Art of Loving* (New York: Open Road Press, 2013), 98.

the oppressed is painfully obvious to those who suffer oppression and to those who listen to their voices. The psychic cost of oppression to people with privilege is isolation and alienation. The attempt to control people and nature through overwhelming power inevitably cuts a person off from meaningful connection and fulfilling mutual relationship.

Despite its irrationality, many people feel an attraction to faith in power. Pursuing security and happiness, human beings commonly seek to be in control, to maximize pleasure and avoid pain.

The alternative, faith in life, leads a person to seek vital, mutual relationship with people and the world. Faith in life connects a person to the prophetic stream, the energetic flow that activates human creativity and growth. This faith enables a person to relate to others in love. However, this faith also comes with a cost. Practicing faith in life requires significant surrender. One must surrender the comforting illusion of control and relinquish the sense of certainty and invulnerability that people crave. Faith in life leads to an adventurous and creative life journey in which little is certain and much is beyond one's control. Fromm writes, "To have faith [in life] requires *courage,* the ability to take a risk, the readiness even to accept pain and disappointment."[2] This risky faith in life animates the liberation journey.

Individuals must make a choice. A person must choose, moment to moment, between two alternatives, either to seek safety through power and control or to embrace vulnerability and the liberation journey. When we choose faith in life, accepting vulnerability and uncertainty, the liberation journey opens before us.

The liberation journey toward deeper mutual relationship leads to an ever-widening circle of loving concern. Fromm places the expanding circle of love at the center of thinking about loving:

> If I love, I am in a constant state of active concern with the loved person, but not only with him or her. . . . To love means to have a loving attitude toward everybody, if to love is a character trait, it must necessarily exist in one's relationship not only with one's family and friends, but toward those with whom one is in contact through one's work, business, profession. There is no "division of labor" between love for one's own and love for strangers. On the contrary, the condition for the existence of the former is the existence of the latter.[3]

---

[2]   Ibid.
[3]   Ibid., 100–102.

Martin Luther King Jr. had a similar understanding of love. He proclaimed that love—concern for the welfare of another human being—naturally extends to every person in our society, especially to people who are poor, to people who are incarcerated, and to people who have immigrated to our country.

Loving a stranger feels different from the kind of love to which we are accustomed. The love for a stranger does not arise from familiarity or personal attraction. King used the Greek word *agape* to define the unsentimental love that he offered all people:

> In speaking of love at this point, we are not referring to some sentimental emotion. . . . "Love" in this connection means understanding, redeeming good will. . . . We speak of love which is expressed in the Greek word agape. Agape means nothing sentimental or basically affectionate; it means understanding, redeeming good will for all men, an overflowing love which seeks nothing in return. It is the love of God working in the lives of men.[4]

In their exploration of love, King and Fromm arrive at the same conclusion. Love cannot be restricted to intimate relations with family and friends. Love must flow into one's community and beyond. Both King and Fromm thought that love is the power that can transform society from a system of oppressive institutions to a community of caring relations.

The practice of loving might seem too soft to be effective in radically changing a society. King thought otherwise. In his speeches and writings King frequently articulated that the liberation journey required a "genuine revolution of values."[5] For King, the core discipline of this revolution was to practice love. Early in his ministry, King proclaimed,

> The only way to ultimately change humanity and make for the society that we all long for is to keep love at the center of our lives. . . . Along the way of life, someone must have sense enough and morality enough to cut off the chain of hate. This can be done only by projecting the ethics of love to the center of our lives.[6]

---

[4] Ibid., 8.

[5] Martin Luther King Jr., *A Testament of Hope: The Essential Writings and Speeches of Martin Luther King Jr.*, ed. James Washington (New York: Harper Collins, 1991), 242.

[6] Ibid., 8, 13.

Near the end of his life, King said,

And I say to you, I have also decided to stick to love. For I know
that love is ultimately the only answer to mankind's problems.
I'm not talking about emotional bosh when I talk about love; I'm
talking about strong, demanding love. . . . I have decided to love.
If you are seeking the highest good, I think that you can find it
through love.[7]

For King, agape has the power to transform and liberate because it is
rooted in God's love. Agape is "the love of God working in the lives of
men."[8] Like the prophets, King saw God's love flowing within historical
reality, moving creation toward deeper mutual relationship: "The Holy
Spirit is the continuing community creating reality that moves through
history. He who works against community is working against the whole
of creation."[9] In the prophetic tradition, King saw the power of God's
love at work in human society, empowering people to create a beloved
community that includes all people, especially those most in need. For
King, divine love working through human beings compels a person to
welcome the stranger, to understand the foreigner, to engender the welfare of the other. This powerful love is the force that draws people into
liberating dialogue.

King's claim that the ethics of active love is the only practice powerful enough to transform society is not mere piety. Research studies have
shown that King's strategy—the power of love in the form of nonviolent
resistance—is far more effective than violent resistance for achieving a
desired social change.[10] There is nothing soft or powerless about love.

bell hooks, an African American womanist[11] writer, was an avid student of Martin Luther King Jr. She expanded on King's thinking about
the application of the "love ethic" in public affairs. In her book *All about
Love*, hooks argues against separating personal and public life in our
thinking about loving. She observes that the practice of domination in
public life inevitably perverts loving in the home:

---

[7]   Ibid., 250.

[8]   Ibid., 8.

[9]   Ibid., 20.

[10]   Moises Velasquez-Manoff, "How to Make Fun of Nazis," *New York
Times*, August 17, 2017.

[11]   "Womanist" is a term coined by Alice Walker to refer to a black feminist
or feminist of color. See her essay, "In Search of Our Mothers' Gardens," in *In
Search of Our Mothers' Gardens* (New York: Open Road Press, 2011).

A commonly accepted assumption in patriarchal culture is that love can be present in a situation where one group or individual dominates another. Many people believe men can dominate women and children yet still be loving. [However] psychoanalyst Carl Jung insightfully emphasized the truism that "where the will to power is paramount love will be lacking.[12]

hooks's insight into the way that domination in public life bleeds into the home is worth pondering. When people, especially men, are accustomed to giving commands and to resolving differences in the workplace and in public life through domination rather than through respectful dialogue, they are likely to apply the same ethic to home life. Similarly, domination in public interactions breeds a pattern of alienation in relationships, a subtle but chilling barrier in the human heart that affects one's life at home and at work.

Like Fromm and King, hooks asserts that love, to be love, must expand beyond the home into the public arenas. hooks insists that oppression cannot be ended until loving practice becomes a civic norm.

The "politicization of love" is the primary way we end domination and oppression. . . . Domination cannot exist in any social situation where a love ethic prevails. . . . Concern for the collective good of our nation, city, or neighbor rooted in the values of love makes us all seek to nurture and protect that good. If all public policy was created in the spirit of love, we would not have to worry about unemployment, homelessness, schools failing to teach children, or addiction. Were a love ethic informing all public policy in cities and towns, individuals could come together and map out programs that would affect the good of everyone.[13]

The politicization of love is the pathway of the liberation journey. As love begins to shape the priorities and policies of civic life, a society can evolve, becoming increasingly organized by the power of relationship. As a consequence, the need for the power of force would progressively recede. Along this liberation path, the wisdom of relationship rather than the power of select elites informs societal structures.

Once we have embraced loving as the central practice of the liberation journey, it is not difficult to imagine what the "politicization of love" would look like in our society. Our schools would move toward

---

[12]   bell hooks, *All about Love* (New York: Harper Perennial, 2001), 40.
[13]   Ibid., 76, 98.

the liberation pedagogy of Paulo Freire. Teacher monologues would cease, and dialogical investigation would flourish. Teachers would model and teach deep listening skills. Classes would involve the students in critical thinking and problem solving, in creating knowledge rather than passively receiving it.

Businesses would become employee-owned cooperatives, allowing the workers to take responsibility for their work and for each other. The workweek and work year would be shortened to allow time for an abundance of family time and community connections.

Quality health care and decent housing would be guaranteed for all. Quality education, at all stages of life, would be affordable and available to all who seek it.

Our prison population would be limited to those who are truly a danger to our society, and the mission of the penal system would be devoted to rehabilitation instead of punishment.

Extraordinary efforts would be made to protect and restore the environment for present and future generations.

Immigrants would be treated with respect. Diversity of all kinds would be honored and treasured throughout society.

A vibrant communal life would offer people a vast array of learning, creative, and civic opportunities. Every member of society would feel woven into a rich fabric of relations.

One can easily envision the fruits of a society that places relationship and loving at the center of its public and private life. At the same time, we are challenged to believe that the imagined loving society can be realized. The support offered in this book is the explication of the twin prophetic assertions: creation is on a liberating journey with God, and this learning journey moves ever toward mutual relationship. Insight into this venerable journey, into the mighty flow of the prophetic stream, serves social change agents in two ways. It informs us that liberating transformation is more than possible; it is the way of creation. And these prophetic insights challenge us to devote ourselves to participate in this journey. As we grasp that a journey in love and toward love is the deepest ground of our lives and of creation itself, we will feel more empowered to partake in that journey.

CHAPTER 20

Enacting a Love Ethic

All the prophets, ancient and modern, understand that societal transformation requires a change in culture. Imperial premises, values, and norms must be uprooted and replaced with relational priorities and practices. According to Fromm, King, and hooks, people can create a more relational society by placing a love ethic at the center of civic life.

At present, capitalist interests shape American civic life and culture. A megabillion-dollar advertising industry bombards us with messages designed to define our priorities, desires, and expectations. Every day, our commercially driven culture addresses people as consumers rather than citizens. The psychologist Mary Pipher observed that social values that were once formed in the rich relational context of family and community are now decisively influenced by electronic mass media:

> Children learn these things from ads: that they are the most important person in the universe, that impulses should not be denied, that pain should not be tolerated and that the cure for any kind of pain is a product. They learn a weird mix of dissatisfaction and entitlement. With the messages of ads, we are socializing children to be self-centered, impulsive and addicted.[1]

As a society, we have not acted to resist the enormous power of commercial culture to shape our personal and civic values. We have accepted the multiple ways the marketplace sets public priorities. There have been some notable exceptions of groups, largely from marginalized communities, that have attempted to raise up relational values, such as human rights, as public priorities. The civil rights movement,

---

[1] Mary Pipher, *The Shelter of Each Other: Rebuilding Our Families* (New York: Ballantine Books, 1996), 15.

the feminist and gay rights movements, and more recently, the resistance at Standing Rock and the Black Lives Matter movement have mounted challenges to the ethics of the market. Artists of all kinds have also used their creative media to project their values and priorities onto the public square.

Churches and synagogues could serve as incubators for an alternative culture. Unfortunately, too many religious institutions have been either totally absorbed into the values of contemporary mass culture or they have limited their critique to issues such as the environment or abortion and have failed to significantly challenge the commodifying ethic of a market-driven commercialized culture.

This civic passivity is largely the consequence of a consumer culture that discourages widespread creativity and civic involvement. An inactive public enables the dominance of the marketplace and established elites. Unfortunately, most citizens have learned to view themselves as consumers of culture rather than cocreators with other citizens of civic culture.

A hands-off approach to the making of culture and policy will not bring a fundamental change in societal values and priorities. Most elites have too much to gain from the status quo. The needed changes will arise only from ordinary citizens, energized by a vision for an alternative society, rising up to create a loving culture and to shape policies congruent with that culture.

In recent years, political institutions in the United States have become increasingly gridlocked, failing to address pressing problems in the areas of a livable wage, comprehensive health insurance, mass incarceration, environmental degradation, quality education, racial discrimination, and more. Hard-won advances in areas such as civil rights, labor conditions, protection of public lands, environmental protection, and financial regulation have been reversed. In the face of this compounding failure of political institutions, many citizens who had heretofore not participated actively in the civic life of their communities now realize that they cannot leave the work of the change they seek in the hands of others. These citizens have learned that only their active involvement in civic, cultural, and political organizations will transform our society. They now understand that the responsibility of each citizen goes beyond voting to include an ongoing involvement in civic life. As a result, thousands of citizens have become involved in political life for the first time, running for public office, joining action groups, and participating in initiatives of all kinds.

This renewed passion for civic activity is an important and hopeful development. A robust relational culture will develop when large numbers of people strengthen the civic fabric of their communities by working alongside their fellow citizens in committees and projects as well as resistance initiatives. The politicization of love requires the active involvement of many ordinary citizens.

This effort to transform society by enacting a love ethic must include sustained attention to a widespread malady that rarely receives the attention it deserves—the plague of loneliness in our society. One recent study revealed that over 42 million Americans over age forty-five reported suffering from chronic loneliness.[2] Another study revealed that the experience of loneliness is more common in people ages eighteen to twenty-four than among the elderly.[3] Several studies reveal that chronic loneliness is associated with greater risk of cardiovascular disease, dementia, depression, and anxiety.[4] This widespread loneliness is a consequence of a commercially driven culture that places more value on production and consumption than on relationship.

Our society has not addressed loneliness as the significant social problem that it is. Instead, contemporary life offers countless ways to temporarily avoid loneliness. Psychologist Anne Wilson Schaef observes widespread addictive behaviors in our society as people self-medicate, in part, to alleviate the pain of isolation. She describes both ingestive addictions (alcohol, food, and drugs) and process addictions (work, shopping, gambling, and sex). For Schaef, contemporary society itself has become an addict; behaviors that numb awareness or distract attention are becoming more common than human connection.[5]

These addictive behaviors offer only temporary relief from the pain of loneliness. What can ultimately alleviate this pain is societal attention to loneliness as a significant problem. Great Britain has begun to address loneliness as a serious public health issue. The Loneliness Project, headed up by a "minister of loneliness," will coordinate the efforts of governmental agencies and nonprofit organizations to develop policies and programs that address the problem.[6]

A national approach to alleviate loneliness addresses the problem on many levels, including the architecture of our cities and neighborhoods,

---

[2]   Alastair Jamieson, "Britain Appoints 'Minister for Loneliness' to Tackle Social Isolation," January 17, 2018, www.nbcnews.com.

[3]   Jane Brody, "To Counter Loneliness, Find Ways to Connect," *New York Times*, June 25, 2018.

[4]   Ceylan Yeginsu, "U.K. Appoints a Minister for Loneliness," *New York Times*, January 17, 2018.

[5]   Anne Wilson Schaef, *When Society Becomes an Addict* (San Francisco: HarperOne, 1988).

[6]   Yeginsu, "U.K. Appoints a Minister for Loneliness"; see also www.the-lonelinessproject.org.

the availability of social groups and meeting places, the opportunity to learn relationship skills, and the media messaging about relationships.

American society was once rich in groups where people could find the warmth of human connection. Almost every community had sewing circles, multiple civic organizations, and sports clubs. Sociologist Robert Putnam has documented the severe decline of these associations in his book *Bowling Alone*.

There are currently some spaces where people can make friends and find community. Twelve-step groups are one such place. Most communities have civic clubs, such as Rotary, Elks, Kiwanis, and Lions Clubs, but membership has been waning in recent years. Religious communities could be an ideal place for people to form meaningful relationship. Some faith communities are intentional about welcoming people, making sure that no one walks into a gathering without being greeted and embraced. To rebuild a relational culture, we need to reinvigorate the small circles where people can gather together.

Our society also has a great need for safe places where people can speak honestly about their lives, their struggles and joys, and particularly their deep yearnings. Ideally, every religious community would provide such safe spaces. Parker Palmer's book *A Hidden Wholeness: The Journey toward an Undivided Life*, delineates the need for such groups and provides guidelines for how to facilitate them.[7]

In Beit Midrash we have aspired to be such a haven for the human soul. Almost every week our study of Scriptures leads us to explore the depths of our lives by the light of our learning. This opportunity for heartfelt connection and meaningful conversation is what makes Beit Midrash more than a class. Heartfelt sharing turns Beit Midrash into a spiritual community.

Over the years in Beit Midrash I have seen that when people in community explore truths about their experience, including the grief of their loneliness and their profound yearning for connection, they become aware of the vital role that relationship plays in their life. They recognize more fully what they have always sensed to be true—that they are woven into a rich fabric of relationship.

A society that values relationship would also provide support for learning relational skills. Many school districts in our country have made social-emotional learning (SEL) a primary goal of their educational program. Second Step, one widely used SEL curriculum approach, teaches emotional regulation and other skills that support both the students'

---

[7]   Parker J. Palmer, *A Hidden Wholeness: The Journey toward an Undivided Life* (San Francisco: Jossey Bass, 2004).

relational well-being and their ability to learn.[8] Adults can benefit from social-emotional learning as much as children. On the road to a more loving society, we need to provide many opportunities for relational learning.

As people develop relationship skills and find more opportunities for meaningful relationships, their awareness of the importance of relationships in their lives will grow. As a result, they will take steps to reform the commercially driven nature of our society.

Addressing the loneliness in our society is a part of the cultural change we need. A love ethic also needs to be applied to every other aspect of our society that limits the flourishing of all people. How do ordinary citizens like you and me radically transform our society? How do we work to enact a love ethic? For most of us, the transformation is made through an accumulation of small acts, just as a river's mighty flow is fed by the gathering of many small tributaries.

The three aspects of prophetic experience provide a pathway for cultural change—guidelines for action toward a more relational and loving society. The first of those prophetic aspects is being imbued with God's love. The prophets' experience of God's loving concern for the world gave them the resources both to call out the injustice of their day and to transcend the limitations of the current society to envision an alternative future. In our effort to enact a loving society, we can begin by nurturing loving in our lives. For some people, feeling loved by God is the foundation of loving in their lives. For others, loving begins with reciprocal love among family and friends. All of us can nurture the love that already flows in our lives and then look for opportunities to widen the circle of loving. As Fromm and King observed, love, by its very nature, desires to expand into every relationship in our lives. A society rooted in loving and a passion for justice will see more clearly the opportunities to enact a love ethic than an activism rooted in a passion for justice alone.

The second prophetic aspect is to call out injustice, to *name* the oppression we witness. Naming involves a detailed description of how people and other living beings suffer, and a careful analysis of the systemic causes of that suffering. In our day, we need to name mass incarceration, predatory lending, stagnant wages, housing discrimination, a broken health care system, inadequate drug rehabilitation programs, loneliness, an oppressive immigration system, an underfunded public education system, a discriminatory legal system, and other systemic causes of suffering. Naming the oppression brings it into clear focus and heightens public awareness and understanding of it.

---

[8] See www.secondstep.org.

Proclaiming and analyzing oppression naturally flows into the two other parts of naming: (1) investigating and articulating the primary assumptions, values, and priorities that support that oppressive practice; and (2) exploring and articulating the alternative values of a more loving and relational practice or policy. These investigations can lead people or a community to examine their personal or communal life to determine what values and priorities they are living out.

On a personal level, the exploration of values begins with an inquiry into how we are treating people and indeed all life. Do we commonly practice loving, giving caring attention to others? I am personally challenged by this practice. I don't naturally treat everyone I meet during the day with caring attention. I need to remind myself to give my full attention to the cashier at the market or a casual acquaintance encountered on the street.

I am a white male who assumes, too often, that the world is set to benefit me. I can become annoyed when I wait more than ten minutes for a lunch date or when someone does not return repeated phone calls. When I take a step back and notice my annoyance, I receive valuable insight. I see the psychic world of privilege I inhabit, and how I cover over old feelings of rejection and unworthiness with expectations that my felt needs will be met in a timely way. As I become aware of these expectations, I notice the times that they lead me to value my own comfort at the expense of my relations with other people. When I recognize these assumptions and values, I lay the groundwork for the opportunity to change my behavior and live out values that are truer to the person I want to be.

Communal organizations, including civic groups, religious congregations, political associations, arts initiatives, and governmental agencies, can undertake a similar investigation of the assumptions and values that direct their activities. Such a clear-eyed examination clarifies whether the priorities that shape an organization's agenda are in alignment with the intention to enact a love ethic.

This focused exploration of assumptions and values leads to the third aspect of prophetic experience: envisioning an alternative future. The Hebrew prophets were visionaries; they were not political strategists. Their analysis did not include a roadmap to a more just future. Instead, they offered people a vision of an alternative society combined with the clear conviction that a more equitable and just polity was within the people's reach.

After we name the negative consequences of systemic oppression, we must take the next step forward and begin to envision an alternative future. Like the prophets, our vision does not need to imagine the full pathway to a more equitable, just, and loving society. In envisioning, we articulate the direction toward an alternative future and the first step in that direction. The Quivira Coalition in New Mexico provides a good example. The founders of the Quivira Coalition, a rancher and two conservationists, were dismayed by the unceasing legal and ideological battles over the disposition of western lands. In the beginning, these founders did not know exactly what policies and practices would bring an end to the conflict. But they did have a vision; they imagined farmers, ranchers, conservationists, and scientists sitting together in dialogue with the intention of naming the core issues of the grazing conflict between ranchers and environmentalists and then envisioning a way forward that met the needs of both groups. From this dialogue among diverse stakeholders, policies and practices emerged that served the needs of all involved. The Quivira Coalition has been successful, in part, because its approach was rooted in the three aspects of prophetic work. First, they grounded the dialogue among conflicting groups in a common love: a deep love for western lands. Second, they clearly named the oppressive problem: the unceasing conflict between ranchers and environmentalists that was hurting both groups. They also identified the core issues, the values that were at the heart of the problem. Finally, they envisioned an alternative way forward and took action in that direction.

The visionary founders of the Quivira Coalition are not alone. Many people are acting prophetically now and can inspire our prophetic action.

Rahwa Ghirmatzion came to this country as a child refugee from Sudan via war-torn Eritrea. This background fuels her passion for helping disadvantaged people settle into a home. But as the executive director of People United for Sustainable Housing (PUSH) in Buffalo, New York, Ghirmatzion's vision goes far beyond building homes. Understanding that vibrant communities nurture human flourishing, Ghirmatzion focuses on developing community capacity and local leadership as the most effective way to build both affordable green housing and networks of human connection. Through an extensive block-by-block campaign and monthly community meetings, PUSH has energized neighborhood residents to participate in direct-action and legislative campaigns that have brought new resources to Buffalo's West Side. As a result, PUSH has reclaimed eighteen neglected houses and redeveloped them for low-income occupants. At the same time, PUSH has placed over twenty people in full-time jobs that contribute to preserving or restoring the environment. PUSH's success testifies to the power of relationship-based change and to the power of love practiced in the public arena.[9]

---

[9] See www.pushbuffalo.org and Jane Kwiatkowski Radlich, "PUSH Buffalo Names New Executive Director," *Buffalo News*, May 30, 2018.

Esteban Kelly is the executive director of the Federation of Worker Cooperatives, a national organization that supports worker-owned and cooperatively managed businesses. Kelly is also the cofounder of the Anti-Oppression Resource and Training Alliance, where he works to identify and combat the roots of oppression, and cofounder of the Philadelphia Area Cooperative Alliance, an organization that brings together cooperative enterprises in the Philadelphia area to learn from each other and grow together. With these three initiatives, Kelly has been deeply involved in naming and uprooting worker oppression and in creating relationally based alternatives. Worker co-ops in the Philadelphia alliance include construction, solar installation, taxi service, childcare, bookkeeping, and more. The alliance also includes school, housing, food, and credit co-ops. Each of these cooperative businesses serves to democratize power in the workplace, build community, and distribute benefits more equitably.[10]

Rev. Dr. William J. Barber II is one of the leaders of the Poor People's Campaign: A National Call for Moral Revival. This work is rooted in Barber's understanding that racism is an intended cultural artifice that has been consciously injected into American society to create division between disadvantaged white people and people of color in order to perpetuate the political control of white elites. Barber's Poor People's Campaign is designed to overcome the artificial division between poor white people and poor people of color. Barber's "fusion politics" brings people from different backgrounds into dialogue to learn about each other's needs and envision how a fusion of poor people from different backgrounds and their allies can overcome a system that has impoverished people of all races. At its heart, Barber's Poor People's initiative is a relationship campaign. He continually articulates that the needed change must emerge from grassroots community building, people coming together in relationship as trusted allies to pursue a common goal.[11]

Christian Picciolini is a former neo-Nazi skinhead leader who left the white supremacist movement and later cofounded Life After Hate, an organization that helps "radicalized individuals disengage from extremist movements."[12] Picciolini understands that people attracted to the white supremacy movement lack the resiliency to reject the movement, in part, because they have imbibed our culture's "faith in power," the belief that a sense of worth, purpose, and belonging can be gained through domination. Picciolini's analysis leads him to conclude that shaming people who have fallen into white supremacy or preaching to them reinforces

---

10 See https://usworker.coop/about/board-staff/.
11 See https://www.poorpeoplescampaign.org/.
12 See https://www.lifeafterhate.org/.

the power dynamic that made them vulnerable in the first place. Instead, Picciolini invests in people. He nurtures people's capacity to fulfill the human need for dignity, purpose, and belonging in healthy ways. Life After Hate offers counseling, job training, and other services that help people find meaningful engagement in life. Life After Hate teaches compassion by extending compassion. Rather than telling their clients that they should not hate an African American, a Muslim, or a Jew, the organization brings their clients into relationship with people from groups that they have hated, trusting dialogue between people to break down the barriers of prejudice.

All these initiatives are prophetic because they grow out of love; they include a clear-eyed naming and analysis of the roots of oppression, and they envision and enact an alternative future by offering people a relational way forward. Each of these efforts enacts love in the public sphere.

While you and I might not think of ourselves as prophets, we have within our grasp the ability to act prophetically: to face the causes of suffering boldly and to work with a spirit of love to seek a more fruitful future. We may already find ourselves in communal places where we can enact these virtues. We may belong to clubs and associations. We may live in families and work in groups. Perhaps we are members of religious congregations and cultural organizations. Each of these groups can be a place for honest conversation about the need to replace market values with the ethics of love. Each of these gathering places can be a rich opportunity to investigate what the practice of agape would look like in any given situation.

Similarly, many of us belong to political groups, labor groups, or business associations, or we participate in social action initiatives. We live in school districts, congressional assembly districts, and political wards. We can transform the workings of each of these entities by asking what values the people want to place at the center of their collective effort, and by periodically evaluating the group's performance in terms of those values.

Most of us carry our own prophetic visions. We see something broken or lacking in our community, and we have visions or initial intimations for how to address the need more effectively. We can become involved, bringing the ethics of love to bear into our communal life. This work becomes prophetic when we are aware that we are working to put in place not only a particular policy or practice but also the cultural values on which that policy rests. The prophet addresses both the immediate situation and the ethic that supports it.

When people bring their prophetic activism into the public sphere, conflict between different interest groups is inevitable. That conflict can be either creative or destructive. Conflict becomes creative when disparate groups work *with* each other in the spirit of dialogue rather than trying to impose their way on others.

Cultural transformation requires dialogical creativity among diverse civic groups. Fundamental societal change will emerge from people working on different issues—such as immigration, racism, workers' rights, and the environment—coming together in dialogue to bring forth a broad vision for social change. Rev. William J. Barber II's fusion politics in North Carolina has demonstrated the power of diverse groups working together dialogically.[13]

As we seek a creative approach to civic conflicts, the virtues of dialogue—curiosity, courage, vulnerability, respect, and empathy—can direct our efforts. We practice curiosity by inquiring with real interest into points of view that differ from our own. Courage can lead us to speak sensitively a truth that others may resist. We practice vulnerability when we speak about love in a setting in which people do not commonly address matters of the heart. Respect leads us to strive to see the full humanity of every party to the conflict. Empathy enables us to place ourselves in the shoes of people whose position is different from our own.

Freire wrote that love is dialogue and dialogue is a form of love.[14] Dialogue and enacting love are the way forward on the liberation journey. These two intertwined practices are the way we walk, the way we make the road toward a relational society. We begin to take back our civic culture from the marketplace when we continuously engage in interpersonal and communal activity in this spirit.

---

[13] See William J. Barber, *The Third Reconstruction* (Boston: Beacon Press, 2016), 201.

[14] Paulo Freire, *Pedagogy of the Oppressed* (New York: Continuum, 2000), 89–90.

CHAPTER 21

The Exquisite Lightness of Being

Prophetic testimony points the way forward to a more relational society. Still we often have doubts—as people did in the days of the Hebrew prophets—that our efforts to transform our society can overcome the powerful entrenched interests that hold the status quo in place. The marketplace ethic and the commodification of global capitalism seem to us so unshakeable that we may question our capacity to bring about an alternative future. The Cain and Abel story speaks a subversive truth about the apparent power of established institutions, a truth that can help us overcome our doubts.

In Hebrew, the name *Kayin* (Cain) comes from the verbal root that means "to possess." The name *Hevel* (Abel) comes from the root that means "unsubstantial" or "evanescent." Understanding the Hebrew roots of these names, we can see that the confrontation between Kayin and Hevel embodies an elemental tension that lives within each of us.

Unsubstantial Hevel embodies the *lightness of being*; his life is like a breath that comes and goes. Hevel's *lightness* signifies the fluid vitality and the vulnerability of aliveness. In his name and premature death we see that a person cannot hold on to a breath or a life. We cannot hold on to our loved ones, our possessions, our accomplishments, or our own life and truly live.

Life is a moving steam of energy, a gift wholly given to us. We cannot create it nor can we successfully clutch it. We can only receive life and allow it to flow through us. Life is like Hevel; it is ephemeral, coming and going continually. To live well, we need to learn to accept and embrace Hevel, the fleeting nature of life.

As Buber teaches, this transitory flow is always relational; genuine life consists of a multitude of ephemeral meetings, encounters in the moment, relational happenings that come and go.

Yet Kayin also lives in each of us. We want to take hold and possess (*kayin*). We naturally grasp to hold on to all that is sweet and good, and when we have held it close, we do not easily let it go.

Inside each person there dwells these twins, Kayin and Hevel.[1] Hevel is animated when we are present to the flow of life. Kayin is the aspect that seeks security and control. Hevel is the aspect that connects to life. Kayin strives to keep us safe. The challenge to human beings, the art of living in faith to life, is to accept and live with the tension between Kayin and Hevel, to embrace both the vulnerability of being alive and the desire to be in control of our lives.

The dynamic between Kayin and Hevel mirrors the tension between the royal and prophetic narratives in the Bible. The biblical kings and Kayin are useful to the life force; they provide structure and stability. But the prophetic narratives and Hevel are more essential to the life force because they carry the transforming stream. Problems arise when the Kayin aspect, personified by the figure of the king, can no longer tolerate the ever-evolving and vulnerable qualities of Hevel.

Early in Genesis the tension between the brothers is too much for Kayin to bear. As the story goes, God attended to Hevel's offering and does not attend to Kayin's. God is not favoring the Hevel quality in a person. Rather, God is addressing a truth about the human psyche. Uplifting connection to Spirit does not come easily to the Kayin quality, the aspect of human nature that seeks to possess. God tells Kayin that he will be uplifted as he "supports *tov*" (vitality).[2] To experience connection to Spirit, Kayin must grow beyond the desire to possess. He must also value the qualities present in Hevel. He does not need to become Hevel; he needs to accept and appreciate him. He must be Hevel's brother. But Kayin is not mature enough to accept such vulnerability. Instead, Kayin slays Hevel. He becomes the strongman who would slay all that is vulnerable, transient, and beyond his control.

Kayin's transgression is deeply ironic. In the absence of the quality expressed in Hevel, the moment-to-moment vitality of life, Kayin cannot find satisfaction and uplift in life. Seeking always to possess life and never to simply receive it, he is doomed to wander across the face of the earth.[3]

Unaccompanied by his brother, Hevel, Kayin is the very face of human greed. Kayin's desire to possess can never be satisfied. Posses-

---

[1]   In the midrash the Rabbis point out that Eve only conceives once before she gives birth to Kayin and then Hevel. They conclude that the boys were twins.

[2]   See Gen 4:7: "הֲלוֹא אִם־תֵּיטִיב שְׂאֵת" [if you cause טוב (*tov*/vitality) uplift].

[3]   See Gen 4:3–12.

sions can never fulfill the yearning of the human soul for life. Kayin is the I of the I-It attitude, a necessary but unfulfilling aspect of human nature. Left alone, Kayin always wants more. Driven by the pain of radical dissatisfaction, Kayin naturally becomes locked in an endless cycle of seeking to possess.

At the heart of Kayin's suffering is his perception of scarcity. For Kayin, either he or his brother will be uplifted. He cannot hear God's promise that his offering can also be raised up. When one's attention is fixed on possessing material goods, one can never be fulfilled. Therefore, there are never enough material possessions to go around.

Alienation is the inevitable consequence of following in the footsteps of Kayin. As greed feeds one's desire to possess and weighs one down with more and more material goods, one becomes cut off from the exquisite lightness of being, from the life-giving flow of the prophetic stream. The ultimate cost of avarice is alienation from people and from life itself. In hooks's understanding, "Greed violates the spirit of connectedness and community that is natural to human survival."[4]

The Hebrew prophets, buoyed by the movement of the prophetic stream, saw the dominance of Kayin present in the Israelite kingdoms. The king and the elites embodied Kayin; they attempted to make themselves substantial by dispossessing the common farmer. Ironically, the ostensibly substantial institutions of kingship and Temple are also vulnerable. Cut off from the life-giving and transforming energy of the prophetic stream, they will inevitably fall of their own weight.

On the other hand, the apparently insubstantial alternative visions of the prophet will eventually take some form; will take on substance, because prophetic vision is rooted in the life force itself. The unstoppable creative power of the prophetic stream moving within creation will ultimately bring down all that constrains its expression and will enliven all that opens to its flow.

In our day, we need to embrace such prophetic vision. We need to see that the apparently substantial predatory institutions of global capitalism will ultimately fall of their own weight because greed alienates a person and a society from the exquisite lightness of being. As with every other imperial system in human history, the deeply unjust aspects of contemporary economic, social, and political structures will eventually self-destruct. As the prophet Walter Brueggemann proclaimed, "They are doomed!"[5]

---

4 bell hooks, *All about Love* (New York: Harper Perennial, 2001), 117.

5 Brueggemann made this pronouncement in a sermon he gave at Temple Beth Shalom, Santa Fe, in October 2014.

With prophetic vision we can see that societal transformation is not just possible, it is sure and certain. Once we comprehend that a radical change of the current order is inevitable, we will be empowered to undertake the second prophetic move—to envision and enact an alternative future.

CHAPTER 22

The Art of Stars and Stones

I live in the high desert of northern New Mexico, not far from the Rio Grande. I love the days I spend rafting down that river. The flow of the river speaks to me, addressing some deep and tender place inside. The tones of the river are sometimes expansive and vast, slow-rolling syllables talking to me in some primordial language, communicating sensate wisdom about expanding, opening up, connecting across limitless reaches. At other moments, the river's speech is staccato—rapid and jarring—calling forth the energy for responsiveness and resiliency in the face of change. As it follows the twisting course of an ancient rift in the arid desert, the river sings the song of life, a multioctave melody of unfolding possibility.

Prophecy is a river. Prophecy is an energetic flow, an animating stream that threads through all that is. The nonverbal language of this flow is *possibility*: the possibility of bringing forth new forms of life, the possibility of taking the next step on a journey, the possibility of making another exodus. This prophetic stream speaks to all creation, addressing each form in its own language, exclaiming the vocabulary of potential—the potential to evolve, to expand in awareness, to grow in relationship.

In humans, the prophetic stream speaks most directly to the imaginative faculty. Human imagination, unfettered by settled norms, lifts a person above the limitations of the present moment and enables the envisioning of a radically alternative future. The sparks of such imaginative fire naturally arise in human awareness. Every human being has moments of imagining alternatives to the established circumstances of one's life.

The human journey—for the individual and the species—involves cultivating the fruits of imagination. One of our ancestors was cutting into the carcass of an animal with a sharp stone when he imagined the

possibility of chipping off stone flakes to expose a sharper cutting surface. Later, one of his descendants was noticing sparks fly off the stone
when the image of fire flashed across her awareness. And so on. The
voice of possibility within them became a creation in the world.

That voice speaks differently within each of us, often in surprising
ways. As a youth, I found myself fascinated by the eighteenth-century
French salons, often presided over by influential women who gathered
people in their homes to discuss the day's cutting-edge topics. I yearned
to participate in such conversations and imagined that someday I might
hold such a gathering. The Beit Midrash is the child of those imaginings.

Imagination is the first human receptor for the prophetic stream. Walter Brueggemann coined the term "prophetic imagination" to capture the
unlikely confluence of playful *imagination* with morally earnest *prophecy*.[1] In Brueggemann's understanding, prophecy does not foretell the
future; prophets imagine an alternative future. Imagination brings forth
images that break through the inertial weight of the status quo. The
unreasonable inventiveness of imagination provides the wings of possibility to accompany the grave moral critique of prophecy. The vividness
of an image points to possibilities that rational analysis cannot foresee.

The ministry of the shepherd Amos is a good model for inventive
imagination. Accepting the charge to announce the impossible, Amos
walks to Beth El to confront the apparently impregnable king and high
priest. In the presence of the high priest and the community, Amos pro-
nounces his vision of a God who stands atop a wall saying, "I will set a
plumb line in the midst of my people" (7:7–8). Amos's imaginative vision
proclaims that the social and religious structures that look like sturdy
walls are not upright and will soon fall.

The prophet Deutero-Isaiah was likewise a messenger of the impossible. On behalf of the downtrodden Jews in Babylon, he proclaims God's
intention to act in totally unexpected ways and release the people from
the grip of Babylonian exile: "Thus said the Living Presence . . . Remember nor recall the former things, nor consider things of old. Behold I will
do a new thing; Now it shall spring forth; shall you not know it? I will
make a way in the wilderness, and rivers in the desert" (Isa 43:1, 18–20).

Prophetic imagination is not pure fantasy; it emerges in response to
the movement of the prophetic stream. The prophet senses the river of
liberating energy at work within the world, subverting and transforming

---

[1] The dynamics of prophetic imagination are powerfully developed in Walter
Brueggemann's seminal works *The Prophetic Imagination* (Minneapolis: Fortress Press, 2001) and *The Practice of Prophetic Imagination* (Minneapolis: Fortress Press, 2012). Brueggemann's insights in these books and many others have
affected my own thinking immeasurably.

the seemingly immutable structures of society. In Brueggemann's words, "This [prophetic] act of imagination knows and trusts that the world is open and supple and that every attempt to freeze it into absolute certitude or into unchanging power arrangements is an illusion."[2]

A challenge facing every prophetic figure is how to engage the imagination of the people, how to lift up the people to see the real possibility of an alternative future that the prophet sees. The Hebrew prophets met this challenge by speaking in images. The prophets were not only visionaries; they were masterful poets, using poetic imagery to express their message, as in these passages from Hosea and Micah:

> Therefore, behold, I will allure her, and bring her [Israel] into the wilderness, and speak tenderly to her. And I will give her vineyards from there, and the valley of Achor [desolation] for a gate of hope; and she shall sing there, as in the days of her youth, and as in the day when she came out of the land of Egypt. (Hos 2:16–17)[3]

> They shall beat their swords into plowshares, and their spears into pruning hooks. Nation shall not lift up sword against nation, nor shall they learn war any more. Every person shall sit under the vine and under the fig tree, and none shall make them afraid. (Mic 4:3–4†)

As in the times of the Hebrew prophets, the challenges of liberating work in our day are both practical and imaginative. Certainly, change agents need to do practical civic work. At the same time, social activism needs to be energized and guided by compelling imaginative visions of an alternative future.

Art is the language of the imagination. Art opens the human awareness to possibility and encourages adventurous thinking and visionary creativity. Artistic expression enables people to sense and see what might otherwise go unnoticed. Painting, poetry, and performance enable people to envision what a society built on an ethic of love might look like. The arts provide the first sketches, the evocative music, and the poetic language that point to what is emerging, to what can be.

Moreover, art creates the fabric of culture. Artistic creations give people a lived experience of cultural values. All the arts—music, theater, literature, folk art, dance, and the fine arts—provide people the opportunity to inhabit a created world in which fresh sensibilities and perceptions as well as emerging values can be explored.

---

[2] Brueggemann, *The Practice of Prophetic Imagination*, 146.
[3] Hos 2:14–15 in KJV.

Art has played an energizing and guiding role in every liberation movement as far back as biblical times. When the Hebrew slaves put the blood of a lamb on their doorposts, they engaged in both a political act and in performance art. The Hebrew people were symbolically representing their resistance, and enacting their transformation, their break from Pharaoh's power.[4]

The Bible devotes a full book, the Song of Songs, to poetic images exploring the liberating power of relationship. The following passage evokes a lover's summons to liberation, an invitation imaged in the springtime emergence of sweet possibilities:

Arise my love, my beautiful one, and come away.
For, behold, the winter is past,
The rain is over and gone;
The flowers appear on earth;
the time of the singing bird has come,
and the voice of the turtledove is heard in our land;
The fig tree puts forth her green figs,
And the vines in blossom give forth their scent.
Arise my love, my beautiful one, and come away. (Song 2:10–13)

In America, dating from colonial days, the arts have inspired and strengthened people intent on resisting and overcoming oppression. African American slaves turned to song, composing and singing blues and spirituals such as "Swing Low, Sweet Chariot" and "There Is a Balm in Gilead" to withstand the crushing degradation of slavery and maintain a sense of human dignity.[5] Songs like "Follow the Drinkin' Gourd" and "Wade in Water" guided fugitive slaves who sought their freedom via the Underground Railroad. From the 1830s to the 1860s, art was widely employed to raise awareness during the Abolitionist movement. Visual artists such as William Blake created paintings that highlighted the horrible degradation of slavery. Harriet Beecher Stowe's bestselling novel of the nineteenth century, *Uncle Tom's Cabin*, fueled the emancipation movement of the 1850s.

The arts played a key role in the civil rights movement a century later. Plays, paintings, and photographs vividly communicated African Ameri-

---

[4] The slaughter of a lamb was an abomination for the Egyptians. In committing such an abomination and marking their homes with the lamb's blood, the Israelites were declaring their freedom from fear of Pharaoh and their trust in the God of liberation.

[5] James Cone, *The Cross and the Lynching Tree* (Maryknoll, NY: Orbis Books, 2011).

can suffering, while songs like "We Shall Overcome," "Oh Freedom," and "A Change Is Gonna Come" energized courageous resistance.

Art animated the labor, feminist, and gay rights movements, amplifying the emotional power of claims for equality and common humanity. The labor movement still sings "The Ballad of Joe Hill," "Solidarity Forever," and "We Shall Not Be Moved." In the 1970s a number of artists like Holly Near, Meg Christianson, Chris Williamson, and Margie Adams wrote songs that lifted and empowered the feminist movement. The AIDS Memorial Quilt galvanized the movement to confront the AIDS epidemic and protect the bodies and the rights of gay people.

For Bill Clinton's inauguration, the poet Maya Angelou delivered a poem, "On the Pulse of Morning," in which she spoke as a prophet would, naming both the brokenness of her day and the expectancy of a bright new future. She recalled African slaves "sold, stolen, arriving on a nightmare praying for a dream." In the same breath, Angelou proclaimed new possibilities and called for a response: "Lift up your eyes upon the day breaking for you. Give birth again to the dream." Like the Hebrew prophets, Angelou roots her poem in nature imagery. The poet gives voice to Rock, River, and Tree, who thereby invite the human community to return to deep mutual relationship with all of creation.

Martin Luther King Jr. articulated his imaginative vision in the form of a dream, a dream that still lives in the American consciousness:

> I have a dream that one day this nation will rise up and live out the true meaning of its creed: "We hold these truths to be self-evident, that all men are created equal."
>
> I have a dream that one day on the red hills of Georgia, the sons of former slaves and the sons of former slave owners will be able to sit down together at the table of brotherhood.
>
> I have a dream that one day even the state of Mississippi, a state sweltering with the heat of injustice, sweltering with the heat of oppression, will be transformed into an oasis of freedom and justice.
>
> I have a dream that my four little children will one day live in a nation where they will not be judged by the color of their skin but by the content of their character.
>
> I have a *dream* today![6]

---

[6] Martin Luther King Jr., *I Have a Dream: Writings and Speeches That Changed the World*, ed. James Melvin Washington (San Francisco: Harper, 1986), 102–6.

King offered people a clear and powerful vision of a better future. He had seen the promised land, and he knew that the people would get there.

The arts have always led the way in the liberation journey, giving metaphoric flesh and bone to inchoate yearnings and intuitions of an alternative future. The forward movement of the liberation journey toward a more relational culture requires images, stories, and songs that activate resistance and social innovation, celebrate human dignity, promote relationship, and envision a better future. Strong support for art and artists is vital to the cultural transformation to a more relational society.

In most people's minds, the word "artist" evokes the idea of a limited number of people who dedicate their lives to making art. In truth, all of us are potential artists, and more of us need to fulfill that potential for the forward movement of the great liberation journey. The narrative arc in the book of Exodus emphasizes this truth. At the outset of Exodus, Pharaoh enslaved the Hebrew people and set them to work building his storehouses. In the final chapters of Exodus, the liberated people are still building. The difference is that the former slaves have now become free women and men constructing the Holy Tabernacle. The evolution from slaves to holy artists suggests the centrality of widespread creative activity in the liberation journey.

The Torah highlights the widespread involvement of the community in building the Tabernacle. Responding to Moses's call for materials, "every person whose heart and mind were uplifted and everyone whose spirit was willing brought the Living Presence's offering for the work of the Tabernacle" (Exod 35:21[†]). A great many people brought their gifts for the Tabernacle.

Equally important, the people's giving knows no bounds. The entire project is suffused with a spirit of generosity. Ultimately Moses needs to tell them to stop; the people had brought more than enough precious materials for the building.

In Pharaoh's scarcity economy there is never enough. Pharaoh continually pushed the slaves to make more bricks for his building projects. By contrast, the former slaves experienced abundance as they brought their gifts for the Tabernacle. This shift in consciousness is made explicit in the text. The word "uplifted"—"every person whose heart and mind were uplifted"—signifies a shift from *moach ha-katnut* (small-mindedness) to *moach ha-gadlut* (great-mindedness). As Rashi observes, these Israelites possessed "a spirit of generosity."[7] They experienced abundance and gave

---

[7] Rashi on Exod 35:21.

generously. Unlike Pharaoh's storehouses whose purpose is to constrain and contain, the Tabernacle, as an artistic endeavor, brings forth abundance because it taps into the prophetic stream, an energetic flow that speaks the language of possibility.

In contemporary life, perceived scarcity is often used to justify a society's failure to provide generous resources to fund the arts. For example, in New Mexico, the former state auditor Tim Keller has repeatedly observed how "the myth of scarcity" has been employed in the state since colonial days to rationalize the failure of the government to meet its citizens' needs. He then presented hard evidence to demonstrate that claims for scarcity are indeed a myth.[8] A society devoted to the wellbeing of all its members, a culture founded in a love ethic, will need to see through the scarcity myth to perceive the depth of resources available to support the flourishing of all.

The spirit of inclusivity that animated many Israelites to bring gifts for the Tabernacle also pertained to the people who participated in building the sacred structure. Every wise-hearted Israelite had a hand in the building: "All the women who were wise-hearted did spin with their hands. . . . And Moses called every wise-hearted man, in whose heart the Living Presence had put wisdom, everyone whose heart stirred him up to come to the work to do it" (Exod 35:25; 36:2).[9]

The whole community was included in the creative enterprise. This inclusive approach to creative work is a vital aspect of the liberation journey. In an imperial society, only a few people are recognized as artists. By contrast, a culture that values human beings appreciates each person's creative potential.

Creativity runs at the core of human nature. Life itself demands creativity. All individuals are challenged to create their own distinctive sense of meaning and purpose, their own distinctive way of being in the world. Each wise-hearted woman, man, and child brings unique gifts to meet life's opportunities and challenges and thereby possesses unique experiences, dreams, and insights. These dreams and insights emerging

---

[8] New Mexico State Auditor (Timothy Keller), "The Myth of Scarcity: Structural Challenges in Economy and Public Funds," PowerPoint presentation, www.saonm.org.

[9] The heart, in biblical thought, is the cognitive organ. "Wise heart" connotes clear thinking well rooted in heartfelt feelings. A wise-hearted person is emotionally connected to what she is thinking skillfully about. To grasp the full implications of "wise heart," we can recall that in the Bible "wisdom" (*hochma*) is a relational and practical term. Rooted in heartfelt thinking, wisdom gives an individual practical knowledge for how to work skillfully with a given material. The people who constructed the Tabernacle brought *hochma* to their artistic work.

from the ordinary people are all needed for sacred work—to imagine and enact the way forward on the pathway toward a more mutually relational society. In the exodus story, Moses does not create the sacred sanctuary for the community. The offerings of many people are joined together to create the common space that will hold the people together and carry them forward.

The spirit of inclusivity is important for the liberation journey today. A radical shift away from a culture of domination and acquisition and toward a culture that values love and dialogue cannot be imposed from the top. It must arise from the ground, from the yearnings of ordinary people for a different way of life. The liberation journey must be shaped and energized by a spirit of inclusion, the wisdom to include the experiences, dreams, and innovative initiatives of as many people as possible in the creative process.

In our day people across the globe are coming together in small groups, in myriad ways, bringing their offerings to create new entities that support human flourishing. Initiatives like Rahwa Ghirmatzion's PUSH Buffalo and Estevan Kelly's Philadelphia Area Cooperative Alliance are beginning to bring forth the new culture that we need for a more relational society. These initiatives are little stars of possibility glowing amid the dark night of the oppressive societal cultures in which we live. These emerging stars are the expression of the prophetic stream in our time.

These creative enterprises are a form of art: social art. Social artists work creatively with people and the natural world to innovate positive social change.

All art is the outgrowth of the artist's imaginative engagement with that person's own perceived reality. Art is the fruit of disciplined dialogue, of hearing the flowing voice of the creative river and responding to that voice. An artist, in imaginative dialogue with the artist's inner or outer world, seeks to give words, voice, color, shape, movement—or societal form—to that encounter.

The artists of the Tabernacle, wise-hearted people, were masters of this sort of dialogue. In biblical thought the "heart," or "*lev*," is the cognitive organ. Wise *lev* connotes clear thinking well rooted in heartfelt feelings. A wise-hearted person is emotionally connected to what she is skillfully thinking about. The Tabernacle artists worked in continual dialogue between their hearts and what building the Tabernacle called forth from them. These masters of sacred art are models for what is needed for the liberation journey. They were mindfully attuned to the promptings of their own wise hearts in dialogue with the opportunities and challenges presented in the external world.

Art is dialogical. Conversely, dialogue is an art—a disciplined, imaginative engagement. To be in dialogue with an other—whether that other is a human, a tree, a stream, or an intuition—a person must listen imaginatively. The voice of the other contains a perception of reality that is in some way, perhaps ever so subtly, wholly new to the listener. To receive this newness, the listener must suspend the matrix of perception—all assumptions of how things are—and exercise the imagination to formulate in the *lev* the new in-formation. The listener must sift through and integrate many streams of multisensory data to create the reality of the other. Realizing the presence of the other at a given moment is a creative act. Authentic dialogue is an art.

Mutual relationship requires dialogue. In this way mutual relationship is also an art. It arises from a creative and imaginative exchange of information, including the in-formation of one's physical presence. As in all art, genuine mutual relationship requires sustained attention to the other.

Going a step further in understanding the central role of art in the liberation journey, we can affirm that every consciously lived moment in a human life is a creation, a work of art. Flourishing human beings are continually creating their lives, bringing forth potential into reality. This understanding is implicit in the biblical notion that humans are created "in the image" of a creating God. Human beings are created to create their lives. A life is rich to the extent that one is artfully engaged in the process of bringing forth.

Similarly, every human collective, culture, and society is rich in aliveness to the extent that its members are collectively bringing forth potential into reality. This ongoing, creative bringing forth is energized by the prophetic stream, continually calling each individual and every collective to make an exodus from the status quo toward a promised land where the collective and all its members are more free to flourish.

Art arises from the flow of the prophetic stream. We human beings first recognize this flow when we give sustained attention to whatever we find most fascinating or disturbing. Fascination and disturbance are the way that the prophetic stream flows into our lives to activate our awareness and our imagination. Each of us is unique in what we find fascinating and disturbing. The disruption of fascination and disturbance breaks through settled ways of thinking and grabs our attention, potentially focusing it on something that is emerging but not yet fully present in our awareness. When we give sustained attention to what fascinates or disturbs us, we begin to notice patterns or themes of interest and concern. Our living becomes creative and prophetic when our wise *lev* becomes engaged. In this engagement, we skillfully apply our imagination to bring forth the potential that lies in those themes. We create art. Some of us make art in the familiar sense of the arts—dance, theater, painting, music, and literature. Others create art in the sense of innovative responses to life's capacity to flourish.

Every person is, potentially, a unique artist in life. Each of us has particular sacred offerings to contribute to the liberation journey. Alice Walker brings forth the image of a stone pile to capture the way the small contributions of ordinary people can change "the course on the planet":

> It has become a common feeling, I believe, as we have watched our heroes falling over the years, that our own small stone of activism, which might not seem to measure up to the rugged boulders of heroism we have so admired, is a paltry offering toward the building of an edifice of hope. Many who believe this choose to withhold their offerings out of shame. This is the tragedy of our world. For we can do nothing substantial toward changing our course on the planet, a destructive one, without rousing ourselves, individual by individual, and bringing our small, imperfect stones to the pile.[10]

Each little stone glows with potential for a more fruitful future. These radiant stones are the little stars I imagine glowing amid the dark of night. As mainstream institutions increasingly fail to meet people's needs, energy will flow toward these little stars, feeding them with increased strength and vitality. These stars have the potential, in time, to connect with each other, to form patterns, to become the foundation of an alternative future.

We live at a time when technology makes possible a gathering of small stones that would have been unimaginable even twenty years ago. In former times only the art of a small number of artists received public notice: only a few poems and stories were published, only select songs were played on the radio, only a few paintings hung in galleries. Today the internet has dramatically democratized art. In the twenty-first century, millions of people, unacclaimed artists, are at work every day creating art and then disseminating these images, poems, movies, and songs worldwide.

Similarly, creative initiatives no longer need the backing of major institutional lenders. internet-based crowdfunding sites like Go Fund Me

---

[10] Alice Walker, *Anything We Love Can Be Saved: A Writer's Activism* (New York: Ballantine Books, 1998).

and Kickstarter enable social entrepreneurs to raise significant money from many small contributors. In 2017 almost a billion dollars was raised in the United States via crowdfunding.[11] In our day, ordinary people, lifted by the energy of the prophetic stream, can bring their small stones to create visions for and movements toward an alternative inclusive culture.

Examples are as numerous as the stars visible on a clear night.

Dave Isay, a radio documentarian, loves to hear and record people's stories. Inspired by the stories he heard, Dave created a "story booth" in Grand Central Terminal in New York City, a quiet place amid the hubbub where people could tell and record their stories. Dave's mission was to preserve and share humanity's stories in order to build connections between people and create a more just and compassionate world. Now, hundreds of stories later, surveys indicate that people who have listened to these stories demonstrate a dramatic increase in the following qualities:

- Feeling more connected to people with different backgrounds
- Thinking people different from themselves are an important part of society
- Having more understanding of immigrants, Latinos, African Americans, and people with a disability or serious illness
- Seeing the value in everyone's life story and experience
- Being more positive about society and more interested in imagining how society could be improved

In discussing the mission of StoryCorps Isay wrote, "We do this to weave into the fabric of our culture the understanding that everyone's story matters."[12]

Artist Judy Baca wanted to empower young people, minorities, women, and LGBTQ people through art. She recruited hundreds of teenagers, many from the juvenile justice system, to help her paint a half-mile mural illustrating "The History of California" as seen through the eyes of people whose perspective has rarely been recognized. The sweeping mural narrative includes Chumash Indians, the arrival of the Spanish (from an indigenous point of view), the mass deportation of Mexican Americans during the Great Depression, interned Japanese Americans, a black activist protesting racially restrictive housing covenants, and family members isolated from each other by the Los Angeles freeways. The

---

[11]   See www.statista.com.
[12]   See storycorps.org.

mural ends with Martin Luther King Jr. sitting at the back of the bus gazing at a smiling Rosa Parks who is sitting in the front row.

Poet Marie Howe also uses her art to engage people in creating a culture in which every human being matters. With the understanding that "art helps to let the heart break open [to connection with other people] rather than [remain] closed,"[13] Howe determined to bring poetry to everyone in New York. She created "The Poet Is In," an initiative in which published poets sit in a booth in public places and write poems for people upon request. Recently, Howe expanded her project to inspire people to write poems in chalk on the sidewalks in New York City.

Walidah Imarisha and adrienne maree brown brought together an anthology of speculative short stories that envision positive social change. Their collection, *Octavia's Brood*, includes several genres—sci-fi, fantasy, horror, and magical realism. All the stories exercise utopian imagination. They imagine more relational societies and worlds without violence, prisons, or exploitive capitalism. The book's title honors the literary work of Octavia Butler, one of the early figures in developing afro-futurism, an aesthetic that infuses the cultures of the African diaspora into science fiction and fantasy. Afro-futurism often envisions utopian societies shaped by African diasporic culture and black technological innovation.

Some of the bright stars of our day come from social art—creative initiatives that engage people and the natural world to bring about societal transformation. Rick Lowe's work offers an example of a project that combines fine art and social art. Lowe has transformed a deteriorating neighborhood in Houston into a visionary public art project. In the early 1990s Lowe organized a group of fellow artists to purchase twenty-two old shotgun houses in Houston's predominantly African American Third Ward and turn them into Project Row Houses (PRH), a site that combines arts venues and community-gathering centers. Since 1993 PRH has served as the anchor of a revitalized neighborhood, providing arts education for youth, studio residencies for emerging artists, a mentorship program for young mothers, an organic gardening program, and an incubator for historically appropriate designs for low-income housing on land surrounding the original row houses. In collaboration with local residents, artists, church groups, architects, and urban planners, Lowe pursues his overarching goal of working with the creativity of the people in a community to revitalize a neighborhood and create beauty while resisting gentrification.

---

[13] Marie Howe, "The Poetry of Ordinary Time," On Being podcast, August 28, 2014, onbeing.org.

Wes Jackson's imagination was also fired by a desire to live in a more harmonious relationship with the land. The native perennial and polycultural grasses in the Great Plains fascinated Jackson, a farmer. In his mind's eye, he could see those perennial grasses replacing the commonly used annual grains that require farmers to disrupt and fertilize the soil every year. Jackson created the Land Institute to develop seeds and practices that would enable farmers to plant perennial grains that help build and protect the soil. The Land Institute brings human ingenuity and the creative ways of the natural world together in dialogue. As resourceful human ventures that work with the creative energy of the natural world, the Land Institute mirrors the way that God *worked with* creation to bring forth new life. In this way, the Land Institute is the fruit of the prophetic stream.

These wise-hearted and creative initiatives represent just a few of the imaginative projects that are growing exponentially in number around the globe. We should not be surprised. Meeting a deep challenge with sustained attention and an imaginative response is not a new experience for human beings. Bringing imagination to bear on complex problems goes to the heart of what it is to be human.

Historian Yuval Harari has observed the central role of imaginative dialogue throughout human history. He points out that humans started their journey on earth as a very small, rather weak species about 200,000 years ago. For 130,000 to 150,000 years, humans lived in very small clans as hunter-gatherers, primarily in Eastern Africa. Then, relatively suddenly, humans exploded out of Africa. Over the next 50,000 to 70,000 years, Homo sapiens rose to a dominant position on the planet. What enabled this relatively unremarkable animal to attain such power?

Harari argues that what makes humans special and powerful is the human capacity to work together both flexibly and in large numbers. Some animals, such as bees and ants, have the ability to coordinate large numbers of workers, but they lack flexibility. Other animals, such as apes and whales, have the ability to cooperate flexibly, but only in small numbers of individuals who have direct contact with each other. Only humans can cooperate both flexibly and in large numbers. This ability to work adaptively and in number has given human beings the ability to irrigate vast territories, to build cities, and to create civilizations.

What inherent capacity enables humans to cooperate flexibly and in large numbers? Harari thinks imaginative dialogue is that capacity, specifically the ability to create and share stories. Harari asserts that only a commonly held and cherished story can bind a large group together. Human affiliations of any size—whether religious, ethnic, or political—are constituted by a story that holds people together. Only humans use imaginative language and imagery to create these large social units. All other animals use their communication systems to describe some aspect of physical reality. From the beginning, the human journey has been an artistic venture.

Harari calls the imaginative and collaborative storytelling break-through that enabled humans to cooperate in large numbers the "Cognitive Revolution." The Agricultural Revolution, the Industrial Revolution, and now the Information Revolution followed the Cognitive Revolution. Humankind is still in the earliest stages of the Information Revolution, yet we are already witnessing the potential for the Age of Information to become the Age of Interconnection. For example, the World Bank estimates that in 2012, 75 percent of humanity had access to a cell phone. While imperial regimes are certainly making every effort to limit popular access to certain information, the growing inter-connectivity within every country and across the globe has the potential to nurture more cooperative and consensual ways of coming together in society.

A mutually relational future is far from guaranteed. The prophetic stream brings forth movement in the direction of mutually fulfilling relationship but does not assure it. No daunting, inspiring journey could carry such assurance. In this evolving creation, human beings are challenged to be the prophetic artists of an alternative future, challenged to make the imaginative and risky journey, step by step, toward the promised land of mutually fulfilling relationships for all.

We can be encouraged—we can take (wise) heart—in knowing that our species was created for this purpose, to venture forth on this journey. Humans possess the requisite qualities for the adventure: the ability to enter into dialogue and to enact love, the capacity to imagine and collaborate. We are called by our human nature and by the nature of creation to participate in the exodus journey, called not only because it is just and not only because we seek a more inclusively fulfilling society, although those goals are worthy enough. Humans are called to the exodus journey because that liberating pathway alone enables us to fulfill our humanity as imaginative artists, people who continually bring forth their human potential.

The Scriptures teach the direction of the journey—inclusive, mutually fulfilling relationships, and the prime directive, to enact love. Dialogue and art are the dynamic of the journey, the way we move forward. Wise-minded people across the globe are listening for what is needed and beginning to create the culture(s) that enact love—the art, social justice initiatives, practices for healing and reconciliation, social innovations, alternative economic structures, and the like. Every human being on the planet is called to participate.

In the words of the poet Denise Levertov,

We have only begun to love the earth
We have only begun to imagine the fullness of life.
How could we tire of hope?
—so much is in bud.
How can desire fail?
—we have only begun
to imagine justice and mercy,
only begun to envision
how it might be
to live as siblings with beast and flower,
not as oppressors . . .
Not yet, not yet—
there is too much broken
that must be mended,
too much hurt we have done to each other
that cannot yet be forgiven.
We have only begun to know
the power that is in us if we would join
our solitudes in the communion of struggle.
So much is unfolding that must
complete its gesture,
So much in the bud.[14]

---

[14]   Denise Levertov, "Beginners," in Robert Creeley and Paul A. Lacey, eds., *The Selected Poems of Denise Levertov* (New York: New Directions, 2002), 137.

CHAPTER 23

The Love That Binds Us

In response to the disintegration of the kingdom and the Temple, the Hebrew prophets stepped forward to reweave the frayed relational ties among the people as well as between the people and God. To do this, the prophets lifted up three intertwined aspects of relationship: dialogue, love, and covenant. Among these qualities, for the prophets, covenant is the foundation. In biblical thought, a covenant articulates the terms of a committed and abiding relationship. When parties enter into a covenant, they express to each other their intention to maintain the relationship over time. This articulated commitment to sustained relationship supports the trust and vulnerability that nurtures the other two relational qualities: dialogue and love.

The Bible conceived of the covenant with God as a contract between a ruler and his subjects, a contractual arrangement that was familiar to the people of the time. The covenant served as an accessible metaphor that expressed God's committed love for the world and the responsibility that God's love placed upon human beings to care for God's world.

In our time, biblical covenant presents many people with a quandary. For most people living in a democratic society, the king/subject metaphor has lost its power and meaning. It is perhaps even distasteful, with overtones of oppressive tyranny that are entirely false to God's intent that all creation flourishes. For this reason, the traditional covenant no longer speaks to many people and thus no longer binds them. However, like the people in biblical times, contemporary people need support in apprehending God's love for the world and the vital role that loving plays in life's flourishing on earth. So it is important to seek out an understanding of covenant that can speak to contemporary sensibilities. What is the covenantal understanding that will support the unfolding of the mutual and loving relationships that are so essential to the prophetic stream?

Our generation is not the first to face the challenge of developing a new understanding of covenant. As we discussed in Chapter 4, the prophets reworked the unilateral, unconditional covenant that God made with Abraham. They conceived of a conditional covenant between God and the people Israel. The prophet Jeremiah, living at the time of the destruction of Judah, went further. Realizing that the covenantal experience of earlier generations had failed to bind the people into relationship with God, Jeremiah conceived of a "new covenant." Instead of a written external covenant, Jeremiah imagined God placing the Torah in Israel's "inner most parts" and writing it "on their hearts" (31:32).[1]

Jeremiah articulates the subtle cords of relationship that bind us to the world. These relational ties come with responsibility to care for the world. This internal sense of covenant and responsibility calls upon us to participate in actions that enhance human flourishing.

Over the years, I have sought to strengthen my awareness of relational bonds and responsibilities. During a day, I often pause to quiet my mind and give my full attention to whatever is in my field of awareness. For me, these occasions are times of covenantal awareness. I would like to share with you one such moment:

> I take a break from writing and look up from the computer screen. Looking out the window, I feel the presence of the large juniper just outside my study. In Buber's terms, the juniper "is bodied over against me."[2] Juniper impresses itself upon me. And now a bird's song lifts me up. A small, brown spider crawls in the corner. I am taken with its agility. We are all in relationship. We are participating together in this lived moment.

Abraham Joshua Heschel's teaching leads me to allow this moment to unfold its potential. He writes about cultivating wonder as a way of knowing, as a way of recognizing relationship. I extend to Juniper, Bird, and Spider a wordless wonder as a way of relating. Wonder opens me to the awareness that Juniper, Bird, Spider, and I are all participating together in the unfolding of life in this moment of creation. We are all partners bringing forth this moment of the grand journey. As I soften my heart, I feel the dialogue that is taking place among us and the subtle love that binds us.

When I extend this awareness further outward to include friends and family, I feel the emotional bonds that connect us. I am not speak-

---

[1]   Jer 31:33 in KJV.

[2]   Martin Buber, *I and Thou*, trans. Ronald Gregor Smith (New York: Charles Scribner's Sons, 1958), 8.

ing metaphorically but rather about a felt sense of connection—call it love—streaming back and forth between us.

Expanding further, my awareness touches people in my community who are suffering: the family struggling in poverty, the undocumented immigrant living in fear, the young people I know at the local high school who are not learning in school what they need to know. I feel my connection to them, my caring for them, and an impulse of the heart to ally with them and act with them.

I might rest here, in this circle of caring, but the Torah guides me to love people from whom I feel estranged. In response, I extend my awareness to people in my community whose behavior or worldview disturbs me, and further to people across this country whose speech and actions impede the liberation journey. With some effort to quiet my heart, I feel their humanity, even our kinship. I don't agree with them. I don't step back from opposing their rhetoric or their actions. I certainly don't weaken my resolve to pursue the work of liberation. I simply feel that they are complex, multifaceted human beings like me. We are brothers and sisters. I allow myself to care about them.

Further, in this moment that feels like prayer, I take in my experience of connection to all that lives, and I notice arising in me the desire to respond by giving something of myself to my partners in relationship.

The word "respond" brings me to the heart of what the biblical covenant has come to mean to me. God initially covenanted with Abraham and Sarah to receive God's blessings and to be a blessing. The biblical covenant is mutual and reciprocal—binding God and human beings to care for each other. One essential fault in imperial relationships is a lack of responsiveness or reciprocity. People with privilege can feel entitled to receive from others without a responsibility to give back, entitled to receive without concern for the welfare and the flourishing of other people. Sadly, I occasionally recognize this blind entitlement in myself. Sometimes I fail to recognize that blessings in my life call for a reciprocal response of giving blessing back to the world.

Reciprocal relations create the interactive fabric that nurtures healthy living systems. Multiple layers of giving and receiving by creatures large and small—a gift economy—sustain the world. The well-being of the earth and all that lives on it requires that humans live in reciprocity, that people continually ask what are the gifts that they need to bring to the land—and to all that lives on the land—that life might flourish and delight in itself.

Reciprocal responsibility is not a stolid sense of obligation. To the contrary, responsibility—responding by giving one's gifts—places one in the flow of loving, a relational stream that gives fullness to life. The *tov/* vitality in life comes from participating in the gift economy.

Jeremiah's covenant, written on people's hearts, was not a covenant that addressed isolated individuals. The prophet conceived that God placed God's Torah inside all the people, writing it upon their hearts. This covenantal metaphor indicates that collectively the people would perceive both the cords of loving relationship that bound them to God and to all creation and they would also perceive the responsibilities that emerge from that relationship. Contemporary covenantal understandings likewise need to address communities and communal responsibilities. Religious congregations within the biblical tradition can explore how God's covenant with all of creation as expressed in the Bible is felt in the lives of individuals and in the community. Then, guided by biblical teaching and the best contemporary moral insight, the community can explicate the responsibilities that emerge from that covenantal relationship. Civic groups can articulate the cords of relationship that bind the group to the public good and articulate the responsibilities that flow from those relationships.

Covenantal thinking also requires that individuals, religious congregations, and civic groups investigate the sacrifice and surrender that covenantal relationships require. Sacrifice was the primary cultic practice in the biblical statutes. While most societies long ago abandoned animal sacrifice, we suffer today from a lack of training in meaningful sacrifice and the surrender that sacrifice embodies.

Every flourishing mutual relationship requires a person to surrender the sense that one is more important than the other and to embrace the reality that the needs of one's partner are equally important as one's own needs. In this way, every flourishing relationship requires that one sacrifice some benefit, some activity, some freedom that one values to gift another what that person desires or needs in order to flourish.

We all practice surrender and sacrifice in our closest relationships, especially as parents, partners, and friends. But the willingness to sacrifice usually diminishes significantly as the circle of relationship moves beyond one's intimate associations toward people one does not know and toward animals and plants that one has not intimately encountered. Both biblical covenant and the latest scientific reports make clear that the well-being of humankind demands that we extend our practice of sacrifice, our circle of responsibility and reciprocity, to all life on earth. Most contemporary societies, especially the wealthier nations, have not been willing to make the material sacrifices that ecological well-being requires. This failure to sacrifice is rooted in a misperception, in the misguided belief that a few can hoard the benefits of creation while exporting the sacrifices in the world to others. In our day, we have the benefit of climate research to confirm what the Bible has always taught: the well-being of creation demands mutually beneficial relationship. As the prophets proclaimed, a society that benefits only a few will inevitably fail.

A prime goal of education today, including religious education, must be to correct the misperception that a society that benefits a few can be sustained. We are called to use our imagination and creativity to introduce people to the reality that creation is a dynamic, interrelated being. Then we must inquire into what we must hold onto and what we must sacrifice to live fruitfully within the creation. This reciprocal living is the covenant to which we are all called.

In this understanding of covenantal relationship, God is not an external authority dictating commands; rather, God is present within relationship. Inexplicably, something infinite is present within finite relationships. Unaccountably, the lines of immediate connection extend outward to include all that is.

Martin Buber described how "the extended lines of relations meet in the eternal Thou."[3] In a moment of earthly connection, Buber encountered something vast and eternal. In a moment of meeting, in a territory beyond words, he met a Presence that bound him into relationship with everything.

Heschel uses the words "mystery" and "radical amazement" to point to this Presence. The human soul craves to connect to this mystery. Without this mystery, the world of finite relations feels small, lacking the depth and grandeur that one encounters in these moments of conscious meeting.

My encounters with Buber and Heschel and their evocation of meeting and mystery set me upon a journey, a wilderness trek in search of the Presence that breathes life into all that is. Along the pathways of this journey, I have sought out sacred texts, spiritual teaching, poems, music, art—anything that would guide me toward a more profound sense of connection and responsiveness. I have also sought out good teachers and traveling companions.

This book is the fruit of the journey that I have taken over the last fifty years. I view it as one strand that I hope will be woven with a myriad of other threads to create the fabric of a more relational culture. Through artistic creativity, community building, political activism, social innovation, teaching, child-raising, scientific inquiry, and more, each of us has the potential to be wise-hearted artists of the fabric of a new culture, a way of being in society that nurtures interrelationship and widespread well-being.

---

[3] Ibid., 75.

We are all a part of the great unfolding journey of creation, a journey in and toward love. The prophetic stream runs deep in all of our lives. We are in covenant together with the world, with each other, and with the transcendent. Throughout this book, I have thought about you as my walking companion on this journey. Thank you for your companionship. May our walking—our wondering, our venturing out, our risking, our engaging, our dialoging, our attentive caring, our envisioning/imagining, our organizing, and our loving—singularly and together, add our life force to the great stream that is at work this very moment to bring forth a more universally flourishing and delight-filled world.

Appendix A
SPIRITUAL PRACTICES FOR PROPHETIC ACTION

Spiritual practices cultivate the inner resources that enable us to act with wisdom, courage, and vision. These practices are most effective when we undertake them with intention and discipline. Intention—directing the will—provides clarity about your purpose. Discipline—setting a fixed time and place or a regular routine—maintains the structure that is the foundation for spiritual practice.

As you read through this appendix, pay attention to which practices speak to your heart and soul.

Gratitude

In prophetic understanding, well-being within a person or a society emerges from reciprocal relationships. The practice of gratitude nurtures this vital reciprocity. When we practice gratitude—as we notice and appreciate the many gifts and blessings we receive—we see more clearly the stream of goodness that flows into our lives. In response to this flow, we naturally want to give back, to participate in the reciprocal gift-giving that is the world. This awareness of gifts received can also lead us to an awareness of people who are less fortunate and to the structures in society that benefit some and harm others. Practicing this awareness can energize us to take prophetic action to expand the circle of benefits to include more people.

The Rabbis teach that one should look for one hundred opportunities each day to say, "I am grateful for. . . ." A day is full of receiving gifts, including the gift of opportunities to give back. These small cycles of reciprocity serve to connect us to the world, not a static world of objects, but a dynamic world of subjects that are continually exchanging gifts. Attention to the continual flow of gifts can heighten our awareness of the larger economic, social, and political systems that benefit us, an awareness that can lead us to ask if these systems adequately benefit all the members of society and all parts of the earth's fabric of life.

To practice gratitude, notice when something good happens and acknowledge your gratefulness. Also, pause occasionally to look into your present experience to find something for which you are grateful. When you recognize a gift you are receiving, appreciate the good feeling that accompanies that gift—be that a boost in vitality, comfort, strength, or joy. Then quietly smile and express your gratitude. At the end of a day, you can also write down the phrase "I am grateful for," and then list moments, people, or events for which you give thanks, such as the great conversation you enjoyed with a friend, an invigorating hike to the lake, a relative's good medical report, or some beautiful music you heard this evening.

Reverence

Prophetic imagination is rooted in reverence. The practice of reverence attuned the prophet to the sublime, an attunement that enabled the prophet to be aware of God's involvement in the world. We can also attune to the sublime and perceive God's involvement in the world by practicing reverence.

Reverence involves observing the world with wonder. Heschel taught that wonder is a way of knowing. Wonder arises when a person observes that the fullness of a being or event that one encounters is in some way inexplicable, in some way beyond rational explanation.

The world is full of such wonders. When Moses saw the burning bush, he took his shoes off, for he was standing on holy ground. The Rabbis observe that Moses saw the "awesome sight"[1] in a lowly desert bush, implying that if the divine Presence can be witnessed in a desert bramble, then the awesome and mysterious are also present in every other aspect of nature. Too often, the busyness of a day or the constant flow of internal chatter creates mental blinders that impede our perception of wonder in the world.

Practicing reverence involves actively looking for wonder in everyday occurrences and standing in amazement before that wonder. Whatever is going on in your life, when you intentionally look with the eyes of wonder—or listen, taste, or touch with wonder—the sublime aspect of the moment is revealed. When you feel confined by thoughts that narrow your field of vision, you can shift your perspective by looking for the wondrous in the present moment. Uttering a simple prayer or scriptural verse can help you make that shift. I sometimes use a phrase from

---

[1] Exod 3:3.

Psalms, such as, "How magnificent are your works, Living Presence" (92:6), or "The whole earth shouts for joy before the Living Presence" (100:1)—or I simply say, "Reverence."

Lovingkindness

Only love truly liberates, truly moves a person or a society forward on the journey toward mutual relationship. In the face of the human-caused suffering in the world, one's anger often fuels social activism. Righteous indignation may awaken a passion for justice, but anger alone does not lead to wise and sustained action. As Martin Luther King Jr. taught, "The only way to ultimately change humanity and make for the society that we all long for is to keep love at the center of our lives."[2] The love at the center of our lives does not originate in us. This love flows through us. We are finite practitioners of the Infinite Love that flows through all that is. Practicing lovingkindness supports us in opening awareness to the loving flow that is essential for the liberation journey.

Many people cultivate lovingkindness through a blessing practice. To begin, set aside a period of time in which you will not be disturbed. Start by thinking of four blessings that you would like to give and receive, such as love, joy, health, and peace. Take a moment with each blessing to feel in your body the sensation that you associate with each blessing. Then bring to mind someone whom you love and internally think, *May [person's name] be blessed with love. . . . May [name] be blessed with joy. . . . May [name] be blessed with health. . . . May [name] be blessed with peace.* If you wish, you can repeat the cycle. Next, place attention on yourself and repeat the cycle of four blessings. Then think of someone for whom your feelings are relatively neutral and repeat the practice. Finally, think of someone whom you find difficult and repeat the practice. You can substitute any other qualities that you would like to use in this blessing practice.[3]

Prayer

Prayer can provide a variety of resources for the liberation journey, such as connecting our hearts to our deepest yearnings and concerns for the world and to God's loving concern for the world. Prayer is also a

---

[2] Martin Luther King Jr., *A Testament of Hope: The Essential Writings and Speeches of Martin Luther King Jr.*, ed. James Washington (New York: Harper Collins, 1991), 13.

[3] I learned this practice from Rabbi Jeff Roth who adapted it from the Buddhist metta practice.

way of entering into dialogue with God, the sort of dialogue that animates the liberation journey. In prayer we speak our heart to God, and in prayer we listen for how God is leading us forward in life.

Begin your prayer practice by dedicating a time when you are free from distraction so that you can attune yourself to the depths of your life. You can speak prayers from a spiritual lineage or give voice to the appreciations, concerns, and yearnings of your own heart. Rebbe Nachman of Bratzlav taught a particular way to bring forth what is in your heart. In Rebbe Nachman's practice, you find a quiet spot, preferably outside, and speak your deepest feelings out loud to God, without ceasing. In this practice, after a few moments your heart naturally spills over with words that carry deeply held concerns, hopes, desires, and visions. After finishing whatever prayer form you practice, allow some time to listen for God's response.

Meditation and Contemplation

Meditation and contemplation help us cultivate the inner spaciousness that gives us greater capacity to face oppression and suffering and take positive action in the midst of a broken situation. Meditation and contemplation nurture the inner calm that enables us to act wisely. These practices also help us perceive hidden potential, to see more clearly into the depth of a situation, into the roots of what is and into the possibility of what might be.

Many religious traditions include meditation and contemplation practices. The meaning of these terms varies among traditions. As I use these terms, *meditation* focuses attention on a specific sensory input. *Contemplation* directs one's attention toward a given external situation or internal emotion and tracks thoughts and feelings that arise about that situation or emotion.

Here are instructions for one form of meditation: Set aside a period of at least ten minutes to sit or walk silently. Select something specific for your mind to focus on, such as your breath, a mantra, the sounds you hear, or a candle flame. When thoughts arise, briefly notice that you are thinking and gently return to your point of focus. Meditation teachers often use the image of clouds moving across a blue sky to communicate the sense of letting passing thoughts arise and go as one directs one's attention to the spaciousness one perceives when one's mind is gently focused on a selected object.

Contemplation focuses attention on a specific situation, relationship, or emotion. When your mind wanders, gently bring your attention back to the subject of contemplation. As you contemplate this subject, gently notice the feelings and thoughts that arise in you. If you wish, you can focus on one of those thoughts or feelings and observe what arises in your awareness.

In both meditation and contemplation, you disengage from the superficial verbal chatter in the mind and direct attention to the depths of your awareness. In this way, you come into immediate relation with your inner life. Both these practices quiet the internal and external noisiness in life and enable you to perceive the movement of the liberating stream that continually speaks the nonverbal language of Exodus, the possibility for more flourishing into life.

Discernment

We human beings recognize the flow of the prophetic stream in the depths of our lives when we give sustained attention to whatever we find most fascinating or disturbing. Fascination and disturbance are the ways that the prophetic stream flows into our lives to activate awareness, critical thinking, and imagination. The disruption of fascination and disturbance breaks through settled ways of thinking and grabs our attention, potentially focusing it on something that is emerging but is not yet fully present in our awareness.

To practice this kind of discernment, pay attention to what disturbs you and to what fascinates you. In attending to what disturbs you, look deeply into the roots of what upsets you. Then be on the lookout for the inchoate visions that arise as you search for a more fruitful way forward. In exploring what fascinates you, attend to the deep yearnings that are often moving within fascination. Living becomes prophetic when you bring wise *lev*—when you apply heart and mind, imagination and analysis—to what disturbs and fascinates you, in order to discern what action and engagement these creative disruptions are calling for. Our discernment can take a further step forward when we share the fruits of this practice with a friend or a circle of like practitioners.

Soul Friendship

Clarity about the deep roots of what disturbs and fascinates us often emerges out of sustained conversation with a good friend. Our souls are relational entities. The vitality of our souls comes alive through relationship, through accompaniment and companionship. Dialogue is the currency of such companionship. Heartfelt dialogue with a soul friend helps to illuminate the presence of soul within. In sustained conversation with a trusted friend we best discern the work that our souls yearn to engage in the world. As we find words to articulate our soul's deep desires, the next steps of our liberation journey come into view.

Sacred Study

Studying sacred literature challenges us to find God's Presence in the written word and thereby to see more clearly God's Presence in and concern for the world. Studying a liberation text like the Bible helps us see oppressive systems more clearly and to think deeply about alternative ways that would support the flourishing of all. Sacred study supports us in the three prophetic attributes: an awareness of God's love, the courage and clarity to name oppression, and the ability to envision an alternative future.

Sacred study can be especially powerful when engaged in a communal setting. Speaking aloud the insights we receive in study helps to clarify our thinking and gives these insights more full-bodied presence in our awareness. Hearing other people reflect on the same thought or the same text adds more body to these insights. The relational context of communal study creates an environment in which we naturally feel more accountable to practice what we are learning into our life.

Communal study, in the form of the two weekly Beit Midrash groups I lead, has been the wellspring for many of the insights in this book.

Sabbath Keeping

Sabbath provides the balance between work and rest, a day of renewal that both reconnects us to our purpose and invigorates our engagement with the world. On the Sabbath we cease our labors. We take a step back and appreciate the beauty of the world exactly as it is. In the very midst of the brokenness in the world, we look for what is vital, whole, and beautiful. We engage in activities that connect us to the deep fabric of life and to the Creator that animates that fabric.

Stop doing. This is the initial and most challenging aspect of Sabbath practice. Sabbath keeping is a subversive act in the midst of a culture that places supreme value on human production.

Sabbath keeping supports our contact with the prophetic stream by providing the time and psychic space in which the deep and often subtle movement of that stream can be felt and contemplated. Sabbath is an expansive time. Heschel called Sabbath, "a palace in time," a time that enables us to perceive and celebrate profound and vitalizing aspects of life too easily missed in the hurry of 24/7 pursuit.[4]

---

4   I recommend several books that explore Sabbath keeping: Abraham Joshua

To keep Sabbath, set aside a twenty-five-hour period,[5] or at least a good part of a day. Create a sacred time container by cleaning and shopping in advance. Start your Sabbath with a ritual such as lighting candles. Avoid commerce, smartphones, emails, the internet, and any work-related task. Fill your Sabbath with rest, friends, community, connecting to nature, prayer, beauty, and joy.

Prophetic Action

Prophetic action itself is a spiritual practice. Wisdom, courage, and vision are qualities of spirit. When we embody these qualities in action, we express spirit. The prophets, animated by God's love for the world, denounced oppression and articulated an alternative future. When we act in love to oppose entrenched powers and promote new possibilities for human flourishing we become channels for the prophetic stream flowing into the world.

Heschel, *The Sabbath* (New York: Farrar, Straus and Giroux, 1951); Walter Brueggemann, *Sabbath as Resistance* (Louisville, KY: Westminster John Knox, 2014); Wayne Muller, *Sabbath: Finding Rest, Renewal, and Delight in Our Busy Lives* (London: Bantam, 2000).

[5] The Jewish Sabbath is twenty-five hours.

Appendix B
CHAPTER REFLECTIONS

Reflection is a way to explore what a concept means to you and to integrate this learning into how you live. Reflection is different than analytical thinking. The reflective process invites you to search your experience to learn how you relate to a given insight. Reflections are most effective if you take time to slowly ponder the questions and carefully attend to your responses. This learning process may be enhanced by journaling your responses or sharing the process with a friend.

Chapter 1: A Journey in Love

Lifted by the Prophetic Stream

Allow yourself to feel or imagine that you feel the Living Presence's love and concern for the world. . . . Imagine that this love fills you with the courage to call out a difficult truth. . . . Now feel what that courage feels like inside you. Courage is a quality of the heart. Let the sense of that courage arise and live in your heart. . . . Now think of a present situation—personal or societal—that disturbs you. What truth could you speak about that situation? . . . Imagine that you can envision a radically alternative way forward. What do you see?

Chapter 2: The Prophets and Deuteronomy

A Time for Change

The Prophets denounced the growing gap between rich and poor in their day as well as the premises and values that supported that inequity. What are some of the premises and values that support the inequity of our day and stand in the way of change toward a more equitable society?

Chapter 3: The Liberation Journey

River of Life

What are the major stepping-stones in your life journey: times of change, challenge, hardship, celebration, setbacks, and steps forward? Make a list. . . . On a different piece of paper, draw the headwaters of a river, placing your first stepping-stones along the flow of the river. As you add stepping-stones, draw the next section of the river's flow to reflect the course of your life. When is the river tranquil, and when challenging? . . . When does the river flow straight and when does it meander? . . . Place new stepping-stones along the river as it continues to flow. . . . As you look at the entire river, what themes emerge?

Chapter 4: The Way of Relationship

Devotion and Obedience

There are times in life when obedience is important, and times when obedience is problematic. This reflection offers you an opportunity to explore how obedience and devotion live in your life. Think of a time in your life when you were obedient. Recall what was happening in your life. How did you feel about what you were doing? . . . How did you feel about the person or institution to whom or which you were obedient? . . . How did you feel about yourself? . . . Now reflect on a time when you behaved with deep devotion. How did you feel about what you were doing? . . . How did you feel about the person or institution to whom or which you were devoted? . . . How did you feel about yourself? . . . What is the difference between your experience of obedience and that of devotion? . . . Did the religious upbringing of your youth call for obedience or devotion? . . . What is the role of obedience and devotion in your present relationship to God or to whatever you hold to be of the upmost importance?

Chapter 5: Telling the Essential Story throughout Time

Creation, Exodus, Today

Imagine that the present moment is a continuation of the exodus journey. Visualize the people leaving Egypt, and then link that emancipation to more recent liberation movements, such as the abolitionist, suffrage, and civil rights movements. Feel how all these movements continue to move forward in your heart. . . . Now, reflect all the way back to the creation of the universe and imagine the entire journey of the universe as a vast evolving process of unfolding potential. . . . Imagine that the creative journey of the universe flows into your life at the present moment. Imagine that the same creative power that stands behind both the universe journey and the exodus journey carries you forward today. How is your life today propelled by this same creative energy?

Chapter 6: Headwaters

Liberating Light

The Jewish morning prayer "Fashioner of Light" portrays God emanating a divine light that continually vitalizes the world from within. Imagine this light flowing through your body. Feel it moving in your heart area, up toward your neck and head, streaming out along your arms and through your hands, moving through your pelvis, legs, and feet. . . . This divine energy moves within all that is to bring forth something new, to liberate some potential into what it could be. How have you experienced this potential being liberated in you?

Chapter 7: Journey Partners

Be a Blessing

Abraham was called to be a blessing. What is a blessing that you are called to bring forth into the world? . . . What vulnerability and risks do you need to accept to be that blessing? . . . What uncertainty and ambiguity? . . . What inner and outer journeys are required of you along the way of living that blessing?

Chapter 8: Rivalry and Resolution in Genesis

Sibling Rivalry

In what relationships do you experience sibling rivalry? . . . Does the perception of scarcity play a role in this rivalry? . . . Does your experience of this rivalry in some way affect other relationships or diminish your vitality or limit your flourishing? . . . What shift in thinking would help you step out of the rivalry and move toward healing? . . . What can you do to decrease the competition? . . . Who in your life is a model of resisting the force of sibling rivalry and attempting to nurture positive relationship?

Chapter 9: Exodus

Power over and Power With

Think about an initiative in which you are or have been involved. In what ways is that initiative employing power over to accomplish its goals? . . . In what ways does the initiative employ the powers of nurturance, relationship, trust, and adaptability to accomplish its goals? . . . What are the advantages and limitations of each approach?

Chapter 10: Force and Transformation

When to Use Force

Think about a situation that concerns you in which force is currently being used, either within your community, in US society, or internationally. . . . How effective is this use of force in creating positive change? . . . Are there nonviolent approaches that might be more likely to lead to lasting transformation in this situation?

Chapter 11: The Reluctant Prophet and the Unprepared People

Journey of the Unprepared

Think of a significant challenge that you took on for which you felt unprepared. . . . Did this challenge also require you to venture off the beaten path? . . . What enabled you to take on this challenge despite your feelings of inadequacy? . . . How might you use that same resource in a current challenge that you are facing?

Chapter 12: Head for the Hills

The People behind the Text

The Hebrew Bible is the legacy of people seeking a more egalitarian society. How does this understanding of the origins of the Bible affect your relationship to the biblical text? . . . How does this understanding affect the role the Bible might play in your participation in the liberation journey?

Chapter 13: A Scribal Tradition

Listening to Different Perspectives

By including diverse and sometimes conflicting texts, the Bible is inherently self-critical. What is your capacity to welcome different points of view? . . . Who in the text of your life brings a challenging voice or a different worldview? . . . What is your attitude toward perspectives that differ from your own? . . . How might you benefit from listening to dissenting points of view?

Chapter 14: A Mighty Stream

We Are Relationship

Think about the relationships in your life. With whom do you have the strongest relationships? . . . What is the quality of your relationship with the earth and nonhuman beings? . . . To serve the vitality of your life, what relationships might you strengthen? . . . How might you give mutual relationship a higher priority in your life?

Chapter 15: A Listening Lineage

On Listening

Think about the past day and recall your interactions. When did you listen well? . . . When were you distracted? . . . When did something someone said trigger you so that you stopped listening? . . . How did you soothe yourself or how could you have soothed yourself so that you did or could return to listening? . . . Did you listen to the Living Presence, and if so, how did you listen to the often-wordless Voice that draws you out into the wilderness of new possibilities?

Chapter 16: We Make the Road by Walking

Life as a Learning Journey

Think about each decade of your life, starting from your teenage years. Write down one major learning for each decade. . . . Identify a significant failure in your life. . . . Alongside the inevitable suffering, what did you learn? . . . How can you approach future "failures" in a way that supports learning?

Chapter 17: Dialogue Is the Way

The Dialogue Virtues

Recall a rewarding dialogue experience. . . . In what ways did the practice of dialogue virtues—curiosity, courage, humility, vulnerability, and empathy—contribute to the dialogue? . . . Think of a frustrating conversation, an exchange that felt more like an argument than a dialogue. . . . How did the absence of one or more dialogue virtues contribute to the outcome of that conversation? . . . What virtue would you like to strengthen to enable you to engage in more fruitful dialogue?

Chapter 18: Dialogue against Oppression

Dialogue across Difference

How have you sought to have conversations and relationships with people from different racial, ethnic, religious, or socioeconomic backgrounds than yours? . . . How can you seek more relationships with people from different backgrounds than yours? . . . What could you say to yourself that would help you exercise courageous imperfection in these conversations?

Chapter 19: The World Is Built with Love

Faith in Power and Faith in Life

What aspects of your life predominantly reflect faith in power? Write them down. . . . What aspects predominantly embody faith in life? Write them down. . . . Is there an aspect of your life that you would like to shift toward faith in life? . . . What would that shift look life? . . . What are steps you might take to move toward faith in life? . . . Now think about these same questions in relation to social policy.

Chapter 20: Enacting a Love Ethic

Social Activism Rooted in Loving

From the place of loving inside you, what is a societal challenge or opportunity that you are called to name and address? . . . How does or could a love ethic guide your activism in that area? . . . Groups or organizations can also act from a love ethic in their work. How does or could a love ethic guide the activities of a work team, coalition, or organization to which you belong?

Chapter 21: The Exquisite Lightness of Being

Kayin and Hevel

Think about a societal institution that you believe limits rather than supports flourishing. . . . What aspects of that institution embody Kayin, the will to control and possess? . . . How does this Kayin orientation make that institution less responsive and vital over the long run? . . . Now think about an organization or association that you belong to. . . . What aspects of that organization embody Kayin qualities? . . . What aspects embody Hevel qualities? . . . How well does the organization work with the balance between Kayin (control/stability) and Hevel (vulnerability/responsiveness)? . . . How does that organization's orientation in regard to Kayin and Hevel affect its vitality?

Chapter 22: The Art of Stars and Stones

Fascination, Disturbance, and Creativity

Identify one subject or issue that currently fascinates or disturbs you. . . . How are you responding to that fascination or disturbance? . . . What is the role of imagination and creativity in your response? . . . How could imagination and creativity, yours and others', enhance your efforts to bring positive change into the world now?

Chapter 23: The Love That Binds Us

The Prophetic Stream in Your Life

The prophetic stream runs deep in all of our lives. We are in covenant together with the world, each other, and the Living Presence. How is this stream flowing in your life? . . . What is it activating you to do next?

Selected Readings

Abramsky, Sasha. "This Washington State Ballot Measure Fights for Both Jobs and Climate Justice." *The Nation*, August 13–20, 2018, 20–23.

Ackroyd, Peter. *Exile and Restoration: A Study of Hebrew Thought of the Sixth Century BCE*. Philadelphia: Westminster Press, 1968.

Albertz, Rainer. *A History of Israelite Religion in the Old Testament Period*. Vol. 1. Translated by John Bowden. Louisville, KY: Westminster/John Knox Press, 1994.

Alter, Robert. *The Art of Biblical Narrative*. New York: Basic Books, 1983.

Angelou, Maya. *The Complete Collected Poems of Maya Angelou*. New York: Random House, 1994.

Arendt, Hannah. *The Origins of Totalitarianism*. New York: Harvest Book Harcourt, 1968.

Baden, Joel. *The Historical David: The Real Life of an Invented Hero*. New York: HarperOne, 2013.

Barber, William J. *The Third Reconstruction*. Boston: Beacon Press, 2016.

Bateson, Mary Catherine. *Composing a Life*. New York: Grove Press, 2007.

Bellah, Robert, et al. *Habits of the Heart*. Berkeley: University of California Press, 1985.

Bergson, Henri. *Creative Evolution*. Mineola, NY: Dover Publications, 1998.

Berman, Joshua. *Created Equal: How the Bible Broke with Ancient Political Thought*. Oxford: Oxford University Press, 2011.

Berry, Thomas. *The Dream of the Earth*. San Francisco: Sierra Club Books, 1988.

———. *The Universe Story*. New York: Arkana Publishing, 1984.

Biddle, Mark E. *Deuteronomy*. Macon, GA: Smyth and Helwys Press, 2003.

Biss, Eula. "White Debt." *New York Times Magazine*, December 2, 2015.

Boggs, James, and Grace Lee Boggs. *Revolution and Evolution in the Twentieth Century*. New York: Monthly Review Press, 2008.

Brown, Frances, S. R. Driver, and Charles A. Briggs. *The Brown-Driver-Briggs Hebrew and English Lexicon of the Old Testament*. Peabody, MA: Hendrickson, 1996.

Brown, William. *The Seven Pillars of Creation: The Bible, Science, and the Ecology of Wonder*. Oxford: Oxford University Press, 2010.

Brueggemann, Walter. *A Commentary on Jeremiah*. Grand Rapids: Eerdmans, 1998.

———. *The Practice of Prophetic Imagination*. Minneapolis: Fortress Press, 2012.

———. *The Prophetic Imagination*. Minneapolis: Fortress Press, 2001.

Buber, Martin. *Between Man and Man*. Translated by Ronald Gregor Smith. Mansfield Centre, CT: Martino Publishing, 2014.

———. *Israel and the World: Essays in a Time of Crisis*. New York: Schocken Books, 1976.

———. *I and Thou*. Translated by Ronald Gregor Smith. New York: Charles Scribner's Sons, 1958.

———. *I and Thou*. Translated by Walter Kaufman. New York: Touchstone, 1970.

———. *A Land of Two Peoples: Martin Buber on Jews and Arabs*. Edited by Paul Mendes-Flohr. Chicago: University of Chicago Press, 1983.

———. *The Prophetic Faith*. New York: HarperTorchbooks, 1960.

Carr, David. *Reading the Fractures of Genesis*. Louisville, KY: Westminster John Knox Press, 1996.

Christensen, Duane L., ed. *A Song of Power and the Power of Song*. Winona Lake, IN: Eisenbrauns, 1993.

Cone, James. *A Black Theology of Liberation*. Maryknoll, NY: Orbis Books, 2010.

———. *The Cross and the Lynching Tree*. Maryknoll, NY: Orbis Books, 2011.

Davis, Ellen. *Scripture, Culture, and Agriculture*. Cambridge: Cambridge University Press, 2009.

Dever, William G. *The Rise of Ancient Israel*. Washington, DC: Biblical Archaeology Society, 1992.

Diangelo, Robin. *White Fragility*. Boston: Beacon Press, 2018.

Ellis, Mark. *Toward a Jewish Liberation Theology*. Maryknoll, NY: Orbis Books, 1987.

Engler, Mark, and Paul Engler. *This Is an Uprising*. New York: Nation Books, 2016.

Finkelstein, Israel, and Neil Asher Silberman. *The Bible Unearthed*. New York: Free Press, 2001.

Freire, Paulo. *Pedagogy of the Oppressed*. New York: Continuum, 2000.

Friedman, Richard Elliott. *The Exodus*. San Francisco: HarperOne, 2018.

———. *Who Wrote the Bible?* New York: Harper Collins, 1997.

Fromm, Erich. *The Art of Loving*. New York: Open Road Media, 2013.

———. *The Sane Society*. New York: Open Road Media, 2013.

Goldbard, Arlene. *The Culture of Possibility: Art, Artists and the Future*. San Francisco: Waterlight Press, 2013.

Gottwald, Norman K. *The Tribes of Yahweh: A Sociology of the Religion of Liberated Israel, 1250–1050 BCE*. Maryknoll, NY: Orbis Books, 1979.

Harari, Yuval Noah. *Sapiens: A Brief History of Humankind*. New York: Harper Collins, 2015.

Harrison, Beverly Wildung. *Making the Connections: Essays in Feminist Social Ethics*. Edited by Carol Robb. Boston: Beacon Press, 1985.

Havel, Vaclav. *Living in Truth*. London: Faber and Faber, 1989.

Heschel, Abraham Joshua. *God in Search of Man: A Philosophy of Judaism*. New York: Farrar, Straus & Giroux, 1976.

———. *The Prophets*. New York: Perennial Classics, 1962.

hooks, bell. *All about Love*. New York: Harper Perennial, 2001.

Howard-Brook, Wes. *Come Out, My People! God's Call out of Empire in the Bible and Beyond*. Maryknoll, NY: Orbis Books, 2010.

Isaacs, Alick. *A Prophetic Peace: Judaism, Religion, and Politics*. Bloomington: Indiana University Press, 2011.

Kierkegaard, Søren. *Fear and Trembling and the Sickness unto Death*. Translated by Walter Lowrie. Princeton, NJ: Princeton University Press, 1941.

Kimmerer, Robin Wall. *Braiding Sweetgrass: Indigenous Wisdom, Scientific Knowledge, and the Teaching of Plants*. Minneapolis: Milkweed Editions, 2013.

Klein, Naomi. *No Is Not Enough*. Chicago: Haymarket Books, 2017.

King, Martin Luther, Jr. *I Have a Dream: Writings and Speeches That Changed the World*. Edited by James Melvin Washington. San Francisco: Harper, 1986.

Kook, Rav. *Orot HaKodesh*. Jerusalem: Maggid, 2015.

Lacey, Paul, and Robert Creeley, eds. *The Selected Poems of Denise Levertov*. New York: New Directions, 2002.

Lang, Bernhard. *Anthropological Approaches to the Old Testament*. Philadelphia: Fortress Press, 1985.

Lederach, John Paul. *The Moral Imagination: The Heart and Soul of Building Peace*. New York: Oxford University Press, 2005.

Leibowitz, Nehama. *Studies in Shemot [Exodus]*. Jerusalem: World Zionist Organization, 1976.

Levenson, Jon. *Creation and the Persistence of Evil*. Princeton, NJ: Princeton University Press, 1994.

———. *The Love of God: Divine Gift, Human Gratitude, and Mutual Faithfulness in Judaism*. Princeton, NJ: Princeton University Press, 2015.

Maimonides, Moses. *Mishna Torah*.

Malcolm X. "The Ballot or the Bullet," www.sefaria.org/texts/Halakhah/ Mishna.

Martin, Courtney E. "Transforming White Fragility into Courageous Imperfection." On Being blog, June 26, 2015.

Mindell, Arnold. *Working with the Dreaming Body*. Portland, OR: Lao Tse Press, 2014.

Moe-Lobeda, Cynthia. *Resisting Structural Evil: Love as Ecological-Economic Vocation*. Minneapolis: Fortress Press, 2013.

Nelson, Richard D. *Deuteronomy*. Louisville, KY: Westminster John Knox Press, 2002.

Oliver, Mary. *A Thousand Mornings: Poems*. New York: Penguin, 2013.

Palmer, Parker. *Healing the Heart of Democracy*. San Francisco: Jossey Bass, 2011.

———. *A Hidden Wholeness: The Journey toward an Undivided Life*. San Francisco: Jossey Bass, 2004.

Perdue, Leo, Joseph Blenkinsopp, John Collins, and Carol Meyers. *Families in Ancient Israel*. Louisville, KY: Westminster John Knox Press, 1997.

Pipher, Mary. *The Shelter of Each Other: Rebuilding Our Families*. New York: Ballantine Books, 1996.

Power, Samantha. *A Problem from Hell: America and the Age of Genocide*. New York: Basic Books, 2013.

Putnam, Robert D. *Bowling Alone: The Collapse and Revival of American Community*. New York: Simon and Schuster, 2000.

Rankine, Claudia. "The Condition of Black Life Is Mourning." *New York Times*, June 22, 2015.

Rifkin, Jeremy. *The Empathic Civilization*. New York: Penguin Press, 2009.

Schaef, Anne Wilson. *When Society Becomes an Addict*. San Francisco: HarperOne, 1988.

Shor, Ira, and Paulo Freire. *A Pedagogy for Liberation*. Westport, CT: Bergin and Garvey Publishers, 1987.

Slessarev-Jamir, Helene. *Prophetic Activism*. New York: New York University Press, 2011.

Solnit, Rebecca. *Hope in the Dark*. Chicago: Haymarket Books, 2016.
Soloveitchik, Joseph. *Abraham's Journey*. New York: KTAV Publishing, 2008.
Swimme, Brian. *The Universe Is a Green Dragon*. Rochester, VT: Bear and Company, 1984.
Tigay, Jeffrey H., ed. *The JPS Torah Commentary: Deuteronomy*. Philadelphia: Jewish Publication Society, 1996.
Turkle, Sherry. *Alone Together*. New York: Basic Books, 2011.
Ufford-Chase, Rick. *Faithful Resistance*. n.p.: n.p., 2016.
Unger, Roberto. *The Religion of the Future*. New York: Verso Press, 2016.
Unger, Sebastian. *Tribe: On Homecoming and Belonging*. New York: Twelve, 2016.
Van der Jagt, Krijn. *Anthropological Approaches to the Interpretation of the Bible*. New York: United Bible Societies, 2003.
van Gelder, Sarah. *The Revolution Where You Live*. Oakland, CA: Berrett-Koehler Publishers, 2017.
Velasquez-Manoff, Moises. "How to Make Fun of Nazis." *New York Times*. April 17, 2017.
Walker, Alice. *Anything We Love Can Be Saved: A Writer's Activism*. New York: Ballantine Books, 1998.
Ward, Stephen M. *In Love and Struggle: The Revolutionary Lives of James and Grace Lee Boggs*. Chapel Hill: University of North Carolina Press, 2016.
Weinberg, Matis. *Frameworks Shemot*. Boston: Foundations for Jewish Publications, 1999.
Zornberg, Avivah Gottlieb. *The Beginning of Desire: Reflections on Genesis*. New York: Doubleday, 1995.
———. *The Particulars of Rapture: Reflections on Exodus*. New York: Doubleday, 2001.

Index

Aaron, brother of Moses, 96,
  113
Abel, son of Adam, 65, 66, 68,
  179–80, 218–19
Abigail, wife of David, 107–8
Abraham, prophet, 35, 83, 84,
  98, 215
  covenant with God, 31, 32,
    200, 201
  descendants of, 65, 69
  family conflicts, 66, 70–72, 76
  Hagar and Ishmael, banishing,
    62–63, 67–68
  homeland, God calling out of,
    40, 57, 58, 153
  journey of, 55–58, 60–63, 93,
    127
  Lot, relationship with, 67, 75,
    78
Adam and Eve, 58
afro-futurism, 194
agape, 165, 166, 177
Akiba, R., 53
All about Love (hooks), 166–67
Alter, Robert, 145
Amaziah, high priest, 7
American culture, 77, 142, 152
  civil rights movement, role
    of the arts in, 186–87
  as commercially driven,
    169–71

community life as diminishing,
  129, 172
external achievement,
  emphasis on, 139
loneliness, national approach
  to alleviating, 171–72, 173
segregation in, 158
Amos, prophet, 6, 10, 32
  Amaziah, confronting, 7
  forgiveness from God, asking
    for, 3–4
  on the Living Presence,
    40–41
  plumb line, vision of God
    holding, 4, 161, 184
  sacrificial cults, prophetic
    judgment on, 22–23
  writing prophets, embodying
    qualities of, 5
Angelou, Maya, 187
Ar, son of Judah, 72
Arendt, Hannah, 112
Assyrian Empire, 14, 103

Babylonian Empire
  Babylonian exile, deliverance
    from, 27, 184
  Exodus 2.0, departure from
    Babylon as, 91
  false prophecy on the
    empire, 32

Babylonian Empire *(continued)*
  Isaiah, encouraging return to, 113
  Jewish temple, destruction of, 14–15, 26
  King Cyrus, defeat by, 103
  preservation of Hebrew texts during exile, 119
Baca, Judy, 193
Bach, Johann Sebastian, 50
Barber, William J., II, 176, 178
Bateson, Mary Catherine, 84
Bathsheba, wife of David, 107–8
Batya, daughter of Pharaoh, 81, 82, 83–84
Beit Midrash learning circles, 136, 172, 184, 210
Benjamin, son of Jacob, 73, 74, 78, 79, 84
Berry, Thomas, 43
Biss, Eula, 160–61
Blake, William, 186
Boggs, Grace Lee, 142–43, 157, 162
Boggs, James, 142–43
brown, adrienne maree, 194
Brueggemann, Walter, 134, 151, 185
  doom of the current order, proclaiming, 131, 181
  on elite maintenance of unjust society, 9
  narrative of the prophets, 39
  prophetic imagination, defining, 184
  on the royal consciousness of King Solomon, 109
Buber, Martin, 130, 200, 203
  dialogue in education, 146–47
  I and Thou, 123–24
  I-It attitude, 127, 131

Levinas, influenced by, 125–26
  nonviolence, discussing with Gandhi, 88
  on relational encounters, 146, 179
Bush, George W., 89–90
Butler, Octavia, 194

Cain, son of Adam
  "brother's keeper" question, 65, 73, 78
  Kayin, reflections on, 179–81, 218–19
  sibling rivalry with Abel, 65–66, 68, 71
Canaan, 6, 69, 73
  Abraham, departure from, 62
  collapse of Canaanite kingdoms, 99–100, 102–3
  Joseph, living amongst the Canaanites, 71
  journey from Mesopotamia to Canaan, 66
  social hierarchy in, 101
  Tamar, Canaanite heritage of, 72, 75
Chaldeans, 55, 56
Cognitive Revolution, 196
Cone, James, 158, 159, 162
covenant, new understanding of, 199–203
crowdfunding, 192–93

David, King, 107–8
deep time, 137–38
Descartes, Rene, 126
Deutero-Isaiah, 32, 184
Deuteronomy, 16, 25, 39, 99, 108
  conditional covenant of, 31–32

on exodus as an ongoing
process, 24
Israelite identity and practices,
shifting, 26–27
listening, injunction on, 34–36
monarchic era, texts written
during, 107
on mutual relationship, 29,
33, 37–38
rituals, calling for, 19–20
sabbatical year legislation, 17
Temple cult, curtailing, 22
Temple scroll as early form of,
14
threats to Judah, text written
in response to, 13, 15
Torah, becoming part of, 110
Dever, William G., 101
dialogue, 112, 162, 176, 191,
208
between Amos and God, 4
central role in Scriptures, 145
in conditional covenant, 32,
34–38
between created world and
God, 46, 48
as a form of love, 178
Freiren dialogue, 155–57
genuine dialogue, 151,
152–53
as goal of education, 147
imaginative dialogue as
unique to humans, 195–96
Initiative 1631, dialogue
involved in, 153–54
love as foundational to, 150,
163, 166
ordinary people, dialogue
arising from, 190
people with privilege,
engaging in, 158–61

in problem-posing education,
148–49
prophetic stream, contributing
to, 31
Quivira Coalition as example
of successful dialogue, 175
reflections on, 217–18
as the way of faithfulness, 146
discernment, practice of, 209

Erikson, Erik, 138
Esau, son of Isaac, 68, 69–70,
74, 75, 78
exodus, 26, 98, 143, 188, 190
Amos, calling for remembrance
of, 40
call to the Exodus journey,
196
creation stories, parallels to
Exodus tales, 41, 42, 47, 80
enslavement of Israelites,
Exodus opening with, 75, 79
Isaiah on return to Judah as
a second exodus, 91, 113
Moses' actions as
foreshadowing, 94, 96
as most formative event in
biblical narrative, 99
nonverbal language of, 209
Passover Seder, reenacting
story during, 19–20, 113–14
physical force in liberation
process, Exodus raising
question of, 87–89, 90
in present time, 20–22, 24,
43, 138, 214–15
women, subverting Egypt's
dominance, 83–86
expansive time, 137–38, 210
Ezekiel, prophet, 16, 23, 32
Ezra, the scribe, 110–11

faith in power *vs.* faith in life,
163–64
forgotten debt concept, 160–61
Fowler, James, 138
Fox, Everett, 36
Freire, Paulo, 89, 146
"banking education," 147–48,
152
on dialogue as a form of love,
150, 178
inclusive dialogue as critical,
157, 162
liberation pedagogy, 140–41,
143, 168
possessive consciousness as
objectifying, 127–28
on problem-posing education,
148–49, 150–51
reflection and action, including
in dialogue, 149, 159, 160
right to speak, reclaiming
before dialogue, 155–56
Friedman, Richard Elliot, 111
Fromm, Erich, 127, 163–64,
165, 167, 169, 173

Gandhi, Mahatma, 88
Genesis, 53, 80, 86, 105, 134
chaos, calling humans to face,
47
on creation as a process of
liberation, 45
dominion and subjugation,
God exercising, 50, 87
Egyptian oppression as a
de-Genesis, 79
familial relationships, focus
on, 65–66, 74, 75–76
God and physical world,
partnering to create
humans, 48–49, 51, 52

midwives, mirroring creating
action of God, 81
monarchic era, texts written
during, 107
natural world, God
addressing, 46
sibling rivalry in, 66, 68,
70–71, 73–74, 76, 78, 215
Ghirmatzion, Rahwa, 175, 190
gratitude, practice of, 205–6
Gutiérrez, Gustavo, 121, 123,
131, 134

Hagar of Egypt, 35, 62, 67–68
Hananiah, the false prophet, 32
Harari, Yuval, 195–96
Harrison, Beverly Wildung, 85,
121, 123, 131, 134
Heschel, Abraham Joshua
Hebrew prophets, seeking
alternative vision of, 131
mystery and amazement of
the Presence, 203
"new thinking," addressing,
17
in prophetic listening
tradition, 134
Sabbath keeping, 210
solidarity with God, on the
loss of, 122–23
on wonder and reverence,
200, 206
Havel, Vaclav, 143
Hevel. *See* Abel, son of Adam
A Hidden Wholeness (Palmer),
172
"History of California" mural,
193
hooks, bell, 166, 167, 169, 181
Hosea, prophet, 10, 32, 33, 185
Howe, Marie, 194

I and Thou (Buber), 123–24
idolatry, 25, 38, 125, 128
Imarisha, Walidah, 194
individualism, adverse effects
    of, 129–30
Initiative 1631, dialogical work
    of, 153–54
Intelligent Design, 52
Iraq, US invasion of, 89–90
Isaac, son of Abraham, 62–63,
    68
Isaiah, prophet, 7, 10, 27, 141,
    143
  contingency, contributing to
    understanding of, 32
  on God as creating and
    leading forth, 41–42
  inadequacy, expressing
    feelings of, 96
  Judah, condemning elites of,
    6
  liberation from oppression,
    on God desiring, 8
  listening as connecting
    people to God, 133
  repentance and forgiveness,
    on the process of, 9
  return to Judah as a second
    exodus, 91, 113
  on violence as a learned
    behavior, 25
Isay, Dave, 193
Ishmael, son of Abraham,
    62–63, 67–68
Israel, 7, 36, 114
  Amos and, 3–4, 6
  conditional covenant with
    God, 31–32, 200
  dehumanization of Israelites
    in Egypt, 79–80
  destruction of, 15, 26, 31

E texts of the northern
    kingdom, 109–11
historical period of the
    prophets, 5
listening between God and
    Israel, 36
love between God and Israel,
    33–34
proto-Israelite peoples,
    100–103
resistance to transformation,
    104–5
Tabernacle, Israelites
    contributing to, 188–89
I-Thou relations, 124–25, 127,
    135, 181

Jackson, Wes, 195
Jacob, patriarch, 75, 113, 115
  angel, wrestling with, 69, 74,
    84
  Canaan, resettling in, 66
  Esau, reconciliation with,
    70, 78
  Isaac, attempting to deceive,
    68
  sons of, 71, 73–74, 79
Jacob, Rebbe, of Kefar Hanan,
    51
Jeremiah, prophet, 149, 202
  on doing what is just and
    right, 16, 62
  God of creation and exodus,
    identifying, 41
  inadequacy, expressing
    before God, 96
  new covenant with Israel,
    32–33, 90, 200
  prophetic call to listen, 35
  repentance, calling for, 9
  on sacrificial cults, 22–23

Joseph, son of Jacob, 71, 115
  Benjamin and, 73, 74, 78
  Judah, reconciling with,
    73–75, 86
Joshua, Israelite leader, 113
Josiah, King, 13–14, 31, 110
Judah, kingdom of, 8, 32, 90
  Babylonian exile, 14–15, 103
  destruction of, 107, 119
  disparities between rich and
    poor, 104–5
  J texts of the southern
    kingdom, 109–12
  repentance from House of
    Judah, calls for, 9
  return from exile as a second
    exodus, 113
  societal and political
    instability of the region,
    5–6, 13, 31
Judah, son of Jacob, 79, 93,
  115
  Benjamin, standing up for,
    78, 84
  as a brother-keeper, 76
  Canaanites, living amongst,
    71–72
  Joseph, reconciling with,
    73–75, 86
Junger, Sebastian, 129

Kayin. *See* Cain, son of Adam
Keller, Tim, 189
Kelly, Esteban, 176, 190
King, Martin Luther, Jr., 123,
  134, 188
  in History of California
    mural, 134
  "I have a dream" speech, 187
  love, keeping central, 169,
    173, 207

love ethic, public application
    of, 165–66, 167
  on segregation, 120–21
Kohlberg, Lawrence, 138
Kook, Rav, 52

Laban, father-in-law of Jacob,
  69
Lappé, Frances Moore, 143
Leah, matriarch, 66, 69,
  70–71, 73, 74–75, 78
Leibowitz, Nechama, 94
Levenson, Jon, 62
Levertov, Denise, 197
Leviathan, creation of, 49
Levinas, Emmanuel, 125–26,
  131
Life After Hate group, 176–77
Lot, patriarch, 67, 75, 78
lovingkindness, practice of, 207
Lowe, Rick, 194

Maimonides, Moses, 22, 53,
  55–57
Malachi, prophet, 32
Manasseh, King, 14
Martin, Courtney, 159
meditation/contemplation,
    practice of, 207–8
Micah, prophet, 6–7, 8, 9, 10,
  36, 185
Michelangelo and *Prisoners*
    sculptures, 50
Midrash HaGadol collection, 56
Midyanite women, 94–95
Miriam, prophetess, 81, 82, 84,
  86, 87, 115
mitzvah as a charge of God, 37
moach d'katnut/moach d'gadlut
    as aspects of mind, 127, 188
Moses, prophet, 14, 20, 98

as an infant, 79, 81, 83–84
burning bush and, 95–96, 206
exodus story, retelling before
  death, 19, 113
forgiveness from God,
  pleading for, 4, 35
Hebrews, rejoining community
  of, 76, 93–94
on listening as essential, 96,
  133
Miriam and, 86, 115
Pharaoh, interactions with,
  47, 87, 97
Tabernacle, helping to create,
  188, 189, 190
Torah, on the need to learn
  and teach, 24–25

Nachman of Bratzlav, Rebbe,
  208
ben Nahman, R. Samuel, 48
Nathan, prophet, 108
Noah, patriarch, 59, 60, 80, 111
*Notes from No Man's
  Land* (Biss), 160–61

Octavia's Brood (Imarisha/
  brown), 194
Onan, son of Judah, 72

Palmer, Parker, 172
Passover, 19–20, 22, 113–14
People United for Sustainable
  Housing (PUSH), 175, 190
Philadelphia Area Cooperative
  Alliance, 176, 190
Picciolini, Christian, 176–77
Pipher, Mary, 169
politicization of love, 167–68,
  171
Poor People's Campaign, 176

Powers, Samantha, 88
prayer, practice of, 207–8
Priestly texts (P), 110–12
Project Row Houses (PRH), 194
The Prophetic Imagination
  (Brueggemann), 9, 109
prophetic stream, 11, 47, 86,
  112, 140, 168
  Abraham's journey,
    embodying, 55, 58, 61
  contemporary prophets,
    activating, 120
  creative power of, 49, 131,
    181, 191
  cultivation of relationships,
    89, 90
  deep listening as a method of
    connection, 96
  deep time and, 138
  in Deuteronomy, 13, 38
  discernment and, 209
  dynamics contributing to
    flow of, 31
  effectiveness of, questioning,
    87
  exodus story, identifying with,
    114
  expression of, in the present,
    190
  faith in life, connecting a
    person to, 164
  feminine aspect of, 83–85
  full flourishing into mutual
    relationship, 77
  God empowering, 80
  Land Institute as the fruit of,
    195
  liberation narrative and, 43,
    74
  Moses and, 81, 97, 98
  no assurances from, 196

prophetic stream *(continued)*
  ordinary people, contributing
    to, 193
  possibilities, energizing,
    45–46, 189
  prophetic imagination,
    speaking to, 183–84
  reflections on, 213, 219
  during the Sabbath, 210
The Prophets (Heschel), 17
prophets and prophecy, 29, 32,
    112, 119, 206, 213
  battle of narratives, 39
  characteristics typifying a
    prophet, 93
  developmental psychology,
    prophetic insight akin to,
    139
  dialogue between Israel and
    God, 34–38
  exodus as a process in the
    present, 20–22, 24, 43, 138
  extended sense of time,
    137–38, 140
  historical period of the
    prophets, 5
  injustice, calling out, 115,
    128
  listening, essential practice of,
    133–36
  love between Israel and God,
    33–34
  nonviolent transformation,
    envisioning, 161–62
  prophetic action, spiritual
    practices for, 205–11
  prophetic activism, 177–78
  prophetic counternarrative,
    40, 42
  prophetic experience, three
    aspects of, 173–75

prophetic vision, embracing
    in the present day, 181–82
  relationship with God as a
    learning process, 25, 26–27
  royal power, challenging, 99,
    143, 180
  sacrificial cults, prophetic
    judgment on, 22–23
  scribes, collecting prophetic
    testimonies, 107, 109–10
  seeds, embodying prophetic
    energy of transformation, 48
  theme of prophetic
    understanding, 122–23
  twin prophetic assertions, 18,
    29, 138, 168
  See also prophetic stream;
    individual prophets
Puah, the midwife, 79, 81, 82,
    83, 84
Putnam, Robert, 172

Quivira Coalition, 175

Rachel, matriarch, 66, 69,
    70–71, 74
Rahab, symbol of terror, 41
rainbow covenant, 59
Rankine, Claudia, 159
Rashi (R. Shlomo ben Isaac),
    51, 57–58, 94, 188
Rebecca, matriarch, 35, 66, 68
reverence, practice of, 206–7
royal narrative, 39, 40, 42, 112,
    180

Sabbath keeping, 210–11
sacred study, 219
Samuel, prophet, 104, 113
Sarah, matriarch, 61, 66, 71,
    201

Hagar, banishing, 62–63, 67–68
journey with Abraham, 57, 60
satyagraha (nonviolence), 88
Schaef, Anne Wilson, 171
Scheidel, Walter, 161
Schmidt, Joseph, 139
Sforno, Obadiah ben Jacob, 87
Shavuot, 19, 20, 22
Shelah, son of Judah, 72, 73
Shifra, the midwife, 79, 81, 82, 83, 84
sin, 115, 121, 139
social-emotional learning (SEL), 172–73
Sodom and Gomorrah, 8, 35, 40–41, 61–62, 67
Solomon, King, 80, 109, 113
Soloveitchik, Joseph, 57
soul friendship, 209–10
StoryCorps, 193
Stowe, Harriet Beecher, 186
Sukkot, 19, 20, 22, 25
Swimme, Brian, 50

Tabernacle, 188–90
Tamar, the widow, 72–73, 74, 75, 78
"The Condition of Black Life is Mourning" (newspaper article), 159–60

"The Poet Is In" initiative, 194
Tigay, Jeffrey, 22
Tribe (Junger), 129

violence
force, contemplation on use of, 216
God and, 59, 87, 91
of imperial domination, 37
in Iraq invasion, 89–90
as a learned behavior, 25
nonviolent transformation, prophets envisioning, 161–62
oppressor consciousness and, 127
satyagraha, Buber questioning, 88

Walker, Alice, 192

Yochebed, mother of Moses, 81, 82, 83, 84

Zechariah, prophet, 32
Zornberg, Avivah Gottlieb, 81, 83